Reframing Financial Literacy

Exploring the Value of Social Currency

Reframing Financial Literacy

Exploring the Value of Social Currency

edited by

Thomas A. Lucey
Illinois State University

and

James D. Laney
University of North Texas

IAP

Information Age Publishing, Inc.
Charlotte, North Carolina • www.infoagepub.com

Library of Congress Cataloging-in-Publication Data

Reframing financial literacy : exploring the value of social currency /
edited by Thomas A. Lucey and James D. Laney.
p. cm.
Includes bibliographical references.
ISBN 978-1-61735-719-0 (pbk.) -- ISBN 978-1-61735-720-6 (hbk.) -- ISBN
978-1-61735-721-3 (ebk)
1. Financial literacy--Study and teaching. 2. Finance, Personal--Study
and teaching. 3. Economics--Study and teaching. I. Lucey, Thomas A. II.
Laney, James D.
HG179.R368 2012
332.071--dc23

2 011048228

Library of Congress, Prints & Photographs Division, FSA/OWI Collection, [LC-DIG-fsa-8b31801]

Printed in the United States of America

CONTENTS

SECTION II: EDUCATIONAL ISSUES

FOREWORD TO *REFRAMING FINANCIAL LITERACY: EXPLORING THE VALUE OF SOCIAL CURRENCY*

Mark C. Schug

Reframing Financial Literacy: Exploring the Value of Social Currency could not be released at a better time. Financial literacy has become an important national and international education priority. In light of the "Great Recession" of 2007-2009 and the sluggish recovery since, it seems difficult to understate its importance. John Bryant who served as President George W. Bush's vice-chairman of the President's Council on Financial Literacy is quoted in the *The Economist* (2008) as saying:

> Everybody wants it. Nobody understands it. Money is the great taboo. People just won't talk about it. And that is what leads you to subprime. Take the greed and the financial misrepresentation out of it, and the root of this [financial] crisis is massive levels of financial illiteracy.

Bryant went on to point out that financial education is at the heart of "the civil-rights issue of the 21st century." He called the attempt to help people help themselves out of poverty through financial literacy and economic opportunity the "silver-rights movement."

The interest of the U.S. government in financial education did not end with President George W. Bush's Council. On January 29, 2010, President Obama created the President's Advisory Council on Financial Capability

Reframing Financial Literacy: Exploring the Value of Social Currency, pp. vii–xiii

as the successor to the President's Council on Financial Literacy. The job of the reconstituted Council is to assist the American people in understanding financial matters and making informed financial decisions by improving financial education and financial access.

As noted by several of the authors in *Reframing Financial Literacy: Exploring the Value of Social Currency*, financial literacy has become an international issue. The Organization for Economic Co-operation and Development (OECD) has been promoting the importance of financial literacy for many years. It recommends that it be taught early and often. The OECD is now testing 15 year-olds on their knowledge of personal finances and ability to apply it to their financial problems in 2012. This is the first large-scale international study to assess the financial literacy. It is being conducted as part of the OECD's Programme for International Student Assessment (PISA) program. The results will be released in 2013. Aspects of financial literacy that will be tested include: dealing with bank accounts and credit/debit cards; planning and managing finances; understanding taxes and savings; risk and rewards; consumer rights and responsibilities in financial contracts. The hope of the OECD is that these results will make to possible to compare levels of financial literacy across countries and provide the basis to develop effective national strategies and good practices.

What We Know That May Be So

The teaching of economics and personal finance at the K-12 level has been highly researched and reported upon in the United States since as early as the 1970s. The research has primarily concentrated on curriculum, materials, enrollments, and effectiveness of teaching techniques. A brief overview of two major reviews of literature and national surveys allows us to glimpse current status of economic education and financial education to help establish the context in which *Reframing Financial Literacy: Exploring the Value of Social Currency* is being released.

The first review of research is the chapter by Steven L. Miller and Phillip J. VanFossen in the *Handbook of Research in Social Studies Education* (2008). Almost all of the studies cited by Miller and VanFossen address issues related to economic education. However, the authors acknowledge that personal finance has taken on new importance. In their conclusion, they state that, "in spite of the historic distinction between personal finance (or consumer) education and economic education, it appears possible (even likely) that financial literacy will become an increasingly important part of economic literacy and thus, economic education."

Miller and VanFossen draw several important generalizations regarding the current state of economic education. Three conclusions appear most relevant here. First, it seems clear that the development of the *Voluntary National Content Standards in Economics* (originally released in 1997, revised in 2001) published by the National Council on Economic Education (now the Council on Economic Education, 2009) has played an important role in influencing what economics is taught at the precollege level. Textbooks and curriculum materials are often aligned to the *Standards*. Many states looked to the *Standards* for guidance on developing state standards in both economics and personal finance. The content of national assessments, such as the National Assessment of Educational Progress in Economics' assessment of high school seniors in 2006, was influenced by the *Standards.*

Second, teachers remain poorly prepared to teach basic economics. Miller and VanFossen point out that, with the exception of advanced placement economics, most economics is taught by social studies teachers who have little formal background in economics. Most economics is taught by social studies teachers who have comprehensive social studies certifications. One study found that for those states that specify minimum coursework in the social sciences as part of their licensure rules, the mean number of semester hours in economics was 3.9, slightly more than a one semester course. This lack of economic education presents a problem because studies reveal that students learn more economics from teachers who have more formal preparation in economics.

Third, research dating back several years shows that children as well as adolescents can learn basic economics and personal finance. The question becomes how should economics best be included in the curriculum? Several studies show that high school students who take a high school economics class score significantly higher on standardized tests than students who had not taken economics. Interesting, students in consumer economics courses and students in social studies courses (with or without economics) scored the same on economics pre- and posttests, strengthening the conclusion that economics needs to be taught independently from other courses.

The issue of how best to include financial education in the school curriculum is similar to that facing general economics. In fact, the situation for financial education is made worse because it is not widely regarded as an independent academic discipline. Should financial education be included as a stand-alone course? If so, what grade level is most appropriate? Should financial education be integrated into existing courses such as economics, business, family and consumer education, and mathematics? If so, what grade levels and courses are most appropriate? These are basic questions that need to be addressed.

A second review of research is noteworthy even though it overlaps to some extent the work by Miller and VanFossen. This review was conducted by Michael Watts (2005). It was prepared for the then National Council on Economic Education under a contract with the U.S. Department of Education. It is unique in several ways and well worth reading. Watts, for example, draws upon research studies published since 1990 in six different fields: economic education, studies on long-term behavior effects of economic education, studies from social studies education, studies from business and vocational education, education studies in domain-specific features of learning, and education studies on expert versus novice differences in cognitive understanding.

Two important conclusions can be drawn from the Watt's (2005) review. First, Watts reports that at both the elementary and secondary levels, students of teachers who know more economics, but also spend more time teaching economics and using appropriate instructional materials, are likely to learn more economics. This conclusion may strike many as mere common sense. Nonetheless, it is reassuring that the research literature is so supportive. Closely related to this point, Watts finds (as did Miller and VanFossen) that the "safest" way to improve student understanding of economics is to take a separate economics course. Even here, however, Watts notes that taking one high school economics course does not ensure long-term knowledge retention and almost certainly does not qualify students as economically or financially literate. Once again, the implication is that economics and personal finance should be taught early and often.

Second, while social studies teachers tend to dominate economic education, Watts notes that secondary teachers in the fields of business and vocational education typically have a better formal preparation in economics coursework than do teachers in other fields, including social studies teachers. This is an important finding that does not get nearly enough attention in the bureaucratic struggles that occur in public education that often involve certification rules. It suggests that high school teachers of economics and personal finance should not be a social studies monopoly. This is particularly important in states where economics is a required course for graduation.

Recent national surveys provide additional understanding of the current status of economics and personal finance in today's curriculum. There is evidence that interest in economic and financial education is expanding across the states. Since 1998, the Council on Economic Education has conducted six surveys regarding the state of economic and personal finance education in the 50 states. In 2007, entrepreneurship was added to the survey.

The most noticeable trend in economic education over the last decade has been the continuation of the strengthening of economics and financial education requirements. The 2009 survey reported that economics is now included, at least to some extent, in the educational standards of *all* states. Forty states (the same as in 2007) require that these standards be implemented. The number of states requiring a formal course in economics to graduate from high school has continued to grow from 17 in 2007 to 21 states. Several of these 21 states, such as California, Florida, New York, and Texas, have large populations. As a result, these states make up nearly 65% of the entire U.S. population. Surprisingly, however, the number of states requiring the testing of student knowledge in economics declined from 23 in 2007 to 19 in 2009.

The importance of personal finance in the curriculum has experienced significantly larger growth over the last decade than economics. Courses in personal finance were included, to some extent, in the educational standards of 21 states in 1998, rising to 44 states in 2009. In 1998, 20 of those states required implementation of the finance course standards, while that number has increased to 34 in 2009. The number of states requiring a formal course in personal finance to graduate rose from 1 in 1998 to 13 in 2009, and the states requiring testing of student knowledge in finance increased from 1 to 9 over the decade.

Perhaps due in part to the deep recession of 2007-2009 and the slow recovery since, entrepreneurship education has been receiving more attention both at the college and precollege levels. Yet, by comparison, it is far less emphasized in the curriculum than economics and personal finance. Nineteen states include entrepreneurship in their K-12 educational standards, and four states require it to be included as part of a high school course, usually economics. Four states require an entrepreneurship course for graduation and five states require testing.

Going Beyond What We May Know

Reframing Financial Literacy: Exploring the Value of Social Currency is a book intended to refocus the current questions most widely addressed in the field such as those discussed in the previous paragraphs. Opening a debate regarding the ethical and democratic foundations of economic and financial education is not for the faint of heart as is illustrated by several of the contributors to *Reframing Financial Literacy: Exploring the Value of Social Currency*. The case is made at several points that the debates related to morality of markets and the implications for members of minority groups and women are fundamental but rarely discussed in the literature. This is most definitely the case.

There is some precedent in pursuing such inquires within the discipline of economics. Economics is a moral discipline founded by Adam Smith, who began and ended his scholarly career as a moral philosopher. Much that is important about economics and the current context of financial education cannot be fully understood or appreciated without considering its moral dimensions.

Many regard Smith's *Wealth of Nations* originally published in 1776 as his most celebrated book. However, Smith also wrote *The Theory of Moral Sentiments* in 1759. It was a work on ethics and human nature and was a sensation at the time. In it, Smith traced the development of conscience as being related to our desire to gain approval and our ability to imagine ourselves in the position of others. Smith argued that people are born with a moral sense, just as they have inborn ideas of beauty or harmony. Our conscience tells us what is right and wrong. We have what Smith calls "sympathy."

> How selfish soever man may be supposed, there are evidently some principles in his nature, which interest him in the fortune of others, and render their happiness necessary to him, though he derives nothing from it except the pleasure of seeing it. Of this kind is pity or compassion, the emotion which we feel for the misery of others, when we either see it, or are made to conceive it in a very lively manner. That we often derive sorrow from the sorrow of others, is a matter of fact too obvious to require any instances to prove it; for this sentiment, like all the other original passions of human nature, is by no means confined to the virtuous and humane, though they perhaps may feel it with the most exquisite sensibility. The greatest ruffian, the most hardened violator of the laws of society, is not altogether without it. (p. 1)

Economic and financial education, however, continues to be haunted by old ghosts. *Reframing Financial Literacy: Exploring the Value of Social Currency* revisits some old ones and identifies several new ones. Its primary contribution lies in arguing that economic and financial education deserve to be considered within broader context of societal concerns. Section I of the book takes this on as its primary challenge. Section II addresses more familiar issues having to do with curriculum, instruction, and teacher preparation but does so primarily within the contexts established by the contributors in Section I. While the authors raise more questions than they answer, the editors offer the field a book that is highly informative regarding issues that are rarely, if ever, addressed in the conventional literature.

REFERENCES

Council on Economic Education. (2009). *Economic, personal finance and entrepreneurship education in our nation's schools, 2009: A report card: Survey of the states.*

Retrieved August 22, 2011, from http://www.councilforeconed.org/about/survey2009/CEE_2009_Survey.pdf

Miller, S. L., & VanFossen, P. J. (2008). Recent research on the teaching and learning of pre-collegiate economics education. In L. Levstik & C. Tyson (Eds.), *Handbook of research in social studies education* (pp. 284-304). New York, NY: Routledge.

The Economist. (2008, April 3). Getting it right on the money: A global crusade is underway to teach personal finance. *The Economist.* Retrieved from http://www.economist.com/node/10958702

Smith, A. (1790). *The theory of moral dentiments*. Library of Economics and Liberty. Retrieved August 22, 2011, from http://www.econlib.org/library/Smith/smMS.html

Smith, A. (1982). *An inquiry into the nature and causes of the wealth of nations*. Indianapolis, IN: Liberty Fund.

Watts, M. (2005). *What works: A review of research on outcomes and effective program delivery in precollege economic education*. New York, NY: National Council on Economic Education. Retrieved August 22, 2011 from http://www.councilforeconed.org/eee/research/WhatWorks.pdf

INTRODUCTION

This section explains the writing of the book, orients the reader to our point of view, and provides a rationale for the project. The development of the introduction considers that the reader is contemplating purchasing or borrowing the text or has just acquired it for use in teaching, learning, or research processes.

Because of the work's interdisciplinary nature, it will appeal to a variety of audiences. The primary readers of this work are perceived as university research faculty from various academic disciplines; however, teachers in grades K-12 may find the lessons useful for employment in their classrooms.

This text could be used by the readers in several ways. First, it could be a university classroom resource that provides information and illustrative activities for learning about financial literacy in a broad sense. Second, it could serve as reference tool for those interested in researching ethical issues related to personal finance and related classroom applications. Third, it could be resource of interest to middle level and high school teachers who teach courses in consumer finance, economics, and psychology. It provides content for presentation in classes, as well as lessons for implementation in classrooms. In other words, the text could be used by K-12 teachers as a lesson planning tool for improving their understanding of lesson content.

This book extends current knowledge in the area of financial literacy or personal finance by exploring the association of financial decision-making with social relationships and personal awareness. Current research into personal finance generally focuses on methods of financial communication, influences on financial behaviors, and financial behaviors among social groups (Xiao, 2008).

Reframing Financial Literacy: Exploring the Value of Social Currency, pp. xv–xix

The work responds to Lucey and Cooter's (2008) call for additional research on sociohistoric moral connections to financial literacy. This collection's importance to teaching and learning lies in the complex nature of financial literacy. Commonly considered to be a process of acquiring and accumulating money for oneself, one's family, or one's business, financial literacy possesses a much more sophisticated essence than conservative views present. Financial literacy is a citizenship issue. This broad conception views financial literacy as intricately associated with justice-oriented citizenship and questions the appropriateness of existent social structures that justify wealth distribution through merit-founded argumentation. This perspectives interprets financial literacy as including the much neglected element of stewardship, which needs stronger social application.

This view of financial literacy's complexity does not call for an abandonment of existing financial literacy education efforts. On the contrary, these educational efforts are critical to educating K-12 students about the financial system and its tenets. What this broader conception *does* encourage is augmentation of the content taught and learned to include holistic financial perspectives that respect the impact of financial decision making on the global community.

This view also invites the readership to question the underlying assumptions of existing financial literacy tenets and the principles that support them. For example, a climate of diminishing natural global resources requires difficult choices about allocation and distribution. To what extent does a greed-driven, profit-maximizing environment provide an appropriate system for distributing these resources? Can communities trust corporations to reinvest their profits, rather than fortifying the exorbitant salaries of directors and CEOs and disbursing residuals to shareholders? How appropriate is a market system that condones the purchase and sale of pollution credits to preserve the profits of corporations that devastate the environment and manipulate domestic and foreign policies? At a personal level, how appropriate is it to work for or conduct business with companies whose policies harm the community, employ unfair labor practices, and/or deter democratic efforts—at home or in other countries?

A unique feature of the book concerns the model lessons or activities that relate to each chapter. These supplements were developed by each chapter author (or student assistants, where indicated) to illustrate the meanings of presented topics, provide suggested methods for the reader/educator to apply with his/her students, and facilitate conversations about these topics and/or methods between the reader/educator and his/her students.

Encouraging discussions about the broader issues in policymaking, public, scholarly, and K-12 settings is apt to prompt some controversy. We view discussion and debate as essential in an educational climate that experiences reductionist curricular policies and standards-oriented convictions. Educating a citizenry that cannot articulate the deep principles of its economic and social environments, and cannot objectively legitimatize their origins does not invite authentic informed dialogue. For example, an argument that depends solely on constitutionality to support claims about a social phenomenon limits its contextuality to principles of United States government, but it ignores the broader context. The argument has no more justification than a teacher who punishes a student for contravening classroom rules without learning the context of the behavior. The argument does not lie within the violation, but within the motives and causes of the violation (many of which may be legitimate).

This book presents literature to support an alternative conception of financial literacy because the rules that frame current conceptions do not invite these conversations. Conversations about financial literacy tend to be framed within a choice-based, profit-driven context. Reframing financial literacy invites open conversations about the contexts that guide choices, the biases and influences of resource control on decision making, and the importance of considering the welfare of underrepresented subgroups when making financial decisions. These dialogues represent necessities for bringing about financially equitable settings that respect all global participants.

The book contains two sections. The first section, "Conceptions of Financial Literacy, Citizenship, and Identity," contains works that provide theory and research that concern definitions of financial literacy and their relationship to conceptions of citizenship, morality, and personal-identity.

In the first chapter, Paul Carr argues that systemic processes shape patterns of individual financial choices. Relating financial literacy to conceptions of democracy and related citizenship issues, he points out the threat of militarization to democratic practice and provides suggestions for education policy and practice.

Benjamin Wellenreiter depicts the curricular disconnect between decision-makers and the ostracized Black communities within South Africa. Wellenreiter describes his first-hand encounters with bleak and unconscionable living conditions that persist in a postapartheid era and points out the inappropriateness of current national economic curricula for students in such settings.

Tom Lucey's chapter differentiates financial morality from financial literacy and classicism. It argues for further efforts to define conceptions of financial morality and to broaden related education efforts.

The following two chapters bring attention to the financial literacy needs of populations that are traditionally underrepresented. Vicky Green's chapter provides an account of financial literacy education in

Canada. She addresses the unique financial needs of women and describes the successes of a women's group that employed peer-support to resist consumerist temptations and develop the financial wellness of its group members.

Andrea Johnson provides information about within-community wealth differences among African Americans. Her findings about family influences on African Americans' financial learning and African Americans' misconceptions of college funding costs provide important information for research into intergenerational influences on financial literacy.

Alan Bates and Tom Lucey's chapter describes college students' conceptions of financial morality. It illustrates the concept's abstractness and the students' difficulties in articulating its meaning.

Jennifer Loew's chapter on decision-making of business managers provides evidence that character education, in and of itself, may not be sufficient for application to business contexts. Rather, preparations are needed to prompt managerial awareness of long-term consequences associated with professional decision making.

Valarie Farnsworth describes research that concerns the importance of financial discourse on the economic advancement of marginalized groups and the importance of opening social discourse about financial practice. Her findings call for education processes that recognize that "financial capability is not simply about being informed and knowledgeable, for it also invokes social and cultural ways of being, thinking, and feeling."

The book's second section, "Education Issues," contains works that explore foundational, curricular, and instructional issues related to financial literacy. This section provides examples and processes for consideration in financial education applications.

Cathy Fagan's description of a values-focused financial curriculum in Scotland provides an exemplar for organizing financial literacy efforts in other settings. The historical accounting of policy formation provides a context to the values emphasis in this curriculum.

Wei Wei Chen and Julie Heath describe a study that demonstrates the benefits of financial literacy efforts aimed at educating teachers and ensuring their "buy-in" with learning processes.

Jeff Sanson and Phillip Van Fossen contribute a discussion of technology's role in educating about financial literacy. They provide a rationale for including digital technology in education processes, describe research that concerns the uses of technology for financial learning, and offer examples of relevant classroom teaching applications.

Mary Frances Agnello and Andrea Knapp offer a chapter that describes the importance of fostering social vision within children as part of financial education efforts. Such vision represents a critical component of developing awareness of and sensitivity towards individuals in diverse financial contexts.

Tom Lucey and Jim Laney provide a chapter that describes a project which used art-based classroom instruction and community research to stimulate preservice teacher candidates' interest in exploring economic-related social justice issues with their future students. They remind the reader of the importance of including all voices in community building and the value of employing art as a tool in that process.

The book concludes with Madalina Tanase's chapter, which concerns the teaching of mathematics in Romanian families. She argues that knowledge of mathematics represents a necessity in developing social power and describes the importance of parental guidance of children's learning towards that end.

The chapters in this volume provide information about financial literacy that necessitates discussion and exploration. Taken as a whole, they provide a basis upon which to conceptualize financial literacy, both in theory and in practice. We encourage the reader's thoughtful reflection about the presented issues and contemplation of their social and educational meanings.

ACKNOWLEDGMENTS

The editors appreciate the efforts of Samantha Skarbek, Emily Gorman, Kristen Mills, and Miranda Flemming in the compilation of the index.

REFERENCES

Lucey, T. A., & Cooter, K. S. (Eds). (2008). *Financial literacy for children and youth*. Athens, GA: Digitaltextbooks.

Xiao, J. J. (Ed.). (2008). *Handbook of consumer finance research*. New York, NY: Springer

SECTION I

CONCEPTIONS OF FINANCIAL LITERACY, CITIZENSHIP, AND IDENTITY

CHAPTER 1

CONNECTING FINANCIAL LITERACY AND POLITICAL LITERACY THROUGH CRITICAL PEDAGOGY[1]

Paul R. Carr

It is sometimes easy and even desirable, to disconnect the local from the global. How could supposedly *developed, industrialized* countries be responsible for the shortcomings in the so-called *underdeveloped* or *developing* world? Thinking too critically about the far-reaching interdependence among actions, life-styles, resources, and (constructed) knowledge in connection to many unsightly, often invisible, forms of oppression, inequity, and exploitation that take place around the world can disrupt comfortable and stable feelings, governments, and societies. Complicity in facilitating underdevelopment, conflict, and instability tells much about methods of education, immersion in challenging political leaders for the truth, and, importantly, global engagement with others.

The connection to the economy and financial literacy is clear: the macro pervades the micro, and decisions about war, trade, and international relations from *above* will most definitely have an impact on the individual *below*, thus influencing how individuals tacitly support the broader macro decisions about sending troops abroad, bailing out banks, providing tax-breaks

Reframing Financial Literacy: Exploring the Value of Social Currency, pp. 3–25

for corporations, enhancing or diminishing funding for health care and education, and so forth.

This chapter raises some of these issues at the macro or global level and connects them to the micro or local level, cognizant that the way of teaching about and for financial literacy cannot and should not avoid a critical perspective of the broader landscape, regardless of how diverse, complex, and nuanced that outside world may be or appear to be. The argumentation occurs through the following four sections, which: (1) introduce critical pedagogy as a means to critique, engage with, and act in relation to oppression, marginalization, and disenfranchisement; (2) frame the discussion of financial literacy and political economy within a debate on and around democracy, which directly shapes understanding of power, social inequality, and economics; (3) critique the role and place of militarization in underpinning and disrupting the local and global economy as well as how individuals understand their connection to their society; and (4) link together the preceding sections to make some concluding comments about the saliency of teaching and learning about/for financial literacy. The objective is to frame some considerations for a thicker, more critical educational experience in which financial literacy can become a meaningful component, aiming to counter the neoliberal values, concepts, and actions infused in much of the current educational reforms (Carr, 2010).

Critical Pedagogy and Financial Literacy

What should formal education address with regard to financial literacy? Should the process develop consumers who are able to judiciously compare products, make judgments about investments, detect investment opportunities, maximize profits, and understand the market? Most people would say that this is certainly part of the equation. However, does learning the proverbial "nuts and bolts" without understanding the linkages between power, inequity, hegemony, and the interdependencies that characterize current economic situations provide for a complete learning? Critical pedagogy can help to address this second question and also place into context the first question. Critical pedagogy can also assist to understand the media, government, the judiciary, and the various power structures, which are neither neutral nor devoid of being hegemonically aligned with specific interests. Significantly, it could be argued that these interests do not always coincide with the desires, aspirations, and lives of a great many people—the masses who toil in support of virtues that rarely shift in their direction.

Critical pedagogy offers a framework to understand political literacy and social transformation, in which static representations of power, identity, and contextual realities are rejected (Darder & Miron, 2006; Denzin, 2009; Giroux, 1997; McLaren, 2005b, 2007; McLaren & Kincheloe, 2007). Critical pedagogy is concerned with oppression and marginalization at all levels and seeks to interrogate, problematize, and critique power and inequitable power relations (Macrine, 2009). Giroux (2007) emphasizes that critical pedagogy

> refuses the official lies of power and the utterly reductive notion of being a method. It opens up a space where students should be able to come to terms with their own power as critical agents; it provides a sphere where the unconditional freedom to question and assert is central to the purpose of the university, if not democracy itself. (p. 1)

Critical pedagogy directly, explicitly, and undeniably links the formalized experience in the classroom and the lived experience outside of the classroom, in which bodies, identities, and societal mores influence what takes place in schools (Giroux & Giroux, 2006). Giroux (2007) boldly states that

> Democracy cannot work if citizens are not autonomous, self-judging, and independent—qualities that are indispensable for students if they are going to make vital judgments and choices about participating in and shaping decisions that affect everyday life, institutional reform, and governmental policy. (p. 2)

Significantly, Denzin (2009) identifies the hubs that support the web of a "critical democratic pedagogy": questioning of environments; using both ethical and pragmatic pedagogies; disrupting of conservative ideals; challenging of materialist assimilation; developing broad conceptions of democratic ideals; and exploring methods of hope. Critical pedagogy can become the cornerstone of democracy in that it provides the "very foundation for students to learn not merely how to be governed, but also how to be capable of governing" (p. 3). Thus, the linkage between a robust, meaningful democracy and critical pedagogy is clearly understood through the lens of transformative learning, engagement, and action.

There is a connection between critical pedagogy and the teaching and learning of economics, business and finance, as well as connected disciplines because the latter serve to ingratiate an unrelenting allegiance to the marketplace. What is the marketplace? Who constructs it? Why, how, and in whose interests? And is it, or rather should it be, the only model that receives attention? Every newscast in the U.S. contains either a ticker-tape, a report, an analysis (loosely interpreted), or an actual reporter, who provides such details as whether the "market" is up or down, how much gold and silver are trading for, who made lots of cash, what some of the trends look like, and so forth.

Do most people understand what this market report is all about, how it affects them, why it is pervading the news, and what the implications of understanding or not understanding it are? Graduate students of education at Youngstown State University have echoed generally that they never really considered it or that they did not care about it being there because it had always been there (Carr, 2009). In other words, current environments constantly direct toward the uncritical validation of the worthiness and superiority of the "market," which leads to a number of hegemonic suggestions that capitalism, neoliberalism, and the freedom of capital to dominate political-economic structures are the only options. Therefore, critical pedagogy offers a framework to cultivate and inculcate political literacy and critical engagement, which speaks to the essence of transformative, emancipatory, antioppression education and which greatly extends, and also contradicts, the premise of educational reforms anchored within a neoliberal mindset (Carr, 2010).

Paulo Freire (1973/2005) is ultimately the leading figure around which a broad range of critical pedagogical scholarship and activism has taken place. He theorized that the conceptualization of education based on traditional modes that enshrine the social order—what he labeled as the "banking model"—can be harmful and destructive for society. Emphasizing the way that power plays out in the "banking model," Freire concluded that

> Whereas banking education anesthetizes and inhibits creative power, problem-posing education involves a constant unveiling of reality. The former attempts to maintain the submersion of consciousness; the latter strives for the emergence of consciousness and critical intervention in reality. (p. 81)

Being conscious, able to read the world, immersed in humane acts, and engaged in a meaningful interrogation of the purpose of teaching and learning should be uppermost in the minds of decision makers as much as the populace in general (Macrine, 2009). Condemning those who would question hegemonic practices as cynical, negative, uncooperative, unconstructive (even destructive), and corrupted can only further widen the gap between those who enjoy comfort and those seeking a more just conceptualization of society. Education, which must underpin democracy for it to be relevant and consequential in favor of the masses, is a political project. It needs to be understood as such to challenge systemically entrenched practices, values, norms, and conventions (Freire, 1973/2005; Kincheloe, 2008a, 2008b). Comprehending the dialectical relations between oppressed and oppressor requires a rethinking of the premise of education, one that properly labels banking models of education.

1. Joe Kincheloe (2008a) puts it quite simply: critical pedagogy is the study of oppression. According to Kincheloe (2007), a critical synthesis of critical pedagogy includes the following components:
2. The development of a social individual imagination.
3. The reconstitution of the individual outside the boundaries of abstract individualism.
4. The understanding of power and the ability to interpret its effects on the society and the individual.
5. The provision of alternatives to the alienation of the individual.
6. The cultivation of a critical consciousness that is aware of the social construction of subjectivity.
7. The construction of democratic community-building relationships between individuals.
8. The reconceptualization of reason-understanding so that relational existence applies not only to human beings but concepts as well.
9. The production of social skills necessary to activate participation in the transformed, inclusive democratic community.

The inextricable linkage to the establishment of a more decent society is ingrained in the foundation of critical pedagogical work. The desire to enhance human agency, imbued in a process of theory and action, thus underscoring praxis and the libratory potential of critical engagement, is (and should be) a central consideration, not an afterthought. Political literacy and media literacy provide a mandatory platform from which education can be explored, cultivated, and transformed (Carr & Lund, 2008; Carr & Porfilio, 2009; Davies & Hogarth, 2004; Kellner & Share, 2007). Critical pedagogy can assist in asking questions that are far from the mainstream political process and the corporate media, but which resonate with the lived realities of the majority of people who do not partake fully in the myriad of societal, institutional, political, economic, and cultural decision-making that serve to shape their lives. As a cautionary note, as illustrated by De Lissovoy (2008), critical pedagogy is not disconnected from other critical theoretical frameworks but must be considered from a "compound standpoint," which enhances its relevancy for the multidisciplinary study of democracy.

In introductory political science classes, students are told of a simple definition of politics: "the art of the possible." Years later, one understands that neither "art" nor "possible" are easily digestible or realizable. Other definitions include "who gets what, when, and how," or "how goals are set and influenced," or, even, "how values are determined." Seeking to achieve a consensus can be, in many cases, tantamount to aiming for mediocrity or might underscore oppressive, exclusionary objectives. Can there be a consensus on war, killing, the death penalty, abortion, gay rights, aboriginal land claims, and so forth? Who participates, and to what degree, may determine the parameters of framing the salience of consensus government.

Critical pedagogy reinforces the reality that politics is messy and needs to be that way. Moreover, critical pedagogy decenters the accepted hegemonic wisdom of the ruling classes and asks questions that encourage introspection, interrogation, empathy, and a critical diagnosis of all people as well as their lived experiences-past, present, and future. Epistemology should be reconceptualized, challenging the White, European, male, Christian, heterosexual, middle-class supremacy that has reigned over Western civilization for centuries (Carr & Lund, 2007; Dei & Kempf, 2006). The construction of knowledge must be considered from multiple vantage points and should avoid the deluge of positivistic measures that have been infused into educational research for decades.

Kincheloe's (2008b) model of interrogating what has traditionally been considered truth and knowledge provides a rich tapestry onto which critical thinking can (and should) take place. How may one understand the vastness, richness, and complexity of the human condition without interrogating power? Are manifestations of youth culture through hip-hop, punk, and various forms of rock music emblematic of the resistance that is lived but not formally documented within the formal, mainstream democratic structures and strictures (for example, the mass media, government, education) (Kahn & Kellner, 2004; Macedo & Steinberg, 2007; Malott & Miranda-Carol, 2003)? Why is a class-based critique, such as those provided by radical scholars and neo-Marxists (Hill, 2003, 2008; McLaren, 2005a, 2005b, 2007, and 2008), generally rejected, ignored, or trivialized in mainstream education circles? Indeed, it would appear that in the United States, the words "socialist," "communist," "liberal," "progressive," "radical," "ideological," and so forth, seem to carry with them such significant baggage, such that the mere mention of them is likely to scuttle any discussion related to change (Macedo & Steinberg, 2007; McChesney, 2008). As Kincheloe (2008a, 2008b) has argued throughout a large body of research and practice, epistemology matters:

> Thus, Knower and known are inseparable dimensions indelibly connected to anything we call knowledge. A critical complex epistemology recognizes that any rigorous knowledge work involves studying the construction of the selfhood of the knower and the impact it has on what any group of people claim to know. (Kincheloe, 2998b, p. 227)

Kincheloe (2008b) poses a pivotal question in relation to the essence of knowledge, research, and power: "How, critical researchers ask, can we remain disinterested and anonymous when concerns, values, experiences, ideology, language, race, class, gender, and sexuality help shape everything we do in a study?" (p. 228).

Ultimately, critical pedagogy seeks to provide, as Freire (2004) argues, hope for a more decent life, being, and society to make life meaningful. Indignation, conscientization, radical love, and enlightenment can lead to the unending dialectical process to achieve various measures of freedom, liberation, and humanity. In sum, critical pedagogy is not about acerbic, cryptic, cynical, negative, aimless criticism; it is primarily concerned with the human condition and the critical engagement, analysis, understanding, and literacy that is a fundamental part of the process aimed to uplift, not downgrade, the constructed knowledge.

As Giroux (2009b) argues, despite the trappings of sophistication and technological innovation, society enters a "new illiteracy in American life", characterized by a "civic deficit" and "civic illiteracy" that can lead to an anti-democratic underpinning to an increasingly disenfranchised society. Thus, the present era can be characterized as one in which democratic illiteracy is rapidly usurping the previous capital and democratic fortitude contained within progressive citizenship values and behaviors that were prominently advanced by John Dewey (1916/1997) and other progressives. Being able to interact with the world—its peoples, cultures, values, differences, decision-making processes, and so forth—is no longer a luxury reserved for elites schooled in private vestiges of the colonial past.

Literacy must move beyond employment-based technical skills and seek to problematize the construction of culture by youth (Giroux, 2005), which can tell us a great deal about power and democracy within society. Youth resistance (Giroux, 1997, 2004) must be understood as a reaction to hegemonic forces and not simply the traditional path that needs to be followed (Casella, 2008). How the positioning towards understand oppositional thinking as well as encouragement of such free thought are critical to the shaping of a democratically literate, engaged, and inclusive society (Cook & Westheimer, 2006; Freire, 1998; Portelli & Solomon, 2001). Whether society teaches about the direct and indirect linkages between political decision making and economic policy should be a concern for teachers and students in elementary and especially secondary schools. From a critical pedagogical vantage-point, one might ask: What standards exist for teaching and learning in relation to financial literacy? Who developed these standards, based on what values, epistemologies, realities and resources? And, importantly, how are students encouraged to question, problematize, and critique the desired learning outcomes? In teaching and learning, is there room to identify an unwavering allegiance to neoliberalism as a problem, or must a tightly structured endorsement of the contemporary economic model represent the only viable option?

Being in the moment requires a reshaping of society that problematizes the prevailing epistemological framework and power structure (Kincheloe, 2008b). Education directly and indirectly affects all citizens (Banks, 2008; Banks et al., 2005). The public good is transparently interlocked to what transpires in and through schools; therefore, Paulo Freire's (1973/2005) notion of *conscientization* should represent a fundamental pillar to achieving a more humane evolution to what is grounded within the grandiose ambitions of theoretical-conceptualizations of democracy.

Is a Little Bit of Honey Better Than a Glass of Vinegar?: Using Force to Extract Gain

A simple Google search generates a myriad of links for the word "democracy." There are a plethora of categories, including: direct democracy; Greek democracy; communism; dictatorship; capitalism; monarchy; socialism; and oligarchy. Democracy is linked to numerous concepts, philosophies, systems, governments, movements, operational systems, and as a label for political parties, processes, and other remnants within popular culture. With regard to particular forms of government, a broad range of possibilities are enumerated, including direct, representative, consensus, constitutional, deliberative, liberal, participatory, republican, and social. Democracy is widely and broadly understood to encompass such things as "majority rule," "government by the people," the "will of the people," and is generally thought to be anchored within a system legitimated by elections.

Historically, vigorous philosophical arguments have opposed democracy. Citing Thomas Hobbes (1588-1679) and public choice theorists, Christiano (2008) presents a central argument against democracy, emphasizing that the common person is not sufficiently equipped to grapple with all of the intricacies and complexities therein, and also that a member of the elite is not simply just another citizen.

An analysis of the flaws with democracy that emanate from the European context provides a number of arguments against the contemporary notion of democracy and suggests that the perception of democracy does not mesh with the reality of what electoral democracy has produced. Numerous aberrations have resulted through the ballot-box. Hitler, among others, after all, was "democratically" elected.

One can see how these pivotal discussions from hundreds of years ago remain germane within the present context, especially given the declining levels of voter participation combined with increasing levels of cynicism related to how elections are conducted (Carr & Porfilio, 2009; Cook, 2004; Patterson, 2003). Truths that were once presumed apparent must now be questioned, and the power of national figures, such as former President George W. Bush, must be reexamined, which should make for a more meaningful democratic experience (Denzin, 2007; Gordon, Smyth, & Diehl, 2008; Kellner, 2002, 2007).

Tinder (2004) presents "perennial questions" that remain unresolved over the centuries, highlighting the link between thinking about human nature and understanding of politics. Political theory, while not readily apparent to many, is grounded in basic beliefs. Tinder points out that most political ideas, perhaps all of them, derive from some particular conception of human nature.

> The conservative idea that political authority should be strong and highly centralized, for example, is based on a conception of human beings as selfish and competitive; the liberal notion that extensive social changes can ordinarily be brought peacefully may arise from the premise that human beings are for the most part reasonable. (pp. 3-4)

Tinder (2004) elaborates an intricate model of critical interrogation of values, beliefs, experiences, and epistemology that requires relinquishing commonly held views and perceptions. Similarly, the critical pedagogy of democracy encourages difficult, problematic, uncomfortable reflection in the hope of achieving higher levels of understanding and engagement.

In a general sense, the traditional framing of democracy focused on rights, freedoms, laws, separation of powers, and systems of government that were intended to be representative (Swift, 2002). Many confounding issues related to minority rights still exist—for example, Who is a minority? How can minority rights mesh with the broader aims and objectives of a just society? What is the balance between majority and minority rights? There is not simply one way of forming and sustaining a democracy. Historical, traditional, cultural, economic, and other factors all shape a society's relationship with democracy. Can a monarchy also be a democracy? How could the Founding Fathers own slaves and prohibit women and minorities from voting while simultaneously decreeing that they were creating a democracy? Was the United States intended to be a democracy in the first place (Chomsky, 2008b)? These questions require an interrogation of the values, instruments, practices, and outcomes of how a given society grapples with democracy before an assessment can be made and before the actual democratic rights and freedoms can be proclaimed (Diamond & Morlino, 2005).

Democracy Watch, a leading Canadian nonprofit, nonpartisan group that advocates democracy and democratic reform, cautions that even if a range of participation and accountability measures are respected, "It is still essentially impossible to stop three key undemocratic activities, and as a result these three activities even if they only occur at infrequently will always remain a threat to all societies aspiring to be democracies."[2]: These three activities include corruption, secret lobbying, and abusive investigative powers.

As is echoed elsewhere in the literature, the three provisos described by Democracy Watch highlight some longstanding and important arguments against, or concerns with, the way that democracy is practiced, as opposed to how it is theorized. The notion of accountability must be unpacked related to who determines what, how, by what criteria, and for what ends. Similarly, Dreher, Kotsogiannis, and McCorriston (2004) examine corruption internationally using an economic model, deducing that the loss to economic productivity is substantially a result of corruption. They emphasize the plurality of causes and indicators framing corruption, including political, historical, sociocultural, and economic factors. Wrage (2007) and Lambsdorff (2007) further flesh out the deleterious nature of corruption in all societies, including those considered the most democratic, which raises important ethical, judicial, political, cultural, and philosophic questions about the relationship between elections and democracy.

Some of the most prevalent types of corruption include influence peddling, bribery, extortion, graft, nepotism, favoritism, government appointments and nominations, insider-trading, and organized activities (such as those related to crime-related gangs and the mafia). The concern over corruption in elections, whether related to the infamous 2000 U.S. presidential election, the recent 2009 Afghani elections, or others in developing countries and elsewhere, renders the actual process of determining issues and leaders to be problematic and even suspicious in some cases. Bradley (2005) provides a critique of the 2004 U.S. presidential election, arguing that voter fraud, combined with the almost nonexistent public reaction to it, needs to be appraised rather than maligned as some sort of a conspiracy theory. Diminishing corruption, similar to enhancing and strengthening democracy, requires a more critically engaged populace—one that is complicit in determining the shape, scope, and direction of the society. Equally, citizens are not passively standing by waiting to endorse candidates through lengthy and costly electoral campaigns.

The question of political participation, raised by the seminal work of Dahl (1972) and further addressed by Chomsky (2008a), is a quintessential piece to the democratic puzzle. How can passive, systemic, nefarious disenfranchisement be tolerated and condoned within a nation proclaiming to be democratic (McLaren, 2005a, 2007)? Clarke, Jenson, LeDuc, and Pammett (1984) wrote of the absent mandate that prevails in the aftermath of elections, postulating that no government ever has a clear mandate due to the confused, dispersed, and divergent ways that citizens vote for or against a candidate/party. For example, some may vote based on issues, personal preferences, and/or party affiliation.

Gandin and Apple (2005), Schugurensky (2003), and others have questioned whether traditional forms of inclusive participation are sufficient to build truly democratic societies, especially when one considers the agenda-setting potential of the mass media (Bagdikian, 2004; McChesney, 1999). In contemporary times, one might question the predominance of polyarchy within the context of President Obama winning the Nobel Peace Prize and then presenting a vigorous defense for the intensification of war in Afghanistan at the award ceremony.

Britt (2004) has assembled an arsenal of interconnected criteria that underscores the shift toward more authoritarian, elite-based, and politically-limiting rule within the U.S. He has concluded that there are visible signs of a sociopolitical decline. The word fascism, commonly associated with the horrors of World War II, is based on 14 specific ideological girders (e.g., Powerful and continuing expressions of nationalism; distain for the importance of human rights; identification of enemies/scapegoats as a unifying cause; a controlled mass media; obsession with national security, power of corporations protected; disdain and suppression of intellectuals and the arts) that buttress a governmental and political framework. Each point in this framework, taken individually, would be highly debatable; however, taken as a whole, this collective depicts an environment where dominant group controls communications and laws to affect an intolerant system of social compliance. As an ensemble of arguments, Britt's analysis raises questions about the salience of the Republican-Democrat polyarchy as well as concerns about the impact of citizen voice, resistance, and engagement. Goodall and Wiener (2008) argue that some of the communications strategies, "such as the suspension of reality, propaganda techniques, and the use of movement opinion to subvert, transform, and replace fact" (p. 135), (a) have been promoted by the Republican party and the conservative movement and (b) exhibit some of the characteristics of totalitarianism (Goodall & Weiner, 2008; Steinberg & Kincheloe, 2009). The blurring of the democratic lines, camouflaged by well-organized and publicized elections that often produce less than hospitable regimes, has commonly been overlooked in mainstream politics and the formal school curriculum. Is the United States sliding into a quasi-fascistic state?

The question raised above would be swatted like a fly by the governing elites but needs to be considered. Should such a diagnosis be undertaken based on lived realities? Related to Britt's formulation of democratic extremism, Kaplan (1997) argued some 15 years ago that "democracies are not value-neutral" and, moreover, that they may not be good for everyone all of the time. For example, "Hitler and Mussolini each came to power through democracy. Democracies do not always make societies more civil, but they do always mercilessly expose the health of the societies in which they operate" (p. 1, para. 5). Kaplan further submits that, in many cases, serious harm, conflict, and even genocide occur as a result of what the West has perceived as democratization, often crudely translated into multiparty elections.

The pivotal underpinning of democracy, concerning a meaningful, critically engaged, vibrant, and socially just education, often appears to be missing from the equation of how societies become democratic. As Martin (2005) puts it, "you can't be neutral on a moving bus." Thus, the potential drifting of a nonparticipatory, thin, polyarchical form of democracy, infused with neoliberalism, could blend into a passive or more aggressive form of fascism if political and democratic literacy and participation levels are considered negligible. If voters participate reluctantly, do not fully believe in the electoral process, are ill informed and disengaged, and are troubled by the integrity of the process, then it may be doubtful how their best interests are actually served. Similarly, if conflicts of interest are not easily identifiable, and there is an air of corporate malfeasance, then the actual system in place to ensure democracy may become a barrier to achieving emancipation, liberty, and transformation. Therefore, Freire's (1973/2005) concept of conscientization is a fundamental component to facilitating *bona fide* democratic participation and ultimately political literacy, which folds into the notion of a thicker, more critically-engaged notion of financial literacy.

War, Democracy, and the Political Economy of Financial Literacy

A pivotal concern in relation to democracy is whether or not it can exist, flourish, and function effectively within a mindset of militarization, framed as the military-industrial complex by senior business, government, and military officials (Chomsky, 2008a, 2008b). With such substantial concern about the cost of healthcare, it is nothing short of bewildering that massive funding can be allocated to militaristic ventures without there being a vigorous, even rancorous debate over the moral, ethical, economic, political, and humanistic objectives of such decisions/priorities. With approximately half of the U.S. budget being directed to militaristic purposes, can there be room for meaningful debate on patriotism, the distribution of wealth, the focus of education, and so forth, when this would conflict with the present power configuration?

Bellamy-Foster, Holleman, and McChesney (2008) peg the annual U.S. military expenditure at one trillion dollars and contextualize the pervasive hegemonic effect of what they call the "military/industrial/media triangle," which serves to further entrench inequities constituting the antithesis of democracy. The gravity and salience of having an economy, a political structure, and a societal framework that present and justify the "goodness" and necessity of such an expansive and powerful military presence should find a place within the core of any concept of financial literacy.

It is difficult to calculate the exact number of U.S. bases abroad, as there appears to be an inherent interest in not disseminating a realistic or truthful portrait of the extent of American empire. Chalmers Johnson (2004), who was one of the most knowledgeable scholars of U.S. military development, estimates the number to be somewhere around 750, but Vine and Schwartz Greco (2009) argue that the actual number is extremely difficult to pinpoint.

Johnson (2007) invokes historical comparisons that raise questions about the rationale for such disproportionate military aggrandizement, pointing out that the Roman Empire in 117 A.D. and the British Empire in 1898, when they were both at the height of their imperial power, had similar levels of power worldwide as that exhibited by the U.S. in contemporary times. What is the cost of such grandiose militarization? Vine and Schwartz Greco (2009) have identified many of the intangible, human costs and the related consequences connected to using the military to engage the world, which collectively impose an immense burden on the American people.

Conclusion: Linking Critical Pedagogy, Democracy, Militarization, and Financial Literacy

Democracy takes many shapes and forms and must be continually debated (Held, 2006). The Western world, in large part based on neoliberal conceptions of progress and development, would probably concur with Fukuyama's (1992) conceptualization of his widely cited work *The End of History and the Last Man*. His central hypothesis is that liberal democracy is the most suitable model to advance social and political development. The triumph of liberal democracies over rival political forms confirms that liberal democracy is the form of government which most closely reflects certain timeless and universal human aspirations. Liberal democracy also seems to be the political form which most closely coincides with certain aspects of human nature and certain ideals which have been recurring themes throughout Western political thought. In particular, the origins of the twin ideals of liberty and equality can be traced along a path of intellectual development which extends from ancient Greece through the American Revolution. As the form of government in which these ideals achieve their fullest expression, liberal democracy stands as a monument to Western political thought and to the humanist intellectual tradition.

In postmodern and critical theory, for whom is liberal democracy most suitable? Who benefits? Who determines its meaning? And how does society understand the experiences of those in the opposition or those who have been marginalized by the application of such theoretical models? To this end, Khan (2001) argues that the notion of liberal democracy is Western-based and that what is required is the development of universal democracy and values, which can allow for different conceptualizations and an acceptance of non-Western traditions. Universal values are not abstract philosophical notions without any practical utility. They are the tools and necessities of ordinary life that the state must protect. For example, the right to life, liberty, and security of person is a universal value that no state should arbitrarily revoke or suspend. Likewise, prohibitions against slavery, torture, arbitrary arrest, and exile are universal values that no state can regard with impunity. In more recent years, electoral democracy has emerged as a universal value as the peoples of the world aspire to make their governments accountable and removable.

Through an emphasis on the study of oppression infused in the critical pedagogical approach/perspective/framework, this chapter has sought to expose how conceptualization of and engagement with democracy is grounded in the way society approaches and understands the economy (Carr, 2010). It has sought to illustrate how the broader macrocontext is inextricably linked to international ambitions/actions/encounters, especially in relation to the military. When considering how to teach for and about financial literacy, it is important to ask: What can be done to critically understand social inequalities in society, especially given the precept of hegemonic, normative concepts of democracy and the ever-looming but much underexamined reality of burgeoning militarization affecting all levels of society? Is there a risk in further limiting and marginalizing this discussion, and, if so, who would be most affected?

Would teaching a thicker, more critical, and robust form of financial literacy assist students in seeking a form of liberation and emancipation? It may, but many other factors, premises, and conditions would have to be considered, including the following items:

1. Producing a curriculum that allows for critical inquiry, engagement, and different forms of evaluation that challenge neoliberalism, militarization, and social inequality;
2. Providing training, support, and professional development for teachers to be able to comfortably and effectively teach about and for critical forms of financial literacy;

3. Amending regulations, policies and institutional cultural practices that inhibit critical engagement in schools, including the limited notion of accountability, the overreliance on standardized tests, and other market-based reforms that have consistently pushed minority and other students to the margins;
4. Enhancing community participation in schools so as to be able to illustrate divergent forms of economic development and reality outside of Wall Street and government-based economic policy;
5. Linking financial literacy and economics more directly to other disciplines and areas of study;
6. Revamping the notion of the educational leadership to focus more directly on social justice, equity, and critical engagement as opposed to what is considered "high academic achievement," which has relegated the former concepts to the proverbial back-burner;
7. Recommitting to a more holistic, dynamic, interdisciplinary, engaged, and critical form of education as opposed to elitist interpretations of education that greatly disadvantage poorer, working-class students, families, and communities.

How is the global tethered to the local? Does society engage in critical, alternative, radical, comparative analysis of the economy? Does society question how power works within an economy? Ultimately, this discourse concerns multiple literacies in the broadest sense, including reading and writing literacy, Freire's (1973/2005) "reading the world" or *conscientization* literacy, political literacy, media literacy, and, financial literacy. Following the arguments in this chapter, it would be very difficult to disconnect these disparate and interdisciplinary forms of literacy.

DISCUSSION QUESTIONS

1. How important is financial literacy for one to be able to effectively participate in democracy?
2. In light of the arguments raised in this chapter, what are some of the advantages and concerns that relate to democracy?
3. Given the macro context outlined in this chapter in relation to militarization and hegemony abroad, how can educators best teach about financial literacy?
4. What are some of the concerns with voting/electoral systems within democracy, and how do they relate to financial literacy?

5. How could teaching critical pedagogy assist in helping to shape a more robust, critical, and meaningful form of democracy?

MODEL LESSON

The Different Types of Democracy[3]

Suggested Grade Level: 5th Grade

Objectives:

(a) Given the opportunity to experience different type of democracies, the learner will write a paragraph about the benefits of each and decide which one s/he would prefer and why.
(b) Given the background information of the different types of democracy, the learner will speak critically about each during the class discussions.

Related Standards:

Jump$tart National Standards in K–12 Personal Finance Education

Financial Responsibility and Decision Making

Standard 4: Make financial decisions by systematically considering alternatives and consequences.

Standard 5: Develop communication strategies for discussing financial issues.

Materials:

- Paper
- Pens/Pencils
- White board

Procedures:

(a) Opening Activities

1. Greet the class and introduce the lesson, by asking the students what they know about democracies. Also inquire about what may they know about the different types. (Direct Democracy-when all the citizens who wish to be involved take part in electing officials.

Representative Democracy- when a representative is selected by the people to represent their views. Liberal Democracy—when all the citizens who wish to be involved vote for the leader of the country.)

2. Once the students have begun talking about democracy, explain they vote on something meaningful to them by using the different types of democracy. (The item for which the class will be voting will vary from class to class depending on the students' likes and wants. The item doesn't have to be something the students will actually receive, but the activity may work better if it is a real life experience.) For example, the students may vote on the combinations of items that they think should be available for lunch in the cafeteria.
3. The students begin the activity by casting individual votes on pieces of paper. This process represents one of the types of democracy (Direct Democracy).
4. The ballots are collected but not tallied until the end.
5. The students are divided up by the teacher into groups of 5 or6, depending on class size.
6. The students in each group select one person in their group who they think will best represent their votes. After each group picks its "representative," the selected person listens to the group's wants and casts a vote on behalf of them all (Representative Democracy).
7. For the final activity, each chosen "representative" comes to the front of the class and tells the class what s/he believes the best idea is. The whole class then votes for one of these "representatives"—the one they think best represents their individual views (Liberal/Constitutional Democracy).

(b) Developmental Activities

1. When the class completes the three different types of voting, the teacher writes the results from each voting activity on the board.
2. The teacher asks the students which option they think best represents the wants of the class
3. The teacher initiates a discussion of how each type of democracy that they experienced is a reflection of the democracies in the United States and other countries. (Examples: Direct-Switzerland and the U.S. Representative: Australia, Canada, and United Kingdom. Liberal: U.K., Canada, Japan, Spain, United States, Germany, India, and Brazil.)

4. After the students have found real life examples of the three different types of democracy, the teacher begins asking guided discussion questions, such as the following examples.

    - How does the dictionary define each type of democracy?
    - How would you describe the three kinds of democracy? How would you describe the communication strategies used within each type of democracy?
    - What examples of the three different types of democracy occur in different settings—home, school, workplace, club/organization, community, and so forth?
    - What are some voting and communication strategies that could help improve decision-making in these settings? Students may role play hypothetical financial decision-making situations in these settings.
    - What similarities and differences exist among the three types of democracy? Create a Venn diagram to summarize your thoughts.
    - What would a new system look like that contained the various types of democratic functions?
    - Based on the information gathered in the activities, which of the different types of democracy is most efficient?

(c) Closing Activities

1. After hearing the different ideas discussed in the activities, teacher will debrief the students about the processes that they experienced and the choices made. The teacher should keep in mind all the outcomes of the voting using the different types of democracy. Also s/he should talk about which idea would be the most beneficial and the most responsible.

(d) Summary and Assessment

1. After the lesson activities, the learner writes about the costs and benefits of each democracy type and which one s/he would prefer and why.
2. The assessment measures performance two areas. The first relates to the nature of students' thinking during the guided discussions. The teacher keeps a list of tallies/checkmarks during the discussions as to who participated in a critical way. The learner is also assessed by based on his/her short paragraph about the costs and benefits of each type of democracy and which s/he would prefer

and why. The paragraph is scored on a 5-point scale. A 5 means that he student demonstrated critical thinking skills in the answer and fully answered the questions; a 3 means that the student fully answered the questions but displayed little critical ability (or vice versa); and a 1 means that the student did not completely answer the question nor did s/he use critical thinking skills.

NOTES

1. Parts of this chapter are based on ideas from my book, *Does Your Vote Count?: Critical Pedagogy and Democracy* (Peter Lang, 2010).
2. See Democracy Watch at http://www.dwatch.ca/ .
3. Lesson developed by Kelsey Kaatz

REFERENCES

Bagdikian, B. H. (2004). *The new media monopoly.* Boston, MA: Beacon Press.

Banks, J. A. (2008). *An introduction to multicultural education.* Boston, MA: Allyn & Bacon.

Banks, J., McGee Banks, C. A., Cortés, C. E., Hahn, C. L., Merryfield, M. M., Moodley, K. A., et al. (2005). *Democracy and diversity: Principles and concepts for educating citizens in a global age.* Seattle, WA: Center for Multicultural Education.

Bellamy Foster, J., Holleman, H., & McChesney, R. (2008). The U.S. imperial triangle and military spending, *Monthly Review, 60*(5), 1-19.

Bradley, R. (2005). Paranoia, conspiracy theories, and the presidential election of 2004. *Cultural Studies-Critical Methodologies, 5*(3), 338-345.

Britt, L. (2004). *Fourteen characteristics of Fascism.* Retrieved from http://educate-yourself.org/cn/fourteencharacteristicsfascism02nov04.shtml

Carr, P. (2010). *Does your vote count? Critical pedagogy and democracy.* New York, NY: Peter Lang.

Carr, P. R. (2009). Political conscientization and media (il)literacy: Critiquing the mainstream media as a form of democratic engagement. *Multicultural Education, 17*(1), 1-10.

Carr, P., & Lund, D. (Eds). (2007). *The great white north? Exploring whiteness, privilege and identity in education.* Rotterdam, The Netherlands: Sense.

Carr, P., & Lund, D. (2008). Antiracist education. In E. Provenzo (Ed.), *SAGE Encyclopedia of Cultural and social foundations of education* (pp.48–52). Thousand Oaks, CA: SAGE.

Carr, P. R., & Porfilio, B. J. (2009). Computers, the media and multicultural education: Seeking engagement and political literacy. *Journal of Intercultural Studies, 20*(2), 91–107.

Casella, R. (2008). Security, pedagogy, and the free-market approach to "troubled youth." In B. Porfilio, & C. Malott (Eds.), *An international examination of urban education: The destructive path of neo-liberalism* (pp. 63–79). Rotterdam, The Netherlands: Sense.

Chomsky, N. (2008a). The election, economy, war and peace. Retrieved from http://www.zcommunications.org/the-election-economy-war-and-peace-by-noam-chomsky.

Chomsky, N. (2008b). *The essential Chomsky* (Anthony Arnove, Editor). New York, NY: The New Press

Christiano, T. (2008). Democracy. In E. N. Zalta (Ed.), *The Stanford Encyclopedia of Philosophy (Fall 2008 Edition)*. Retrieved from http://plato.stanford.edu/archives/fall2008/entries/democracy/

Clarke, H., Jenson, J., LeDuc, L., & Pammett, J. H. (1984). *Absent mandate: The politics of discontent in Canada*. Toronto: Gage.

Cook, S. A. (2004, September). Learning to be a full Canadian citizen: Youth, elections and ignorance. *Canadian Issues Magazine*, 1-6.

Cook, S., & Westheimer, J. (2006). Introduction: Democracy and education. *Canadian Journal of Education*, *29*(2), 347–358.

Dahl, R. A. (1972). *Polyarchy: Participation and opposition*. New Haven, CT: Yale University Press.

Darder, A., & Miron, L. F. (2006). Critical pedagogy in a time of uncertainty: A call to action. *Cultural Studies—Critical Methodologies*, *6*(1), 5-20.

Davies, I., & Hogarth, S. (2004). Political literacy: Issues for teachers and learners. In J. Demaine (Ed.), *Citizenship and political education today* (pp. 181-199). Hampshire, England: Palgrave Macmillan.

Dei, G. J. S., & Kempf, A. (2006). *Anti-colonialism and education: The politics of resistance*. Rotterdam, The Netherlands: Sense.

De Lissovoy, N. (2008). Conceptualizing oppression in educational theory: Toward a compound standpoint. *Cultural Studies—Critical Methodologies*, *8*(1), 82-105.

Denzin, N. K. (2007). *Flags in the window: Dispatches from the American war zone*. New York, NY: Peter Lang.

Denzin, N. K. (2009). Critical pedagogy and democratic life or a radical democratic pedagogy. *Cultural Studies—Critical Methodologies*, *9*(3), 379-397.

Dewey, J. (1997). *Democracy and education: An introduction to the philosophy of education*. New York: Free Press. (Original work published 1997)

Diamond, L., & Morlino, L. (2005). *Assessing the quality of democracy*. Baltimore, MD: Johns Hopkins University Press.

Dreher, A., Kotsogiannis, C., & McCorriston, S. (2004). Corruption around the world: Evidence from a structural model. Retrieved from http://129.3.20.41/eps/pe/papers/0406/0406004.pdf

Freire, P. (1998). *Pedagogy of freedom: Ethics, democracy, and civic courage*. Lanham, MD: Rowman & Littlefield.

Freire, P. (2004). *Pedagogy of indignation*. Boulder, CO: Paradigm.

Freire, P. (2005). *Pedagogy of the oppressed*. New York, NY: Continuum. (Original work published 1973)

Fukuyama, F. (1992). *The end of history and the last man*. New York, NY: Free Press.

Gandin, L. A., & Apple, M. (2005). Thin versus thick democracy in education: Porto Alegre and the creation of alternatives to neo-liberalism. *International Studies in Sociology of Education*, *12*(2), 99-116.

Giroux, H. (1997). *Pedagogy and the politics of hope: Theory, culture and schooling.* Boulder, CO: Westview Press

Giroux, H. (2004). Class casualties: Disappearing youth in the age of George W. Bush. *Workplace: A Journal of Academic Labor, 6*(1).

Giroux, H. (2005). Kids for sale: Corporate culture and the challenge of public schooling. In S. Shapiro & D. Purpel (Eds.), *Critical social issues in American education: Democracy and meaning in a globalizing world* (pp. 143-162). Mahwah, NJ: Lawrence Erlbaum Associates.

Giroux, H. (2007). Democracy, education, and the politics of critical pedagogy. In P. McLaren, & J. Kincheloe, (Eds.), *Critical pedagogy: Where are we now?* (pp. 1-5). New York, NY: Peter Lang.

Giroux, H. (2009). The spectacle of illiteracy and the crisis of democracy, truthout (September 15). Retrieved from http://www.progressivevalues.org/article_detail.cfm?articleID=405

Giroux, H., & Giroux, S. S. (2006). Challenging neo-liberalism's new world order: The promise of critical pedagogy. *Cultural Studies—Critical Methodologies, 6*(1), 21-32.

Goodall, H. L., & Wiener, S. (2008). Creating the right reality: Communication message strategies and the Republican party. *Cultural Studies—Critical Methodologies, 8*(2), 135-158.

Gordon, S. P., Smyth, J., & Diehl, J. (2008). The Iraq War, "Sound Science," and "Evidence-Based" educational reform: How the Bush administration uses deception, manipulation, and subterfuge to advance its chosen ideology. *Journal for Critical Education Policy Studies, 6*(2), 173-204. Retrieve from http://www.jceps.com/PDFs/6-2-10.pdf

Held, D. (2006). *Models of democracy.* Palo Alto, CA: Stanford University Press.

Hill, D. (2003). Global neo-liberalism, the deformation of education and resistance, *Journal for Critical Education Policy Studies, 1*(1). Retrieved from www.jceps.com/?pageID=article&articleID=7

Hill, D. (2008). Resisting neo-liberal global capitalism and its depredations: Education for a new democracy. In D. Lund & P. Carr (Eds.), *Doing democracy: Striving for political literacy and social justice* (pp. 33-49). New York, NY: Peter Lang.

Johnson, C. (2004). The Arithmetic of America's military bases abroad: What does it all add up to? HNN *(History News Network).* Retrieved from http://hnn.us/articles/3097.html

Johnson, C. (2007). 737 U.S. Military Bases = Global Empire. *alternet.* http://www.alternet.org/story/47998. (Excerpt from the book *Nemesis: The last days of the American republic,* Metropolitan Books)

Kahn, R., & Kellner, D. (2004). *Global youth culture.* Retrieved from http://gseis.ucla.edu/faculty/kellner/essays/globyouthcult.pdf

Kaplan, R. (1997). Was democracy just a moment? *The Atlantic. 280*(6), Retrieved from http://www.theatlantic.com/magazine/archive/1997/12/was-democracy-just-a-moment/6022/

Kellner, D. (2002). "The axis of evil," Operation infinite war, and Bush's attacks on democracy. *Cultural Studies—Critical Methodologies, 2*(3), 343-347.

Kellner, D. (2007). Lying in politics: The case of George W. Bush and Iraq. *Cultural Studies –Critical Methodologies*, *7*(2), 132-144.

Kellner, D., & Share, J. (2007). Critical media literacy, democracy, and the reconstruction of education. In D. Macedo & S. Steinberg, (Eds.), *Media literacy: A reader.* (pp. 3-23). New York, NY: Peter Lang.

Khan, A. L. (2001). *A theory of universal democracy: Beyond the end of history.* The Hague, Netherlands: Kluwer Law International.

Kincheloe, J. (2005a). Kids for sale: Corporate culture and the challenge of public schooling. In S. Shapiro & D. Purpel (Eds.), *Critical social issues in American education: Democracy and meaning in a globalizing world* (pp. 143-162). Mahwah, NJ: Lawrence Erlbaum.

Kincheloe, J. (2005b). The passion of the right: Religious fundamentalism and the crisis of democracy. *Cultural Studies—Critical Methodologies*, *5*(3), 309-317.

Kincheloe, J. L. (2007). Critical pedagogy in the twenty-first century. In P. McLaren & J. Kincheloe (Eds.), *Critical pedagogy: Where are we now?* (pp. 9-42). New York, NY: Peter Lang.

Kincheloe, J. L. (2008a). *Critical pedagogy: Primer.* New York, NY: Peter Lang.

Kincheloe, J. L. (2008b). *Knowledge and critical pedagogy: An introduction*. London: Springer.

Lambsdorff, J. G. (2007). *The Institutional economics of corruption and reform: Theory, evidence and policy.* New York, NY: Cambridge University Press.

Macedo, D., & Steinberg, S. (2007). *Media literacy: A reader.* New York, NY: Peter Lang.

Macrine, S. (Ed.). (2009). *Critical pedagogy in uncertain times: Hopes and possibilities.* New York, NY: Palgrave MacMillan.

Malott, C., & Miranda-Carol, J. (2003). Punkore scenes as revolutionary Street pedagogy. *Journal for Critical Education Policy Studies, 3*(1). Retrieved from www.jceps.com/?pageID=article&articleID=45

Martin, G. (2005). You can't be neutral on a moving bus: Critical pedagogy as community praxis. *Journal for Critical Education Policy Studies, 3*(2), Retrieved http://www.jceps.com/index.php?pageID=article&articleID=47

McChesney, R. (1999). *Rich media, poor democracy: Communication politics in dubious time*. New York, NY: Free Press.

McChesney, R. (2008). *The political economy of media: Enduring issues, emerging dilemmas*. New York, NY: Monthly Review.

McLaren, P. (2008). Capitalism's bestiary: Rebuilding urban education. In B. Porfilio & C Malott (Eds.) *The destructive path of neo-liberalism: An international examination of urban education* (pp. vii–xv). Rotterdam, The Netherlands: Sense.

McLaren, P. (2005a). *Capitalists and conquerors: A critical pedagogy against empire.* New York, :NY: Rowman and Littlefield.

McLaren, P. (2005b). Critical Pedagogy reloaded: Dispatches from Las Entranas de La Bestia. *Cultural Studies—Critical Methodologies*, *5*(3), 318-337.

McLaren, P. (2007) *Life in schools: An introduction to critical pedagogy in the foundations of education*. Boston, MA: Pearson Education.

McLaren, P., & Kincheloe J. L. (Eds.). (2007). *Critical pedagogy: Where are we now?* New York, NY: Peter Lang.

Patterson, T. (2003). *The vanishing voter: Public involvement in an age of uncertainty.* New York, NY: Vintage Books.

Portelli, J., & Solomon, P. (Eds.) (2001). *The erosion of democracy in education: From critique to possibilities.* Calgary, Canada: Detselig Enterprises

Schugurensky, D. (2003). Civic participation—on active citizenship, social capital and public policy. *Canadian Diversity, 2*(1), 10-12.

Steinberg, S., & Kincheloe, J. (eds). (2009). *Christotainment: Selling Jesus through popular culture.* Boulder, CO: Westview Press

Swift, R. (2002). *The nonsense guide to democracy.* Toronto: New International.

Tinder, G. (2004). *Political thinking: The perennial questions*. New York, NY: Pearson Longman.

Vine, D., & Schwartz Greco, E. (2009). Too many overseas bases. *Foreign Policy in Focus.* Retrieved from http://www.fpif.org/articles/too_many_overseas_bases

Wrage, A. (2007). *Bribery and extortion: Undermining business, governments, and security.* New York, NY: Praeger Security International.

CHAPTER 2

GARBAGE TRUCKS AND DEPOSIT SLIPS

The Disconnect Between Life Experiences and the Economics Curriculum of South Africa

Benjamin R. Wellenreiter

Located on the high plains in the center of Free State, South Africa is the community of Botshabelo. Described as an "apartheid dumping grounds" (Hoogendoorn et al., 2008 p. 166), Botshabelo represents both a scar of the apartheid government of South Africa and a promise for improving economic conditions for Black South Africans. "One of apartheid's most controversial creations" (Tomlinson & Kriege, 1997, p. 691), Botshabelo was devised by the apartheid government of South Africa in 1979 as, "a home for 'surplus' black

Reframing Financial Literacy: Exploring the Value of Social Currency, pp. 27–45

people resident in the 'white South Africa' " (p. 692). Second in population size only to the township of Soweto, Botshabelo serves as a South African variant of the Native American reservation system applied in the United States, and it is described as one of the best examples of the apartheid system in application (Krieg, 1991). Though the formality of the apartheid laws are nearly two decades past, infrastructure deficits with which Botshabelo's citizens live pose significant barriers to political, economic, and financial justice. The postapartheid government has made many strides toward political and economic justice, but much work remains if South Africa is to erase the effects of the mandated economic and financial injustices of the past. Though postapartheid changes to curriculum policy address racial, economic, and financial issues, it is argued that many of these changes do not take into account practical constraints such as lack of teachers and classroom resources (Cross, Mungadi, & Rouhani, 2002). Without coordination between curriculum policymakers and infrastructure policymakers to provide for economically inclusive environments, the gap between what is learned in schools and what is experienced in communities will remain.

Nested within the struggle for political, economic, and financial justice is a need for opportunities to tie together economic and financial literacy concepts with the everyday experiences of underserved South African learners. Providing South Africa's underserved learners with educational experiences that arm them with the tools to better their personal lives and their country is essential in the effort to undo the injustices of apartheid.

Communities in which learners cannot apply concepts learned in the classroom may undermine the idea that economics and financial literacy principles can be applied beyond the school setting. Without access to economic and financial opportunity in their communities, learners may be encouraged by their environment to leave concepts in the classroom. Viewed more broadly, environments in which learners cannot easily tie concepts covered in classrooms to their daily lives may encourage learners to view their school experiences and life experiences dichotomously. An end result may be an environment in which learners in underserved communities receive the message that many economic and financial literacy concepts experienced in schools are to be seen, but not applied, in their lives beyond their formal education.

This chapter explores community infrastructure deficits with which many South African learners live and contrasts these learners' community experiences with the economic and financial literacy curriculum of South Africa. Though this curriculum is designed to provide learners with skills necessary to achieve financial self-sufficiency, many of its goals are difficult to attain because of infrastructure deficits faced in learners' communities.

Using the infrastructure deficits faced by residents of Botshabelo as an example of living conditions for many South African learners outside of school, one can see that many assessment standards of the Economics and Management Sciences (EMS) curriculum of South Africa cannot be well connected to the lives of many learners outside of school. Though the EMS curriculum stresses application of concepts outside of school, underserved learners cannot practice their skills because they have no reasonable access to economic opportunity. Additionally, it can be argued that South African government agencies and private financial institutions need to more strongly dedicate their resources to infrastructure development in these underserved communities. If economics and financial literacy concepts are to be effectively applied outside of school, infrastructure deficits within many of South Africa's communities must be better addressed. Only when the daily lives of South Africa's citizens are improved, can economic and financial justice be realized.

Botshabelo

The landscape along the 33 mile drive from the Free State capital of Bloemfontein to Botshabelo provides little variation for the eye to see. Situated in a high, treeless plain, the local municipality of Mangaung, South Africa, which contains Bloemfontein, Botshabelo, and about a dozen other communities, consists mainly of ranches and mines. Botshabelo seems to appear gradually on this plain. Described as "hidden urbanites" (Mokoena & Marais, 2007, p. 317), Botshabelo and neighboring Thaba Nchu are granted few signs along the main road to indicate their existence. It is only when the scattering of one room tin shacks becomes greater in density that visitors start to recognize they have entered Botshabelo.

Because of the informality of economic development in Botshabelo, precise statistics on population and economic activities are difficult to ascertain. Population estimates of this community range from 195,000 (Tomlinson & Krige, 1997) to 300,000 (Jagals & Griesel, 2003). Estimates of the population of the Mangaung Local Municipality, in which Botshabelo and Bloemfontein are located, place the number of citizens between approximately 645,000 (Naidoo, 2003) and 753,000 (Statistics South Africa, 2007). (See Figure 2.1).

Though population estimates vary, it is clear that Botshabelo lags far behind in economic contribution to the Mangaung Local Municipality, relative to its size. Botshabelo comprises approximately one third of the population of this area, but Naidoo (2003) estimates that it contributes only 7.1% to the overall Gross Geographic Product to the municipality.

Figure 2.1. Nineteen point four percent (19.4%) of homes in Mangaung Local Municipality are described as; "informal dwellings" (Statistics South Africa, 2007, p. 64).

Bloemfontein, with a population only slightly larger than Botshabelo, contributes 87% (Naidoo, 2003).

Under apartheid law, Black South Africans were forced to live in designated areas, such as Botshabelo, and make long commutes to jobs in "White" areas such as Bloemfontein (Seekings, 2000). Placed out of sight from white areas onto lands with little intrinsic economic value, many black South Africans have to use considerable percentages of their incomes and time to get to their places of employment (Behrens & Wilkinson, 2003). Though it is possible to reach economic centers, Seekings (2000) describes the reality for many Black South African communities and their relationship to formal economic opportunity: "Some of these sprawling slum settlements were within commuting distance of cities in 'white' South Africa, albeit at distances which entailed journeys of several hours' duration each way" (p. 832).

As a result of the apartheid government's purposeful focus on economic activity and infrastructure in the White areas, townships like Botshabelo suffered from decades of neglect. The lack of organized community services that persist, such as waste water management systems, solid waste management, and generally poor living conditions, provide evidence of this abandonment. Additionally, because the vast majority of economic activity takes place away from Botshabelo, private-sector financial institutions are reluctant to expand into communities like Botshabelo (Okeahalam, 2007). The absence of basic financial services contributes to the lack of political, economic, and financial prospects for many South African citizens. Deep economic development in communities like Botshabelo is not a top priority for government officials who focus on quantity of services rather than quality of services (Fourie, 2008). Marais (2003) describes the government approach to economic development in these areas seen as lacking economic promise:

> In localities with low development potential, government spending should focus on providing social transfers, human resource development and labour market intelligence. This will enable people to migrate, if they so choose, to localities that are more likely to provide sustainable employment or other economic opportunities. (p. 3)

A policy that focuses on improving human resource development and market intelligence may improve the knowledge and skill base of citizens in underserved communities. Unfortunately, without corresponding policies that address infrastructure deficits of these communities, citizens will likely continue to struggle to meet basic needs. The result is a situation in which citizens may have labor market intelligence, but no means to access the labor market in a meaningful way.

Both government and private investment in underdeveloped communities, such as Botshabelo, are overshadowed by investment in communities that have more developed infrastructures, such as Bloemfontein. As a result, Botshabelo and similar communities suffer from both infrastructure and private-sector financial institutions maintaining their focus on traditionally advantaged areas. Marais (2003) argues that large-scale investment in communities such as Botshabelo may reinforce apartheid spatial patterns because investment in areas with little economic promise may result in sunk costs for individuals living in these communities, if these individuals wish to sell their property and move. Lack of economic and financial development, however, may also reinforce apartheid spatial patterns because individuals who live in these communities often spend significant amounts of time and capital acquiring basic needs and opportunities that might be more easily available with improved infrastructures and more formalized local economies.

While attempting to foster large-scale economic opportunity in locations lacking economic promise risks creating false or temporary advantages, it is important to provide citizens of these communities with adequate infrastructure so they might improve their economic status.

Even minimal infrastructure improvements can form the basis for more economic opportunity.

It is reported that 13.6% of Botshabelo's households have no income, while 42.5% earn less than $850 a month (Naidoo, 2003). The number of indigent households in Botshabelo is estimated to be 46% (Naidoo, 2003). With the driving distance to the economic center in Bloemfontein, compiled with the lack of formal financial institutions and deficits in infrastructure in their immediate community, the learners of Botshabelo have little opportunity to see formal economics in action. Much of the formal economic activity in which citizens of Botshabelo participate takes place in Bloemfontein, away from the eyes and everyday experiences of learners who attend local schools.

Beyond formal economic activities, living conditions of many of Botshabelo's learners outside of school are ramshackle. In summarizing the state of the informal communities of South Africa and the cities they surround, Huchzermeyer (2009) states:

> South African cities are hugely inadequate—shaped by discriminatory and repressive apartheid planning and further expanded by powerful and far from equitable market processes, driving apartheid's planned inequality and exclusion even deeper and effortlessly overriding attempts at urban democratization and integration. (p. 60)

Of most immediate concern to residents of Botshabelo are substandard housing units, lack of easy access to potable water, sewage treatment deficits, solid waste removal deficits, and air pollution (Jagals & Griesel, 2003; Naidoo, 2003; Parnell, 2004). "Informal dwellings," defined as shack or squatter settlements, comprise 19.4% of the homes in Mangaung Local Municipality, compared to the national average of 14.4% (Statistics South Africa, 2007, p 64). Roughly 1 in 5 citizens of this local municipality live in shacks.

Within these inadequate homes, citizens struggle to meet basic needs. Water sanitation in many of these neighborhoods consists of pit latrines or bucket systems (Jagals & Griesel, 2003). In the Free State, in which Mangaung Local Municipality is located, use of pit latrines comprises 22% of home sewage facilities, while 12.7% use a bucket system (Statistics South Africa, 2007). Some 3.2%of homes in Free State have no toilet facilities (Statistics South Africa, 2007). It was found that 23.5% of water samples taken from buckets used for drinking water contained fecal coliforms (September, Els, Venter, & Brözel, 2007). Though it is clear that improvements in water availability and treatment are needed, city-level reforms concerning environmental issues, such as waste water management, solid waste sanitation, air pollution, and land-use, are not being implemented systematically (Parnell, 2004).

Infrastructure deficits are not limited to Botshabelo. Disposal of solid refuse, for example, is a concern for many residents of South Africa. Though Free State exceeds the national average in terms of solid refuse removal at 80.0% (compared to the national average of 61.6%), neighboring states, such as KwaZulu-Natal, have refuse removal rates as low as 11.8% (Statistics South Africa, 2007).

Even in a state where refuse collection is above the national average, Botshabelo still has concerns with the dumping of dead animals in public areas, general surface pollution such as plastic bags, and a large number of curb-side dumps in poorer neighborhoods (Naidoo, 2003). Reflecting the need for a more formal approach to the solid waste disposal issues faced by Botshabelo and the Mangaung Local Municipality is the recommendation that the municipality begin the task of "drafting and promulgation of regulations and guidelines as well as the *formulation* of waste management plans as part of an Integrated Waste Management process" (Naidoo, 2003, p. 166, italics added). This statement acknowledges the lack of current application of waste management procedures. Electricity and other infrastructure services are being addressed, but because these services are prohibitively expensive to many of South Africa's poor, they may still be inaccessible to a significant portion of the population (Naidoo, 2003). Given their ongoing experience with inadequate water services, substandard waste disposal programs, inadequate housing, and remote formal economic centers, the learners who study economic and financial concepts in Botshabelo's schools may have rare opportunities to put them into practice. Many factors within these communities interact to present a bleak prospect for learners who live in Botshabelo and other similar townships in South Africa. Murray (1995) hypothesizes about the likely futures of many of the youth of Botshabelo:

> Their prospects are grim. Formal sector or stable employment is hopelessly beyond the reach of the very many of the youth. Inevitably, they prey on pensioners; they live by their wits from one day to the next; and they hone their skills as best they may in the disparate nooks and crannies of the second economy. (p. 6)

Though Murray's words are 15 years past, more recent investigations into the economic and infrastructure issues facing Botshabelo indicate these words still hold truth (Tomlinson & Krieg, 1997; Turok, 2001).

On their walk to school, many learners who live in Botshabelo see main roads comprised of dirt, one room shacks in which whole families live, solid waste piled along the roads, and individuals struggling to meet basic water needs. What they do not see on a regular basis are garbage trucks, banks, or formal economic opportunity. The psychological distance between their lived experiences and the economic and financial concepts learned in school may be greater than the driving distance between Botshabelo and Bloemfontein.

The EMS Curriculum

After the fall of the apartheid government in the late twentieth century, political and educational leaders of South Africa worked to undo the injustices of the country's education system. The policy implemented works to "redress imbalances generated through historical inequalities" (Department of Education, 1995, Chapter 13, para. 9). The grand goals set forth in the early years of transition, however, became bogged down in political conflicts (Jansen, 1999). Though much progress has been made to provide equal educational access, significant differences in educational achievement remain between learners of different socioeconomic backgrounds (van der Berg, 2008).

The Economics and Management Sciences (EMS) curriculum addresses the economics and financial literacy needs of South African learners. The philosophy of this national curriculum states that the priorities of the economics curriculum "include the significant contemporary economic issues of poverty, redistribution of income and wealth, growth and development, globalization, respect of the environment and human rights" (Department of Education, 2008, p. 7).

Though the stated philosophy of the EMS curriculum places emphasis on economic and financial justice issues, many assessment standards used to measure achievement within this curriculum may currently be beyond the life experiences of many South African learners. Table 2.1 outlines the four EMS learning outcomes and provides examples of assessment standards. Although the sample assessment standards in Table 2.1 emphasize the application of economic and financial principles outside the classroom, the infrastructure and financial conditions within communities such as Botshabelo may prohibit learners from using them on a regular basis. In an environment where many neighborhoods struggle to obtain basic needs such as potable water and solid waste disposal, it may be unrealistic to believe that underserved learners have the opportunity to effectively apply many of these skills. Diverse formal economies, communication technologies, and banking institutions require more advanced infrastructures than many South African communities have.

Revising learning objectives and assessment standards in a way that avoids important economic and financial knowledge and skills would further marginalize underserved learners by withholding skills vital for full participation in the formal economy. Rather than advocating for this additional marginalization, it is argued that government agencies

Table 2.1. Four EMS Learning Outcomes

Learning Outcome	*Example Assessment Standards*
1. The economic cycle—The learner will be able to demonstrate knowledge and understanding of the economic cycle within the context of the "economic problem."	Grade 3: Identifies some business leaders and entrepreneurs in own community and describes their businesses. Grade 9: Discusses the role of the foreign sector in the economic cycle.
2. Sustainable growth and development—The learner will be able to demonstrate an understanding of sustainable growth, reconstruction and development, and to reflect critically on its related processes.	Grade 2: Identifies available resources used to create innovative and marketable products. Grade 4: Identifies the differences in the standards of living of highly developed and subsistence economies. Grade 7: Compares and discusses the difference between savings and investments. Grade 9: Explains the role of savings and investments in economic prosperity and growth.
3. Managerial, consumer, and financial knowledge and skills—The learner will be able to demonstrate knowledge and the ability to apply responsibly a range of managerial, consumer, and financial skills.	Grade 4: Investigates the use and purpose of a savings account. Grade 5: Finds out and discusses how a savings account is opened at a bank and completes deposit and withdrawal slips. Grade 6: Explains the concept of debt and compares the banking and savings facilities offered by different banks. Grade 7: Discusses the use of technology in telecommunication services (e.g., cell phones) and financial transactions (e.g., ATM, internet) in improving administration, communication, and access to information. Grade 7: Draws up an elementary statement of net worth using personal records. Grade 8: Investigates the various methods of savings and investments (e.g., savings accounts, fixed deposits, shares, unit trusts) and calculates returns on a variety of investments.

(Table continues on next page)

Table 2.1. Continues

Learning Outcome	*Example Assessment Standards*
4. Entrepreneurial knowledge and skills—The learner will be able to develop entrepreneurial knowledge, skills, and attitudes.	Grade 7: Participates in a joint venture between the school and the community/parents by taking ownership of producing a product or service.
	Grade 8: Identifies financial institutions and organizations promoting entrepreneurship.

Adapted from "Revised National Curriculum Statement Grades R-9 (Schools)," Department of Education, 2002, Gazette No. 23406, Vol. 443, Pretoria.

responsible for infrastructure development and private-sector financial institutions should focus more resources on these underserved communities. Within the curriculum, focus should be placed on active citizenship that works to empower learners to promote change within their communities.

Though the Revised National Curriculum states that "issues such as poverty, inequality, race, gender, age, disability, and challenges such as HIV/AIDS all influence the degree and way in which learners can participate in schooling" (Department of Education, 2002, p, 2), the assessment standards do not place focus on how learners can affect change in their communities. An example of these assessment standards stopping short of active citizenship occurs in Learning Outcome 2, Assessment Standard for Grade 6 where learners "[identify] steps that can be taken by the government to redress historic imbalances and poverty (e.g., redistribution of resources, gender equity, capacity building, restoring people's dignity, creating opportunity and empowerment" (p. 25). Adding assessment standards in which they critique wealth distribution and apply their understanding of this concept in their own communities would empower learners to take an active role in addressing this issue. While a focus for Grade 5 is on "the impact of apartheid policies on people's lives, ownership, growth and development, and steps taken by government to deal with historical imbalances" (p. 18), little focus is placed on how the individual can influence these imbalances. Overall, more focus needs to be placed on how individuals can work to influence issues of poverty at both the community and national levels.

Government policies that encourage "providing social transfers, human resource development and labour market intelligence" (Marais, 2003, p. 3) should be augmented with policies that more strongly stress infrastructure development within communities of underserved citizens. Promoting economic opportunity in these communities will better allow learners to use economic and financial principles in a more localized fashion, more effectively reinforcing concepts taught in schools.

EMS curriculum documents stress connecting classroom experiences to the greater community. Encouraging teachers to bridge the gap between learners' experiences in the classroom and application of economic and financial concepts in their lives outside of school, the Learning Programme Guidelines emphasizes the following philosophy:

> In keeping with an outcomes-based approach, the teaching of Economics should not be confined to the classroom only but should include interaction with the outside world. This creates opportunities for research and practical work, shifting the emphasis from rote learning to the development of life skills and values. (Department of Education, 2008, p. 7)

Though the philosophy encourages teachers to work to connect curriculum to communities, teachers who work in underserved communities may lack the community resources to facilitate authentic experiences. In Botshabelo, where 46% of households are described as indigent (Naidoo, 2003), skills such as authentically using deposit slips at ATM machines may remain unachievable to learners.

There are many instances within the EMS curriculum materials that make statements pertaining to the application of economic and financial principles. Expanding on the excerpt above, the Learning Programme Guidelines goes on to explain the following:

> Experiential (i.e., active) learning, individual work, group work and continuity are essential components in the teaching of economics.... Continuity is vital to ensure that there is a logical and coherent flow between the activities presented in the Economics classroom. It is therefore important to link that which was done before [to that] which is being done at present to provide consolidation of the application of life skills. (Department of Education, 2008, p. 8)

In acknowledging the potential disconnect between concepts and the ability to apply them, the EMS teacher's guide provides a general statement to teachers about the importance of adjusting educational experiences to the lives of their learners:

> People in both rural and urban areas often find themselves limited in exposure to some other EMS experiences that do not apply to their situations. Teachers need to expand opportunities and exposure for learners through arranging excursions to bridge the gap between theory and practice. (Department of Education, 2003, p. 32)

Providing a specific example of how teachers can create opportunities in underserved areas, the guide further states:

> Where access to factories is not available, for example in rural areas, teachers need to realise that learners could also be taken to brickyards that will expose learners to production. Teachers can also make pamphlets and booklets on production from factories available to the learners. (Department of Education, 2003, p. 32)

An example of an assessment standard to which learners in underserved communities may be limited in exposure is Learning Objective 3, Assessment Standard for Grade 5, in which a learner "finds out and discusses how a savings account is opened at a bank and completes deposit and withdrawal slips" (Department of Education, 2002, p. 27). to fully implement this assessment outside the school environment, a learner must have access to financial institutions and see others actively using these institutions. In neighborhoods where financial institutions may be many miles away, learners whose households lack the means to travel may rarely see this important skill in use and be discouraged from viewing this skill as applicable to their lives outside of school. Only when banks and ATM machines are more readily available, along with infrastructure improvements that allow individuals to spend less time acquiring basic needs, will learners be better able to put these skills to use.

A more general statement about the application of economics and financial concepts occurs in the Learning Program Guidelines for teachers which states: "In keeping with an outcomes-based approach, the teaching of Economics should not be confined to the classroom only but should include interaction with the outside world" (Department of Education, 2008, p. 7). Unfortunately, there are few opportunities beyond the classroom to apply these concepts. Additionally, it may be beyond the ability of individual teachers to provide experiences in which learners can interact with formal economic opportunities. True ability to apply many of these standards outside the classroom requires changes in government and private sector policy that encourages more local economic and financial development.

Another example of the potential inability of learners to use assessment standard skills in their lives outside of school occurs with Learning Outcome 3, Assessment Standard for Grade 7, in which learners "[discuss] the use of technology in telecommunication services (e.g., cell phones) and financial transactions (e.g., ATM, Internet) in improving administration, communication, and access to information" (Department of Education, 2002, p. 40). While learners in underserved communities are certainly capable of such discussions, they leave classrooms and enter communities in which even basic needs, such as access to potable water and garbage collection, are lacking. The ability to see these processes in use outside the classroom is questionable, and the lack of access may promote the idea that these skills do not apply to them. Similarly, Learning Outcome 4, Assessment Standard for Grade 8, in which the learner "identifies financial institutions and organizations promoting entrepreneurship" (p. 45), may be successfully accomplished in the school setting, but it may be difficult to put to authentic use in communities such as Botshabelo.

Broad assessment standards, without government policies to alleviate inequalities, may encourage learners in underserved communities to view economic concepts as marginalizing their lives outside of school. Learning Outcome 2, Assessment Standard for Grade 4, requires learners to "[identify] the differences in the standards of living of highly developed and subsistence economies" (Department of Education, 2002, p. 24). While at school, learners in underserved communities discuss how standards of living can vary greatly between different economies. The learners then return home to neighborhoods where they see subsistence economy at work, without government policy that encourages advancement to more highly developed economic systems. A system in which learners have knowledge of highly developed economies, but little means to interact with them, encourages them to see economic and financial inequalities without realistic ability to act upon them. More congruence between the EMS stated philosophy of working to improve economic and human rights must complement government policies that more aggressively work to accomplish these goals. Though the curriculum approaches issues such as the effects of apartheid policy, poverty, and inequities in wealth distribution, it does not place enough focus on promoting active citizenship in which learners can work at an individual level to address these issues. Additionally, although teachers are expected to find outside learning opportunities for their learners, the curriculum does not provide enough support for communities in which formal financial opportunities are unavailable. Teachers may individually encourage their learners to be active participants in improving their communities, but until the national curriculum places more focus on active citizenship, these efforts will remain isolated.

Learners in South African schools discuss effective entrepreneurship, the complexity of global markets, how resources can be used most effectively, and the impact of government policy on economic advancement. They learn skills related to effective time and resource management, techniques for saving and investing money, and the effective use of telecommunications and other technologies. Unfortunately, for many learners, these skills remain in the classroom because they have little means to practice them outside of school. Going to homes where much time and capital is spent acquiring clean water and managing solid waste, learners in many

South African communities live in at least two worlds. Although learners certainly transfer many of the skills learned in the EMS curriculum to their environments outside of school, other learners are being left behind in the classroom. In a community where garbage trucks are infrequent visitors, how many authentic opportunities does a learner really have to fill out a deposit slip?

Recommendations and Conclusions

A more concerted effort by government officials and private sector financial institutions to focus resources on providing Botshabelo and other communities with basic services, both infrastructure and financial, is necessary if learners are to apply economic and financial skills outside the classroom. Though the philosophy and goals of the EMS curriculum stress practical use of economic and financial concepts, the realistic application of these concepts outside of school is beyond the reach of many South African learners. While teachers are charged with developing experiences to connect the curriculum to the lives of their learners, government policies may be discouraging true integration. It is recommended that government policymakers focus more attention on the infrastructure deficits of communities described as having little economic potential. Additionally, it is recommended that private-sector financial institutions invest more in underserved communities. Doing so will give greater opportunity for learners to authentically practice the skills they learn in the classroom.

The description of the complex issues faced by the citizens of Botshabelo in this chapter is incomplete. Analysis of the effects of government policies upon the short-term and long-term well-being of Botshabelo's residents is likewise insufficient. Experts with more background of the intricacies of government policies and their effects upon communities, the EMS curriculum, and the rich cultures of South African communities may find this analysis wanting. It is hoped this outsider's view of the connection between the infrastructure issues and EMS curriculum provides fodder for discourse between individuals with more understanding of the diverse, but connected, fields discussed in this chapter.

Similarly, description and analysis of the many strengths of the EMS curriculum and the effective practices of classroom teachers use to overcome economic and financial barriers is not included. This chapter is intended to further the discussion of how government policy, economic education, and the lives of learners interact. It is hoped this chapter serves as stimulation in the ongoing work to improve the lives of South Africa's learners.

This writer's visit to Botshabelo, Soweto, and other communities in South Africa, provided the opportunity to visit with learners who are passionate about using skills that would provide them with economic advancement. The teachers with whom he spoke are fully dedicated to eradicating the injustices that remain due to the apartheid-era policies. Both learners and teachers with whom he has conversed, work tirelessly to achieve economic, financial, and social justice. To match the dedication of these learners and teachers, the government of South Africa must do more to ensure citizens who are underserved have more equal opportunity to put important economic and financial concepts to use in their own communities.

ACKNOWLEDGMENTS

The opportunity to visit Botshabelo, Soweto, and other communities in South Africa was provided by the Council for Economic Education Study Tour on Economic Education to the Republic of South Africa, 2009. Funding was provided by the United States Department of Education and carried out in coordination with the U.S. Department of State. The author wishes to thank the following individuals for their assistance: Joanne Dempsey, President, Illinois Council on Economic Education; Ina Combrinck of the South African Foundation for Economic and Financial Education; and Jennifer Freeman of Morton Junior High School.

DISCUSSION QUESTIONS

1. How can environmental factors such as access to potable water and affordable electricity in communities in which learners live influence their conceptualizations and applications of economic and financial concepts?
2. Many assessments include references to experiences that may be beyond the reach of many learners (e.g., questions regarding ATM machines or internet usage). How can wording of assessments potentially marginalize learners who come from underserved communities?
3. What are some strategies classroom teachers can realistically employ to assist learners in overcoming the economic and financial barriers, such as lack of access to formal financial services, in their communities?
4. How should teachers best approach classrooms in which learners have large differences in their exposure to, and experience with, formal financial processes?

5. Who is responsible for increasing social currency among learners in underserved communities? Governments, teachers, private-sector financial institutions, and/or learners?

MODEL LESSON

Community Planning—How Basic Systems Affect Our Lives

Suggested Grades: Middle Level Grades

Objectives:

(a) Learners will describe infrastructure systems that influence their daily lives.
(b) Learners will explain how infrastructure systems interact to maintain current standards of living.

Related standards:

National Economic Education standards:

Standard 2: Decision-Making Learners will understand that effective decision making requires comparing the additional costs of alternatives with the additional benefits. Many choices involve doing a little more or a little less of something: few choices are "all or nothing" decisions.

Standard 3: Allocation-Learners will understand that different methods can be used to allocate goods and services. People acting individually or collectively must choose which methods to use to allocate different kinds of goods and services.
Materials:

- Paper, writing utensil, chalkboard/whiteboard

Procedures:

(a) Opening activities

1. In this activity, learners are given the role of community planner. They create a list of basic infrastructure needs (e.g., road maintenance, water systems, electrical grids, gas lines, garbage

disposal, and telecommunications systems) and prioritize these systems in terms of the importance of maintaining current standards of living. Learners must provide a rationale for their prioritization. Learners are then asked to remove one system and explain how its removal affects other systems and what the standard of living might be like without it.

2. Teacher begins by informing learners they will be discussing the systems that are used to maintain current standards of living. Learners are asked to list systems they use. A beginning suggestion by the teacher may help learners identify these systems.

(b) Developmental activities

1. After the list of infrastructure systems is created, learners are asked to individually prioritize these systems on paper, providing a brief rationale for their ordering. Teacher then places learners into small groups for comparison. Small groups then create a second priority list based upon input from all individuals. Rationales are developed by groups. Each group lists on the chalkboard its priorities for comparison with other groups.
2. Upon completion and comparison of priority lists, groups are asked to remove one system and explain their rationale for removal. Learners are then asked to describe how the current standard of living might change as a result of removal of a system. Learners must explain how removal of one system might affect other systems.

(c) Closing activities

1. Teacher asks learners to explain how lack of access to different systems may affect standard of living. Teacher then asks learners to explain how removal of one system may affect others.

(d) Summary and assessment:

1. Inform learners they are to keep track for two days of their use of the infrastructure systems identified at the beginning of the lesson. Learners create a chart with systems and mark the number of times they used each system over the 48-hour period. At the conclusion of the 48 hours, learners write one paragraph explaining which system they view as most vital. Learners write a second paragraph explaining how other systems may be affected by the removal of the most vital system.

2. Upon completion of chart, learners are asked to describe their experiences with this analysis and explain how the systems might be interrelated.

REFERENCES

Behrens, R., & Wilkinson, P. (2003). Housing and urban passenger transport policy and planning in South African cities: A problematic relationship? In P. Harrison, M. Huchzermeyer, & M. Mayekiso (Eds.), *Confronting fragmentation: Housing and urban development in a democratizing society* (pp. 154-174). Lansdowne, South Africa: Cape Town Press.

Cross, M., Mungadi, R., & Rouhani, S. (2002). From policy to practice: Curriculum reform in South African Education. *Comparative Education, 38*(2), 171-187.

Department of Education. (1995). White paper on education and training. *Government Gazette 357,* (16312). Pretoria, South Africa: Government Printer. Retrieved from http://www.info.gov.za/whitepapers/1995/education1.htm

Department of Education. (2002). Revised national curriculum statement grades R-9 (schools). *Gazette 23406*, (443). Pretoria, South Africa: Government Printer.

Department of Education. (2003). *Revised national curriculum statement grades R-9 (schools): Teacher's guide for the development of learning programmes, economic and management sciences.* Pretoria, South Africa: Government Printer.

Department of Education. (2008). *National curriculum statement grades 10-12 (general): Learning programme guidelines.* Pretoria, v: Government Printer.

Fourie, J. (2008). A note on infrastructure quality in South Africa. *Development Southern Africa, 25*(4), 481-494.

Hoogendoorn, G., Visser, G., Lenka, M., Marais, L., Van Rooyen, D., & Venter, A. (2008). Revitalizing the Bloemfontein CBD: Prospects, obstacles, and lost opportunities. *Urban Forum, 19*(2), 159-174.

Huchzermeyer, M. (2009). The struggle for *in situ* upgrading of informal settlements: A reflection on cases in Gauteng. *Development South Africa, 26*(1), 59-73.

Jagals, P., & Griesel, M. (2003). The impact of urban discharges on the health-related microbiological quality of untreated surface water: Can catchment management solve the problem? *Water Science and Technology, 47*(3), 15-20.

Jansen, J. (1999). The school curriculum since Apartheid: Intersections of politics and policy in the South African transition. *Journal of Curriculum Studies, 31*(1), 57-67.

Krieg, D. S. (1991). Bloemfontein. In A. Lemon (Ed.), *Homes apart: South Africa's segregated cities* (pp. 104-119). London: Paul Chapman.

Marais, L. (2003, September). *Housing in former homeland areas of South Africa: Delivery, issues, and policy in the Free State Province.* Paper presented at the World Congress on Housing: Transforming Housing Environments through Design, Pretoria, South Africa.

Mokoena, M., & Marais, L. (2007). The missing link in cooperative governance and housing delivery: Lessons from Mangaung Local Municipality. *Urban Forum, 18*(4), 311-327.

Murray, C. (1995). Structural unemployment, small towns and agrarian change in South Africa. *African Affairs, 94*(374) 5-22.

Naidoo, R. (2003). *Mangaung state of the environment report*. Bloemfontein, South Africa: Mangaung Local Authority.

Okeahalam, C. (2007). Economics of access in a developing country: An analysis of firm-conduct in financial services. *International Journal of Social Economics, 34*(12), 923-942.

Parnell, S. (2004, October). *Constructing a developmental nation—The challenge of including the poor in the post apartheid city.* Paper presented at the Overcoming Underdevelopment in South Africa's Second Economy. Development Bank of Southern Africa, Midrand, South Africa.

Seekings, J. (2000). Introduction: Urban studies in South Africa after apartheid. *International Journal of Urban and Regional Research, 24*(4), 832-840.

September, S. M., Els, F. A., Venter, S. N., & Brözel, V. S. (2007). Prevalence of bacterial pathogens in biofilms of drinking water distribution systems. *Journal of Water and Health, 5*(2), 219-227.

Statistics South Africa. (2007). *Community survey 2007: Municipal data on household services* [Report No. 03-01-22 (2007)]. Pretoria, South Africa: Author.

Tomlinson, R., & Krige, S. (1997). Botshabelo: Coping with the consequences of urban apartheid. *International Journal of Urban and Regional Research. 21*(4), 691-705.

Turok, I. (2001). Persistent polarisation post-apartheid? Progress towards urban integration in Cape Town. *Urban Studies, 38*(13), 2349-2377.

van der Berg, S. (2008). How effective are poor schools? Poverty and educational outcomes in South Africa. *Studies in Educational Evaluation, 34*(2008), 145-154.

CHAPTER 3

CONCEPTUALIZING FINANCIAL MORALITY

Thomas A. Lucey

The concept of financial morality represents a matter of scholarly intrigue and controversial befuddlement. It contradicts many capitalist notions that would appear to be reasonable at first blush. This conundrum represents an extension of recent arguments that educators should reconsider their approaches to citizenship education. Tupper (2008) argues that citizenship education suffers from influences of tenets that are subconsciously ingrained in patterns of thinking, yet lack justification. They are commonsense; everyone knows that they are true. Carr (2008) provides evidence that teacher candidates interpret democratic citizenship in terms of civic responsibility and obedience (thin conceptions), but lack the vision to consider it as a participatory process that allows for criticism and change (thick conceptions). Financial morality extends the identification of fallacies with commonsense mainstream school curricula (Tupper, 2008) and emphasis on "thin" citizenship (Carr, 2008) to the problematic of financial literacy convention. Financial morality represents the thick view of financial literacy that educators should not ignore.

Financial morality's relevance to education relates to its association with a justice-oriented approach to citizenship education (Westheimer & Kahne, 2004). Instead of the conventional entrepreneurial, profit-maximizing

Reframing Financial Literacy: Exploring the Value of Social Currency, pp. 47–63

basis to financial practice, financial morality employs a stewardship ideal that is antithetical to individualism.

Affecting students' application of moral dimensions to personal finance requires the development of their ability to visualize the concrete *and* abstract consequences of financial decision making and their willingness to make informed, compassionate choices. For example, a concrete outcome can be illustrated by investment in stock of multinational corporations that results in the long-term development of personal wealth. This growth would be evident in increased investment values of one's account statement. Realizing the abstract outcome may involve the knowledge that this wealth enhancement results from expectations of profits generated through practices that mistreat laborers (Baran, 2001/2007; O'Rourke, 2001/2007) or abuse the environment (Kincheloe, 2010).

Is it possible to increase personal wealth while living a moral existence? Is it moral to increase one's wealth through means that require others to labor in inhumane conditions, such as sweatshops? Is it appropriate to purchase fuel from a corporation that pollutes a significant water resource? Is it appropriate to deposit money with lenders who will not provide financial services to a particular area? Is it virtuous to be patriotic when the government enacts laws that support corporate lobbyists who exercise injurious practices to people and environments? These are finance-related, moral questions that schools may examine through inquiry and other means. They broaden students' financial views to include consideration of the systemic origins and consequences of their financial decisions and discussion of alternatives for citizen action.

Morality requires one to focus on the appropriateness of intentions and the outcomes of actions as they impact other people. It also blends the concrete and abstract. A comprehensive interpretation of an action (concrete) requires an interpretation of associated consequences (concrete and abstract) and intentions (concrete and abstract). The morality of a decision about whether or not to purchase a detergent that harms the environment or to purchase goods from companies that mistreat workers relates to various factors that include the consumer's patterns of knowledge, financial resources, and purchase contexts. The "morality" of financial decision-making involves many other factors.

The influences that determine the morality of behaviors are not readily identifiable. Swartz's (2010) call for a sociologically-based framework that relates moral ecology and moral capital demonstrates the relevance of considering morality as a broad, deep, or thick issue that requires authentic accountings to properly conceptualize. The issue requires knowledge of the patterned social contexts and biological nuances that foster various moral traditions comprising the global tapestry of society. Bergman (2002) conceives of moral development as being a series of social negotiations and suggests that this learning/development continues as one discovers new situations. In other words, as one's social networks expand and become more complex, an individual encounters additional behavioral and rationalization variants that shape his or her decision making. Bergman's interpretation extends to financial decisions, for moral financial behavior involves deep thinking about systemic human motives.

Financial morality represents the intersection of financial and moral conceptions. It concerns the extent to which patterns of financial decision-making occur within a moral conception. Whether and how individuals and corporate entities position themselves in relation to this conceptual conundrum bears greatly on the integrity of their financial decision-making. This chapter invites a scholarly dialogue about the abstract and material dimensions of these issues. It explores the nature of financial morality in both its broad and narrow forms by relating it to financial literacy and classism.

These topics are important to the education community because of the existent curricular emphasis on economic-centered production content, rather than human-centered values content. The current reductionist climate, which integrates social studies into literacy and mathematics instruction in the elementary grades, constrains social studies thinking to a narrow perspective that aims at the development of responsible and participatory citizens (Carr, 2008; Lucey, in press; Westheimer & Kahne, 2004). A participatory democracy also requires development of citizens that respect various points of view, and it builds from the different perspectives to create a system where all people are valued. By presenting these topics and a broader perspective on citizenship preparation, this chapter offers an opportunity to examine the concept of financial morality, modify this interpretation, and relate the notion to instructional practice.

Financial Literacy and Financial Morality

This section distinguishes financial morality from financial literacy. Understood in a conventional sense, financial literacy represents an understanding in six areas: financial responsibility and decision making; income and careers; planning and money management; credit and debt; risk management and insurance; saving and investing (Jump$tart Coalition, 2007). A holistic awareness and application of all these areas provides for a comprehensive financial process for earning, protecting, allocating, and growing one's personal wealth. Financial morality requires accounting for immediate and distant human outcomes of financial decisions.

Financial literacy represents a broad concept that involves awareness and application of the aforementioned areas. A financially literate entity builds wealth by creating a plan for acquiring, protecting, and allocating financial resources to reduce financial dependency on others. The aforementioned conventional sextet of financial domains undergirds the patterns of personal relationships and information necessary to accomplish these goals. It is analogous to self-sufficient farming, wherein one grows crops to both feed one's family while generating seed to sustain crop growth. Understood narrowly in the context of financial resources and one's control of them, financial literacy attributes financial status to the outcome of an individual's financial choices.

To what extent are financial decisions matters of choice? The habitual nature of human behavior, as described by Trout (2009), would suggest that financial decisions relate less to choices and more to recurring impulses stimulated by biological imprints and environmental contexts. Jared Diamond's (1999) widely read work, which concerns the patterns of maturity within and among human societies, indicates that access to resources, environmental conditions (e.g., climate and other life forms), and land patterns combine to shape the factors that influence development of human societies. Similarly, the societal contexts of one's biological parents shape his or her patterns of decision making and conditions of individual human development.

Economically speaking, children do not come into life on an even keel with each other. Even within households, the positioning of first, last, or middle child fosters different memories among the children, prompts different treatment from their parents, and provides different responses from siblings. Children enter life in various economic settings and develop patterns of consumer decision-making influenced by various factors (Moschis, 1985). The households in which children develop are characterized by different spending patterns, as related to the amounts of available resources and the patterns of priorities. As a child develops, s/he interacts with various social systems (Bronfenbrenner, 1979). The theory that various cultural elements (e.g., race, religion, gender) influence student behavior (Banks, 2006) provides additional insight into these systematic developmental interactions. Patterns of cultural domination that result from patterns of social judgment related to physical traits and social conditions (such as skin color, economic status, belief systems, and sexual orientation) indicate that each of Bronfenbrenner's social systems contains patterns of judgments that may work to enhance or diminish one's social status.

The argument that financial decisions are matters of choice presumes that one realizes, both rationally and emotionally, all the available alternative options. Rationally, it makes sense to delay a purchase and put money aside in a short-term, interest-bearing account until one has saved the resources for that item. The desire to immediately acquire the item through a short-term credit tool may overrule the argument to delay spending and save. The choice-based theory of financial decision-making discounts the role of emotion and environment in shaping financial practice.

The relationship between social positioning and financial consequence can be seen in Clements, Johnson, Michelich, and Olinsky's (1999) observation that excessive borrowing, financial ignorance, and medical expenses represent the most frequently reported reasons for bankruptcy filings. It could be argued that the patterns found by Clements et al. may have resulted from poor choices; however, these claims ignore the role of fate in these decisions.

Let us consider a poorly compensated employee, who has an employer that does not offer health insurance; s/he may incur medical expenses and use credit cards or other sources of debt to pay off these expenses because s/he sees no other alternative. Let us say the employee had attended poorly funded neighborhood schools. The schools had emphasized a rote curriculum because the teachers had low expectations for their mostly non-college-bound students. Did this employee make bad financial choices that resulted in his or her placement in these circumstances? The claim of poor decision-making neglects consideration of the systems through which this employee developed the narrow range of financial alternatives that s/he perceived. This person did not choose to live in the household and family environment within which s/he developed, and s/he did not choose the school s/he attended or the curriculum s/he was taught.

These familial and educational contexts have significant bearings on a person's emotional and cognitive development patterns. Just as Moschis (1985) explains the various manners by which households influence patterns of consumer socialization, Berliner and Biddle (1995) discuss the effects of schools on patterns of student achievement, and Kozol (2005) describes the disparate learning conditions between affluent and impoverished schools. A stronger emphasis should be placed on changing the social conditions that prompt poor financial decisions, rather than blaming the decision-maker victims of these social conditions.

Stone and Maury (2006) illuminate another commonality among the bankruptcy factors mentioned by Clements et al. (1999). These conditions represent matters that are often perceived as beyond the victim's field of vision. Because a person lacks the vision to perceive the long-term consequences of decisions, s/he does not view the wide array of possible financial outcomes. Financial behavior thus represents less of a choice, in which one decides between a range of alternatives, and more of an unplanned, impulsive reaction to the conditions that fate or luck offers. Creating a participatory democratic citizenry requires that social studies teachers empower their students' social vision by broadening their awareness of the lasting outcomes of financial decisions. For those who are economically marginalized, appropriate instruction may involve explorations of (a) financial net worth (the difference between the values of one's financial assets and liabilities) and (b) the consequences of credit and investment decisions. For those who are economically privileged, it may require study of social problems that result from classist views of financial behavior.

In Relationship to Financial Literacy

Proponents of financial morality view cooperative financial community as the ultimate goal. The concept of financial morality broadens the vision of financial literacy to include a responsibility to the welfare of others. Teachers should use their classrooms as environments to guide their students' sensitivity to others, beginning within their classroom and reaching out to the school and outside community. Thus, students develop an appreciation for financial stewardship that values others for their own needs or spirit. An overemphasis on conventional financial literacy marginalizes efforts to promote moral conduct because obsessions with financial wealth may psychologically blind one to the needs for others and the importance of community.

Within financial literacy, financial morality is not limited to consumer decision-making. Westheimer and Kahne's (2004) framework for good citizenship suggests that consumer-based decisions should include/reflect responsible approaches to financial morality. A person's sense of financial morality occurs within existing social structures and results from processes that others have encouraged. Consequently, avoiding a particular brand of food because of the manufacturer's treatment of laborers does little to seriously challenge the cause of the problem, but it does provide the consumer with an abstract sense of emotional security.

Efforts to affect changes in laws or to engage offending businesses in dialogue represent approaches to financial morality that are indicative of participatory citizens. This sense of morality occurs through stimulation of change within the system and the initiation of programs in which responsible citizens can participate. Initiating a dialogue with legislators may prompt development of a regulation that curbs industry production of toxic atmospheric chemicals. Such laws force offenders to moderate offending behaviors. This moderation reduces the pollution; however, it does not necessarily change the underlying causes of the situation (i.e., shareholder demands for the highest return on their financial investment at the lowest amount of risk).

A justice-oriented approach to financial morality analyzes the social flaws that cause the problem and strives for systemic change. The problem may lie within (a) the capitalist principles that underlie patterns of social thought and (b) profit motive that prompts a disregard for environmental integrity. How does one become engaged in this process? One possible justice-oriented response involves the practice of an antithetical life-style to the offending conditions. What this practice would look like is not entirely clear; however, Crossan's (1994) account of Jesus of Nazareth's antithetical lifestyle to that of first century Rome may provide some clues. According to Crossan, Jesus practiced an egalitarian lifestyle that contradicted the ideals of Ancient Rome. For example, he practiced a mobile ministry, talking to those people he met, thereby challenging the common practice of anchoring business in one location. Similarly, he socialized with all those people who invited him, rather than accepting select invitations based on the social worthiness of the hosts.

What would an egalitarian classroom look like? Conceptualizing teachers as facilitators of learning, rather than as controllers of information, policy, and procedures, offers direction. Extending this view to schools and district structures constitutes a logical extension. In this view, teachers provide opportunities for students to develop critical thinking skills through discussions and solutions of real-world problems. These strategies have been practiced by Atwell (1998) in regards to reading and Brantlinger (2008) in relation to mathematics. The focus involves an authentic exercise of skills in which all individuals are valued for their different strengths. For circumstances where contraventions of community expectations occur, community forums result, in which community members discuss contraventions and decide upon appropriate responses.

Classism and Financial Morality

The concept of classism concerns the stereotyping and discrimination of people based on perceptions of their economic status. It represents a social challenge, for it attributes economic status to patterned decisions and behaviors that are of an individual's or group's own choosing (Koppelman, 2005). Agnello and Lucey (2008) note that the topic of classism is clearly absent from social studies methods courses and social studies texts, reflecting the resistance of educators to informing students about the fallacies of classist thinking. In a democratic society that purports to value everyone's freedom, discrimination based on economic class remains a bastion of bias that education continues to neglect. Economic class is not entirely a matter of choice; stereotyping and abuse based on economic status inappropriately assigns blame to victims for conditions which may not be under their control.

Popular efforts to remedy classist practices perpetuate the difficulty because they base recommendations on perceived traits of people based on economic class. Environmental differences prompt patterns of social judgment. Ruby Payne's (1995) popular framework for understanding poverty derives from unconfirmed observational evidence that perpetuates stereotypes documented by Cozzarelli, Wilkinson, and Tagler (2001). As illustrated by her "quiz" about whether one can survive within a particular economic class, Payne attributes economic status to one's patterns of behaviors. Her work fails to acknowledge that economic status also relates to patterns of social policies and practices towards individuals.

Whereas classism attributes economic class to one's decisions and behaviors, financial morality relates one's decisions and behaviors to economic class. Financial morality includes a conception of sacrifice that conventional financial literacy lacks. The economic class that one inherits when s/he enters life largely determines his or her behaviors and social networks. The judgments of others based on economic status ignore the lack of choice involved with the social contexts that people inherit.

Conventional financial literacy concerns wealth possession, while financial morality concerns itself with wealth and social stewardship, interpreting financial status as partially self-determined. Understood broadly in the context of social resources and their influences on financial decisions, financial morality construes financial status as the result of the controls that others may impose. Historical and current patterns of economic discrimination in the United States that occur against various socioeconomic groups (as described in Anderson, 1988; Cohen, 2003; Conley, 2001; Loewen, 2005, 2007; Morris & Morris, 2000; Zinn, 2003) illustrate the use of financial status to suppress economic opportunities for the less fortunate.

Financial literacy standards and theories noticeably lack a concern for the welfare of those who are affected by one's financial decision making. While financial literacy standards contain an element of charity, as addressed in Standard 5 of the Planning and Money Management competencies (Jump$tart Coalition, 2007), the guidelines involve conditions (i.e., researching organizations and beneficiaries; relating giving to budgets; and evaluating charity budgets). With respect to charitable giving, a conservative view of financial morality includes a judgment of recipient merit. This view/judgment is a form of control that prevents people from exploring their legitimate relationship to community. If potential beneficiaries (individuals or organizations) conform to the conditions established by the donor, they are rewarded with contributions.

The broad view of financial morality concerns wealth detachment. Its relevance to community welfare lies within the emphasis on long-term community wellness, rather than short-term individual gratifications. This conception recognizes wealth accumulation as the product of fate and choice, and it withholds judgments based on one's economic class. Fate and choice relate to a vision and expectation. Financial control and permanence appear associated with a choice-based psychology. Financial acquiescence and temporariness appear connected to a fate-based conception.

Financial morality is antithetical to conventional financial literacy because of its emphasis on holistic outcomes, rather than individual outcomes. This difference between financial literacy and morality may be considered analogous to the distinction between morality and social convention expressed by Nucci (2001).

Interpretive differences of financial morality relate to the contexts from which the observer derives. For example, to one who may be prepared strictly in understandings of finances that require focus on accumulations of financial resources and maximization of return, consideration of the human consequences of financial growth may be seen as nonsensical because success is earned by maximization of return. The human consequence lies with the ignorant who do not understand the financial system.

Social, geographical, generational, and traditional contexts represent factors that influence judgments and behavior patterns (Lucey, 2008; Lucey, Kruger, & Hawkins, 2008; Macintyre, 1984, 1988). Given the plethora of behavioral influences that exist, the challenge of moral judgment may be less one of interpreting correct behavior than one of realizing the contextual pressures on decision-making that give rise to heterogeneous value/belief systems. This is not to say that morality is totally subjective, but that marginalization of various social contexts from which people originate impairs the development of a nurturing, moral community.

Financial morality occurs when those who make financial decisions fully consider the long- and short- term human consequences to others as well as themselves. Admittedly, this definition is vague; yet, it provides a starting point for exploration. McGregor's (2008) example of forsaking lower-priced goods for those produced in humane production settings provides a talking point. In relating this behavior to the idea of "moral intensity" (Izzo, 1997), McGregor recounts six factors (time between consumption and consequences; volume of consumer expectations; consumer beliefs about consequences; attachment to those affected by decisions; consumer beliefs about number of people affected; and social acceptability of action) that affect the intensity of one's moral consumerism. In order to be realized, financial morality requires the elements of cognition (knowledge), affect (motivation and will), and action (ability). Because individuals are exposed, by choice and fate, to various pieces of information, they act to different moral degrees. Financial morality represents an absolute concept in that certain patterns of financially moral behavior are considered to be universally desirable; yet, it also represents a subjective concept that respects the fact that people have experienced various intellectual patterns that (a) shape their interactions with the various systems of information that guide other people's patterns of thinking and (b) prompt contextually-originated values.

Thick and Thin Views

Recent scholarship (e.g., Carr, 2008) distinguishes between thin and thick views of democratic citizenship. Thin views emphasize superficial or routine practices, such as voting, as essential behaviors. Thick views of citizenship involve substantial or system processes, such as political engagement, as core financial behaviors.

A thin view of financial morality involves individualistic interpretation of the motives and consequences for one's decision making. Financially moral behaviors occur because they are perceived as the "right" things to do and because they will result in future individual benefits. For example, investing in the stock of a corporation that is perceived to conduct its business morally may ease one's conscience while providing opportunity for future profit. This conception involves a thin view of spirituality (Lucey, in press) that relates to patterns of personal abilities to counter scientific or social law. In other words, spirituality is interpreted as an abstract, almost magical trait that gives power to change socially undesirable phenomena. Thin efforts include purchasing products and services of companies that are environmentally responsible and humane in their business practices. Thin views of financial morality change only the business parties with which financial decisions are made; they do not change the patterns of practice themselves. A thin view of financial morality relates to one's own acts, and not to the acts of others.

A thick view of financial morality involves holistic consideration of the motives and consequences for one's decision making. It involves a thick view of spirituality (Lucey, in press) that synthesizes a sense of personal identity within the context of others and recognizes the relationship of one's decisions to the community. Thick efforts to be financially moral include involvement in community outreach to challenge the financial system that perpetuates social injustices and classism. These efforts work to organize efforts to counter offending corporations in their patterns of environmental devastation and human abuse by organizing boycotts, labor strikes, and corporate protests. Those with thick views of financial morality extend interpretations of related acts beyond their own financial choices by making the *abstract* issues concrete for themselves and others.

Financial morality represents a broad conception of financial literacy that respects all parties affected by financial decisions. It requires decision-makers to consider outcomes to the entire community so that all stakeholders are valued.

CONCLUSION

This chapter provided an interpretation of financial morality, differentiating it from conventional financial literacy and classism. Instilling broad, financially moral citizenship conceptions through teacher preparation and through exploration in K-12 classrooms represents a necessary practice to accomplish a socially just community.

Much work in clarifying fine points of financial morality remains to be done. Swartz (2010) and McGregor (2008) have initiated the scholarly pursuit of financial morality issues. Their investigations represent more than intellectual curiosities, for they symbolize the heart of a global society. Conceptions of financial morality and its application or avoidance reveal much about human nature. The extent to which the essence of this nature is economic or humane remains to be seen.

DISCUSSION QUESTIONS

1. What may be the historic origins for the concept of financial morality?
2. To what extent do you agree with the author's conception of financial morality? Discuss the premises of your claims. How are they similar or different from the author's premises?
3. To what extent do you view yourself as being financially literate (in a conventional sense) or financially moral? To what extent might it be possible to possess elements of both concepts? Use examples and readings to support your position.
4. The chapter explains the antithetical relationship between financial morality and classism. How would you describe the relationship of classism to conventional financial literacy?
5. What might be done to improve financial morality within the global community? To what extent is financial morality a concept that should be taught in schools?

MODEL LESSON

Money and Responsibility[1]

Suggested Grade Level: 2nd or 3rd Grade

Objective:

(a) To be responsible with one's money and someone else's money
(b) To behave morally or ethically with one's money.

Related Standards

Jump$tart National Standards in K–12 Personal Finance Education:

Financial Responsibility and Decision Making

Standard 1: Take responsibility for personal financial decisions

Planning and Money Management

Standard 1: Develop a plan for spending and saving

Standard 2: Develop a system for keeping and using financial records

Standard 3: Describe how to use different payment options

Credit and Debt

Standard 3: Describe ways to avoid or correct debt problems

Saving and Investing

Standard 1: Discuss how saving contributes to financial well-being

Materials:

- fake U.S. currency bills and change
- cash register
- credit/debit card
- checks

- Teacher Reference: Godfrey, N. S. (1995). *A money adventure: Earning, saving, spending, sharing.* Eaglecliffs, NJ: Silver Press.

Procedures:

(a) Opening Activities:

1. Define and show real money, coins, checks, and credit cards. Discuss how to use them, where/when/how to save money, and how to keep track of spending. Then, as a class, read the book, Neale Godfrey's (1995) *A Money Adventure: Earning, Saving, Spending, Sharing*. Discuss the similarities and differences between your knowledge before you read the book and after reading the book.

(b) Developmental Activities:

2. Give students a list of items that they would need to pay and budget their money for (such as food, gas, cell phone use) and other things that they would need to keep a daily record of (such as lunch, drinks, etc.) Give them a set amount of money to begin with (e.g., $1,000). Help them come up with a table that keeps track of (a) the items acquired or services used (b) the amounts they need to pay and when, and (c) the sources of the goods and services that they purchase, and (d) the effects of their spending decisions on other people. See the abbreviated example table below.

Item	Amount Paid	Manufacture Source	Spending Outcome
Pair of Shoes	$25	Corporation	Profit for Corporation

3. Discuss with students their responsibility for paying money back and paying bills on time and thinking about how other people are affected by their spending. What are the working conditions that prompted the creation of these products? What are the effects on those companies that do not receive payments for their goods? Discuss what the word "moral" means and how that relates to being responsible with their money.

(c) Closing Activities:

1. Facilitate students' play of "store" and "bank" with a cash register, play money, and checks. Provide for transactions that have simple dollar amounts (no decimals).
2. Require students to maintain ledgers that track the amounts of money that they possess and make smile or frown faces as they proceed through the activity.
3. Require all students to participate in the store and bank's community. Observe how patterns of financial decisions relate to the various students.
4. Monopoly would be another great game to play that involves money skills. Alter some of the board locations and create Chance cards to provide consequences for businesses that disrespect the community.

(d) Summary and Assessment:

1. While the students are playing "store" and "bank," check to see whether they are using all forms of money payment correctly and whether they are indeed purchasing items and making payments to pay bills, etc.
2. Debrief the students about their feelings during the experiences. Identify key points during the activity, and encourage students to refer to their ledgers and notes. Ask the students how they feel when others treat them fairly. How do they feel when they treat others fairly? Do students seem to understand that their actions impact not only themselves but all others in the "community" and that there is a need to "play fair" in our play and in real life?

NOTE

1. Lesson developed by Lauren Rivera.

REFERENCES

Agnello, M. F., & Lucey, T. A. (2008). Toward a critical economic literacy: Preparing K-12 learners to be economically literate adults. In D. E. Lund & P. R. Carr (Eds.), *Doing democracy and social justice in education* (pp. 247-266). New York, NY: Peter Lang.

Anderson, J. D. (1988). *The education of Blacks in the South 1860-1935.* Chapel Hill, NC: University of North Carolina Press.

Atwell, N. (1998). *In the middle: New understandings about writing, reading, and literacy* (2nd ed.). Portsmouth, NH: Boynton/Cooke Heinemann.

Banks, J. A. (2006). *Cultural diversity and education: Foundations, curriculum, and teaching.* Boston, MA: Allyn and Bacon.

Baran, M. (2007). Stop killer Coke! In B. Rakocy, A. Reuss, C. Sturr, and the *Dollars and Sense* Collective (Eds.), *Real world globalization* (9th ed., pp. 54-60). Boston, MA: Dollars and Sense. (Original work published 2001)

Bergman, R. (2002). Why be moral? A conceptual model from developmental psychology. *Human Development, 45,* 104-124.

Berliner, D. C., & Biddle, B. J. (1995). *The manufactured crisis: Myths, fraud, and the attack on America's public schools.* Boston, MA: Addison-Wesley.

Brantlinger, A. (2008). Economic inequality and secondary mathematics. In T. A. Lucey & K. S. Cooter (Eds.), *Financial literacy for children and youth* (pp. 276-297). Athens, GA: Digitaltextbooks.

Bronfenbrenner, U. (1979). *The ecology of human development.* Cambridge, MA: Harvard University Press.

Carr, P. (2008). Educators and education for democracy: Moving beyond "thin" democracy. *Interamerican Journal of Education for Democracy, 1*(2), 147-165.

Clements, J., Johnson, D., Michelich, K., & Olinsky, C. F. (1999). Characteristics of bankruptcy filers: Implications for educators. *Journal of Family and Consumer Sciences, 91*(4), 71-74.

Cohen, M. A. (2003). Report on the racial impact of GMAC's finance charge markup policy—In the matter of *Addie T. Coleman et al. v. General Motors Acceptance Corporation* (GMAC). Retrieved from http://www.nclc.org/initiatives/cocounseling/gmacreportbystate.shtml

Conley, D. (2001). Decomposing the black-white wealth gap: The role of parental resources, inheritance, and investment dynamics. *Sociological Inquiry, 71*(1), 39-66.

Cozzarelli, G., Wilkinson, A. V., & Tagler, M.J. (2001). Attitudes toward the poor and attributions for poverty. *Journal of Social Issues, 57*(2), 207-227.

Crossan, J. D. (1994). *Jesus. A revolutionary biography: A startling account of what we can know about the life of Jesus.* San Francisco, CA: HarperCollins.

Diamond, J. (1999). *Guns, germs, and steel: The fates of human societies.* New York, NY: W. W. Norton.

Izzo, G. (1997, May). *A theoretical perspective of the effects of moral intensity on consumers' ethical judgments of marketers' non-normative methods.* Paper presented at the South Western Marketing Association Co5fnference, University of Central Arkansas. Retrieved from http://www.sbaer.uca.edu/research/sma/1997/PDF/07.pdf.

Jump$tart Coalition. (2007). *National standards in K-12 personal finance administration with benchmarks, knowledge statements, and glossary* (3rd ed.). Washington, DC: Jump$tart Coalition. Retrieved rom http://www.jumpstart.org/assets/files/standard_book-ALL.pdf

Kincheloe, J. L. (2010). Consuming the All-American corporate burger: McDonald's "Does it all for You." In J. A. Sandlin & P. McLaren (Eds.), *Critical pedago-*

gies of consumption. Living and learning in the shadow of the "Shopacalypse" (pp. 137-147). New York, NY: Routledge.

Koppelman, K. L. (with Goodhart, R. L.). (2005). *Understanding human differences: Multicultural education for a diverse America.* Boston, MA: Pearson/Allyn and Bacon.

Kozol, J. (2005). *The shame of the nation: The restoration of apartheid schooling in America.* New York, NY: Crown.

Loewen, J. (2005). *Sundown towns: A hidden dimension of American racism.* New York, NY: Touchstone.

Loewen, J. (2007). *Lies my teacher told me: Everything your American history textbook got wrong* (Revised Ed.). New York: Touchstone.

Lucey, T. A. (2008). Economics, religion, spirituality, and education: Encouraging understandings of the dimensions. In T. A. Lucey & K. S. Cooter (Eds.), *Financial literacy for children and youth* (pp. 559-577). Athens, GA: Digitaltextbooks.

Lucey, T. A. (in press). Preservice teachers' conceptions of democratic essence: Interpretations of democratic principles, and their connections to social justice, economic class, and spirituality/religion at a Midwestern institution in the USA. In D. Zyngier & P. Carr (Eds.), *Can education make a difference? Experimenting with, and experiencing democracy in education.* Charlotte, NC: Information Age Publishing.

Lucey, T. A., Kruger, D. P., & Hawkins, J. M. (2008). Grasping the foundational roots of economic perceptions: Pre-Colonial West Africa and the Bantu. In T. A. Lucey & K. S. Cooter (Eds.), *Financial literacy for children and youth* (pp. 316-334). Athens, GA: Digitaltextbooks.

Macintyre, A. (1984). *After virtue* (2nd ed.). Notre Dame, IN: Notre Dame Press.

Macintyre, A. (1988). *Whose justice? Which rationality?* Notre Dame, IN: Notre Dame Press.

McGregor, S. L. T. (2008). Conceptualizing immoral and unethical consumption using neutralization theory. *Family and Consumer Sciences Research Journal, 36,* 261-276.

Morris, V. G., & Morris, C. L. (2000). *Creating, caring, and nurturing educational environments for African American children.* Westport, CT: Bergin and Garvey.

Moschis, G. P. (1985). The role of family communication in consumer socialization of children and adolescents. *Journal of Consumer Research 11*(4), 898-913.

Nucci, L. P. (2001). *Education in the moral domain.* Cambridge, England: Cambridge University Press.

O'Rourke, D. (2007). Sweatshops 101: Lessons in monitoring apparel production around the world. In B. Rakocy, A. Reuss, C. Sturr, and the *Dollars and Sense* Collective (Eds.), *Real world globalization* (9th ed., pp. 139-146). Boston, MA: Dollars and Sense. (Original work published 2001)

Payne, R. K. (1995). *A framework: Understanding working with students and adults from poverty.* Baytown, TX: RFT.

Stone, B., & Maury, R. V. (2006). Indicators of personal financial debt using a multi-disciplinary behavioral model. *Journal of Economic Psychology, 27*(4), 543-556.

Swartz, S. (2010). 'Moral ecology' and 'moral capital': Tools towards a sociology of moral education from a South African ethnography. *Journal of Moral Education, 39*(3), 305-327.

Trout, J. D. (2009). *Why empathy matters: The science and psychology of better judgment.* New York, NY: Penguin Books

Tupper, J. A. (2008). Interrogating citizenship and democracy in education: The implications of disrupting universal values. In D. E. Lund & P. R. Carr (Eds.), *Doing democracy. Striving for political literacy and social justice* (pp. 71-84). New York, NY: Peter Lang.

Westheimer, J., & Kahne, J. (2004). What kind of citizen?: The politics of educating for democracy. *American Educational Research Journal, 41*(2), 237-269.

Zinn, H. (2003). *A people's history of the United States: 1492-present* (Perennial Ed.). New York, NY: Harper.

CHAPTER 4

YOUNG CANADIAN WOMEN'S FINANCIAL LITERACY

Vicki A. Green

This chapter provides a brief history of women's financial literacy and barriers to achieving it. As early as 1999, Waring addressed barriers to women's financial equality along with the concept of time use as an indicator of economic welless in her book, *Counting for Nothing: What Men Value and What Women Are Worth*. Waring's (1999) work was extended by Joo (2008) exploring personal financial wellness, in addition to Fox and Bartholomae (2008) addressing financial education and program evaluation. This chapter explores the challenges that face Canadian women in becoming financially literate, including program offerings in and out of school. It looks at one group of Canadian women, The Smart Cookies, who are successfully helping women to educate themselves about being financially competent. There is greater focus on financial issues because of the 2008 global financial meltdown and resulting worldwide recession. Financial challenges that face so many people at once seem to have raised concerns regarding knowledge, skills, and understanding about financial literacy. This chapter is concerned with Canadian women's financial literacy and how to meet the related financial challenges.

Reframing Financial Literacy: Exploring the Value of Social Currency, pp. 65–78

Canadians Save Too Little

Data and surveys suggest that Canadians may be saving too little, consuming too much, amassing excessive debt, and investing less than they should be in education and skills development. For example, in 1982 Canadians saved 21.2% of disposable income, whereas in 2005 Canadians saved 1.7%. The amount of disposable income that Canadians saved increased in 2010 to 4.6% (Toronto Dominion Band Financial Group, 2010). Since 2002, Canadians have shifted their savings attitudes, with the bulk of savings generated by returns on assets that have been largely debt financed. In addition, survey data indicate that 27% of Canadians fail to pay fully their credit card debts each month (Toronto Dominion Bank Financial Group, 2010).

Canadians Weak in Financial Information

Nearly one quarter of Canadians have been found to be deficient with regard to (a) monitoring their finances, (b) planning ahead, and (c) staying financially informed (Task Force on Financial Literacy, 2010). A survey conducted in 2008 by the Strategic Council on behalf of the Canadian Foundation for Economic Education found 28% of Canadians struggle with financial knowledge (Strategic Counsel/CFEE, 2008), which reinforces the Task Force on Financial Literacy finding. In addition, a 2009 survey for Canadian Securities Administrators found that 35% of Canadians do not have any savings or investments (Toronto Dominion Bank Financial Group, 2010). To improve Canadians financial literacy, the Task Force included the following recommendations: improve fundamental knowledge, encourage savings behavior from youth to adulthood, and provide financial materials to individuals at specific points in life regarding their financial decisions. Individuals face so many financial decisions with high levels of complexity; consequently, they may need some guidance in making these decisions.

In summary, an increase in the percentage of Canadian's debt, poor financial planning, and lack of financial knowledge have long-range implications for Canadians' financial wellbeing. This chapter, focuses on what can be done by a segment of the population, namely Canadian women.

Canadian Women's Financial Background

Canadian women's pay equity has consistently remained at 67-71 cents for every dollar earned by North American men (Waring, 1999). This disproportionate compensation demonstrates that women need be more careful about saving and investing. Increased participation in university education has not substantially altered the reality of Canadian women's income in the workplace (Luong, 2010). On average, women spend 11.5-15% years of their work age years outside the workforce, resulting in lower lifetime wages/income and lower retirement savings. Legislation determining greater equity of opportunity has increased women's capacity for earning and investing money (Mackinnon, Elgquist-Saltzman, & Prentice 1998). However, it is only within the last decade that women have participated more fully in the North American economy (Luong, 2010).

A marked characteristic of the last decade is an economy fueled by debt. More women attend university today than in the past decades (Luong, 2010). Their university and college loans have increased along with women's greater educational and economic participation. "Since 1990, average tuition for a four-year undergraduate program in real inflation-adjusted terms has more than doubled between 1995 and 2005" (p. 1).

Women are willing to participate in education at the university level as their higher incomes and higher levels of education are found to bring about longer life expectancy and long-term health benefits (Luong, 2010). These findings have far reaching implications for women's investment capacity because, statistically, women tend to be financially independent in their later years. Thus, it would behoove the financial industry and educational institutions to provide women with increased opportunities to participate actively in their own financial education. All university students have enjoyed easy access to credit, for there is aggressive credit card selling on university campuses across Canada (Luong, 2010). However, women students in particular need to understand debt prior to obtaining it. Historically, women have earned less than their male counterparts and have interrupted their careers with child rearing and caring responsibilities. Also, it has been found that "helping people with debt problems is a money loser for the banks and other financial institutions" (Task Force on Financial Literacy, 2010, p. 21).

Kiyosaki (2006) reports that roughly 87% of poverty-stricken seniors are women; furthermore, nearly one half of Canadian women over 50 years of age are single and manage their own money, and one out of two marriages end in divorce. Young women tend to believe in the princess myth and fail to realize that no one will provide for them financially throughout their lives. In addition, women may not realize that many types of cohabitation can make them financially vulnerable. Through multiple financial challenges, women have always managed money despite legal and social restrictions. Women have learned about money management through handling basic household expenditures.

There are many Internet resources available to teach women financial knowledge, increase their understanding, and change their financial behavior. However, lost time, wasted money, personal frustration, and lack of trust result from their failure to understand financial and regulatory information. Plain language enables women to act. For example, plain language is needed with respect to credit card statements, interest rates, and repayment plans. How much financial information available to young women today is in the interest of the provider? Yes, online resources exist, but to what extent are these websites and the information contained therein trustworthy? Financial literacy materials must also be made available to young women through accredited, regulated, local, nonprofit organizations and not through those who have a conflict of interest in selling financial products. In Canada, opposition is growing toward financial literacy materials marketed by financial industry providers, while curriculum materials created and implemented through Canadian Ministries of Education are increasingly in favor. This change resulted from the Organisation for Economic Co-operation and Development's (OECD, 2009) establishment of the *International Gateway for Financial Education* to explore, describe, and analyze the effectiveness of programs to improve financial literacy.

In summary, Canadian women want and need clear and simple language from both the private and public sectors in order to budget, save, and pay down their debt. They also want greater monitoring and evaluation of the financial literacy programs currently being marketed to them by the financial industry. They support current trends in Canadian Ministries of Education curricula and financial program initiatives.

Canadian Women and Financial Literacy Programs

Rabbior (2010), President of the Canadian Federation for Economic Education, states, "The challenge for Canadians is to transfer their financial knowledge to affecting financial behavior" (p. 1). He has asked Canadians to describe the attributes of a financially competent person. Rabbior advocates using the term "financial capability" rather than the term "financial literacy" (p. 1). Changing financial attitudes, attributes, and behaviors is more effective than continuing to focus on financial knowledge. He believes the task ahead is better able to be achieved using financial competency than literacy. The Canadian challenge is to redirect an economy of spenders to one of savers. It is paramount for Canadians to know that funds for investment largely come from household savings and not leveraged debt. Rabbior states "that economic capability needs to go hand in hand with financial capability" (p. 1). Financial capability suggests one has the necessary tools with which to make financial decisions, whereas economic capability is needed to understand the greater context. Tools alone do not guarantee good financial decision making. For example, most people understand the importance of establishing and following a budget; however, less than 25% of Canadian households do so. Financial literacy related to content knowledge has not significantly improved financial behavior among Canadians. Content knowledge is forgotten, not applied, or ignored as it is learned out of financially applicable contexts. Direct application and active financial literacy might help as The Smart Cookies (see below) found out with the success of their book, articles, and columns. Canadians need to attend to descriptors and attributes that define a financially capable and responsible person. With greater reflection, Canadians' financial behavior might adapt and change.

Canadian Children and Youth and Financial Education

Financial literacy at the elementary school level needs to be increased and given more emphasis. Program for International Assessment (PISA) results for 2006 reported 4 in 10 Canadian youth lacked language literacy and math skills. However, the recently published 2010 PISA results show improvement in language literacy, mathematics, and science scores in four provinces with the largest Canadian populations (i.e., British Columbia, Alberta, Ontario, and Quebec). Currently, Canadian students' financial literacy is not tested through PISA as it is in New Zealand, for example. Thus, Canadian math scores have been used to estimate students' financial literacy, but different aspects of financial literacy are taught across the curriculum in Canadian schools.

The Toronto Dominion Bank Financial Group Special Report (2010) states that "childhood financial education needs to be prescriptive, preventative, development and delivered on a mass-scale" (p. 10). It should begin early and continue through secondary school. Ministries of Education across Canada continue to discuss the importance of standardized financial curricula for youth in elementary and secondary schools.

Currently, early financial knowledge taught to children in elementary schools explores needs, wants, saving, and spending. Financial literacy can be found throughout the British Columbia curriculum, for it appears in elementary through secondary grade levels and in a number of subject area curricula. Some examples at the elementary grade levels reveal financial literacy is often included in a foundational way and is taught in mathematics; whereas, at the secondary level, financial literacy is prescribed in subjects such as Basic Life Skills and Mathematics. Financial literacy also appears in subject areas such as economics, health and education, family studies, social studies, and business education (Ministry of Education, Province of British Columbia, 2010). However, it must be noted that making financially relevant material interesting and applicable to elementary children can be challenging, and surveys of secondary students suggest that they want to know more about money and the role money plays in their lives (Cappon, 2010; Kramer, Rogers, & Kaznowska, 2010). As much as these students need to know about mortgages and purchases of big items over time, there was consensus among them that financial educational programs need to provide more relevant, reliable, and readable financial information (Kramer, Rogers, & Kaznowska, 2010).

The use of fragmented, cross-curricular financial skill sets aimed at young people across 12 years of schooling is not an ideal way to prepare youth for the ravages that the financial industry perpetuates on financially ill-informed and financially unprepared people. Consequently, specific educational programs are being proposed to ministries of education across Canada to help youth develop financial competencies and be better prepared to manage their financial resources.

Canadian Teacher Education and Financial Literacy

Adequate resources must be set aside for training teachers. United States studies have found that teachers, much like the broader population, struggle with certain financial concepts and knowledge (McCormick, 2009). Education in Canada falls under the jurisdiction of each province and territory. Each provincial Ministry of Education provides the K-12 curricula. The provincial ministries of education need to design and implement financial competency programs across the curriculum and the various grade levels. University education faculties need to introduce courses in financial competency for teachers.

Support incentives to encourage saving and investment over borrowing and debt accumulation are currently being publically addressed by the Bank of Canada, which also provides cautionary information to Canadians who are carrying too much debt. In addition, Canadian commercial banks are instructed not to be too heavy handed toward consumers and their debt. As one might note, a double message is coming from financial regulatory institutions. However, no one, including teachers, can miss the message being sent by the Bank of Canada today—namely that the Canadian central bank is encouraging saving, whereas the Canadian commercial banks seem bent on promoting consumer debt through easy credit. It is also critical to note the importance of providing curricula to teachers who are often unprepared and uncomfortable imparting financial information to their students, especially since many lack the necessary background knowledge and skills. Areas for curricula consideration include budgeting, consumer education, borrowing, and compounding, yet financial literacy courses are not being taught to beginning teachers in Canadian colleges of education.

As mentioned above, students might benefit from specific material on mortgages, but they also need to understand credit cards, cell phone contracts, and ordering movies on cable and songs on iPod. It is recognized that support for teachers is forthcoming from members of the financial industry who are developing curriculum materials for presentation in schools (Task Force on Financial Literacy, 2010). These volunteers need to be transparent, unbiased, and free from conflicts of interest in presenting financial information to teachers and their students. Also, educators should make a concerted effort to minimize the potential for volunteers to exploit the classroom for their own or their employer's benefit. To ensure that volunteers do not participate in a conflict of interest while presenting financial materials to students, The Task Force on Financial Literacy provided background materials available for the teachers' own education. The Task Force on Financial Literacy listed existing financial education sources available to Canadian teachers:

1. Credit Unions, which set up banking services in local schools and have adapted curricula developed in the United States for use in the Canadian context.
2. Volunteers from financial services industries, who share their time and energy to teach important financial literacy concepts to students across Canada.
3. The Canadian Federation for Economic Education has online programs available.
4. Government agencies have available curricula on-line.
5. Provincial security regulators have made available education materials for teachers and students.

This list is not sufficient to educate Canadian teachers on how to provide financial literacy to their students. However, it constitutes an initial effort to identify what exists in the field as Ministries of Education move forward to develop curriculum materials that will be PISA tested. A survey of Canadian university students by the Canadian Alliance of Students Associations (Canadian Student Survey, 2010) revealed a significant lack of financial aid literacy and indicated that students relied on poor sources for financial aid information. The Canadian Student Loans Program is complex and unclear. Students enter into financial contracts at a vulnerable time in their academic lives, and little help is provided to ensure that they understand the long-term financial implications of their financial decisions.

Women students are particularly vulnerable as debt incurred obtaining a university education is difficult to pay off when the realities of their working life are marked by interruptions for child rearing, lower financial remuneration for the same work as men, and longer life spans than men. One wonders why financial literacy programs have not discussed the Canada Student Loan Program in secondary schools, prior to students accessing it.

Canadian Women and Financial Realities: The Smart Cookies

The Smart Cookies, a group of women who became debt ridden through loans for their university studies, are taking action to correct such oversights. The Smart Cookies (2008) exemplify the attributes of financially capable women and recognize the opportunities available for developing these attributes. It was through hard financial lessons and hard work that The Smart Cookies turned their financial lives around. Yes, they got into debt—debt that was too easy to obtain. Further, these five women held university degrees and realized that their financial education had been nonexistent. We need to ask: Who benefits when our highly motivated and educated female youth are able to acquire a burdensome debt from a financial industry (including a government sponsored loan program) that claims to have the female students' best interest and futures at heart? The Smart Cookies have demonstrated that applied knowledge can increase the financial capacity of young women. How did they do so? The five Canadian women met weekly to analyze their spending habits, including credit card statements, bank statements, cell phone plans, bills, and pay checks. They were in debt from over spending, student loans, keeping up with the Joneses, and going out for coffees, drinks, and dinners.

The Smart Cookies and Barrett (2008) identified one of the main reasons young women seemed to reject financial information. Financial knowledge has been seen as belonging to males and as being difficult to understand. Farnsworth (this volume) discussed "the dichotomies of public/private and rational/emotional" (p. 160) that have been used to denote male and female lives. Males' lives a have been constructed so that men occupy a public and rational environment, whereas women have historically occupied emotional and private realities. Waring (1999) discussed the inequality of women's financial lives based on time use and the prevalence of unpaid women's work in nurturing and caring tasks that are seen as private. Similarly, Farnsworth identified financial capability as belonging to the private sphere. The young women who formed The Smart Cookies belong to a generation brought up on easy credit and the problems caused by "live for today and tomorrow will take care of itself." The Smart Cookies have learned about their finances and therefore are defined as financially competent. A financially competent person is one who has knowledge, understanding, and skills and who accepts responsibility for financial decision making. The financially competent person understands credit and money management, including taxes, pensions, benefits, and savings. Too many people abdicate their financial responsibilities to others and do not accept the outcomes. For example, in many families, the control of money and financial decisions may rest with one person. Educators should help students develop financial networks and talk about their decisions and problems, thus developing students' self-confidence to control their own financial decision making. Farnsworth states

> teaching young people about financial capability is not simply about imparting technical knowledge about the choices and products available. The split between the rational and the emotional is a myth that allows for the pretence that these are not also moral choices and decisions. Moreover, the split between public and private, where finance is regulated to the private sphere, detracts from public and social implications of financial decisions and the finance system itself. (p. 161)

Believing strongly in women's financial agency, The Smart Cookies took action. They created a website and published a book to help prevent other young women like themselves from falling into burdensome debt. Financial agencies and government programs should also support the advice they offer. According to The Smart Cookies and Barrett's (2008) suggestions for creating financial competency include the following: "talk less" on your cell phone, "lose the landline" or eliminate your home phone, "cut cable costs," "go paperless" or receive bills online, and be energy efficient (p. 96). In one year, The Smart Cookies' finances improved markedly. In reflection, the Smart Cookies found their financial challenges occurred in an economy that provided easy credit, hyperconsumerism, shopping peer pressure, high tuition costs, student loans, and societal expectations for "living the good life." Fortunately, after a couple of years of following their own advice, The Smart Cookies now see saving their money as thrill seeking. They are unafraid to stick to their own long-term goals, pick up separate checks, entertain at home, and shave pennies off the price of daily consumer items.

The Smart Cookies have demonstrated and provided the knowledge, skills, and attitudes needed to change the spending behavior of young Canadian women to become financially capable and competent. How has this been possible given current research that illustrates that today's women, similar to their counterparts throughout human history, face greater financial challenges than men? Perhaps current research does not reflect the increase in use of social media, the Internet, and the availability of global financial trends. Furthermore, the financial industry has been slow in providing specific materials and information for women. The Smart Cookies isolated the "buyer beware" axiom for young Canadian women and defined for consumers the importance of comparative shopping. One of their suggestions, for example, is for consumers to compare the different prescription fees paid to pharmacies. In addition, The Smart Cookies have demonstrated viable alternatives for Canadian women to withstand peer pressure and to avoid the accumulation of debt acquiring items beyond their financial means.

In the past, generations of Canadian women were brought up in a climate of thrift and savings. The Smart Cookies belong to the first generation of Canadian women to experience the Canadian banking industry's promotion of financial products that did not provide full disclosure. They present relevant and timely material that meets the needs for young Canadian women to educate themselves about financial issues. We cannot ignore the reality that The Smart Cookies have risen to national and international attention with the publication of their book on helping young women become financially capable and with their televised appearance on the Oprah Winfrey show. In the opinion of this author, the financial industry is playing catch-up in our newly wired economy.

DISCUSSION QUESTIONS

1. Is it reasonable for women to continue to accept different levels of pay compared to men? Why or why not?
2. How can women achieve greater financial knowledge in an industry dominated by men?
3. When should children learn about money? How should money be introduced to them?
4. What advice would you give to persons in debt who are living beyond their means?

5. What is the most important attribute of financial competency demonstrated by The Smart Cookies? Defend your choice.

MODEL LESSON

Imagine, Draw, or Cut Out Possible Purchases

Suggested Grade Levels: 6-8
Objectives:

(a) To create a spending plan or develop a saving plan.
(b) To postpone instant gratification.

Related Standards

Jump$tart National Standards in K-12 Personal Finance Education

Financial Education Standards

Financial Responsibility and Decision Making

Standard 1: Take responsibility for personal financial decisions

Standard 4: Make financial decisions by systematically considering the alternatives and consequences.

Materials:

- Magazines and catalogues
- Drawing paper and colored pencils

Procedures

(a) Opening Activities

1. Ask students about recent purchases and whether they were or were not previously planned. (Have you ever bought something you later regretted? Do you spend your money without thinking about alternatives or consequences?) Write examples from students in a semantic web on the board.
2. Ask students what might have helped them reconsider the purchases prior to buying them.

3. Explain to students that they will create collages of possible purchases from magazines, drawings, and catalogues.
4. Define "possible."

(b) Developmental Activities

1. Explain to students that they are to imagine three to four goods/services they would like to buy. Ask for examples.
2. Hand out magazines, catalogues, drawing paper, and colored pencils.
3. Ask students to create collages of their possible purchases. Discuss (a) why it might not be wise to buy items on impulse or to buy everything you want/need at once and (b) the criteria one might use in making decisions about what to buy now and what to buy later. Have students label their possible purchases and ask them to place an ordered value on them based on identified criteria.
4. Help students develop a realistic timeline for their future possible purchases.
5. Place students' collages and timelines around the room to remind them of possible purchases and the desirability of prioritizing their wants/needs, reconsidering possible purchases, and postponing some possible purchases to a later date.

(c) Closing Activities

1. Ask students to explain their first possible purchase and a potential timeline for their future purchases.
2. As students purchase items from their collages over time, ask them to check off the drawings or pictures of these items on their collages.

(d) Summary/Assessment

Note the correlation between students' collages and their purchases for two weeks. Instruct students to write about how creating a collage helped them postpone and/or reconsider purchases. Ask students to write whether their satisfaction increased or decreased with each purchase and why.

REFERENCES

Canadian Student Survey. (2010, March). A project by the Canadian Alliance of Student Associations, in partnership with the Council of Alberta University Students, the Ontario Undergraduate Student Alliance, and the Alliance of Nova Scotia Student Associations. Retrieved from http://www.ousa.ca/wordpress/wp-content/uploads/2010/04/2nd-Report-Canadian-Student-Survey.pdf

Cappon, P. (2010, May 12). *The changing face of literacy: The financial literacy Imperative*. Toronto, Canada: The Canadian Council on Learning/Conseil Canadien Sur L'Apprentissage.

Fox, J. J., & S. Bartholomae (2008). Financial education and program evaluation. In J. J. Xiao (Ed.), *Handbook of consumer finance research* (pp. 47-68). New York, NY: Springer Science Business.

Joo, S. (2008). Personal financial wellness. In J. J. Xiao (Ed.), *Handbook of consumer finance research* (pp. 21-33). New York, NY: Springer Science Business.

Jump$tart Coalition. (2007). *National standards in K-12 personal finance education.* Washingtong, DC: JumpStart Coalition for Personal Financial Literacy.

Kramer, N., Rogers, J., & Kaznowska, E. (2010). The illiteracy of the literate: The lack of financial aid knowledge among Canadian university students. Canadian Alliance of Student Associations. Retrieved from http://www.caus.net/docs/10-05_Survey 3.pdf

Kiyosaki, K. (2006). *Rich women: A book on investing for women*. New York, NY: Warner Books.

Luong, M. (January, 2010). *The financial impact of student loans*. Perspective on Labor and income. Toronto. Retrieved from http://www.statcan.gc.ca/pub/75-001-x/2010101/pdf/11073-eng.pdf

Mackinnon, A., Elgquist-Saltzman, I., & Prentice, A. (1998). *Education into the 21st century: Dangerous terrain for women?* London: Falmer Press.

McCormick, M. H. (2009). The effectiveness of youth financial education. *Journal of Financial Counseling and Planning*, *20*(1), 70-83.

Ministry of Education, Province of British Columbia. (2010). *Response to the task force on financial literacy public consultation document questions*. Retrieved from http://www.financialliteracyincanada.com/documents/consultation/New%20Brunswick%20Securities%20Commission.pdf

OECD Project on Financial Education. (2009). *International Gateway on Financial Education.* Paris, France: Author.

Rabbior, G. (2010, May 11). Presentation to the Task Force on Financial Literacy. Toronto. Retrieved from http://www.financialliteracyincanada.com/documents/consultation/Canadian%20Foundation%20for%20Economic%20Education%20_CFEE-addendum_May%2012.pdf

Rabbior, G. (2010. November 10). *On-line classroom*. Toronto, Canada: Globe and Mail.

Task Force on Financial Literacy. (2010, September). *What we heard: A summary of public consultations.* Retrieved from http://www.financialliteracyincanada.com/documents/Summary-of-Public-Consultations-eng.pdf

The Smart Cookies, & Barrett, J. (2008). *The Smart Cookies guide to making more dough and getting out of debt*. Toronto, Canada: Vintage Canada.

Strategic Counsel. (2008). *Canadian national survey on economics and financial capability.* Prepared for the Canadian Foundation for Economic Education. Retrieved from http://www.cfee.org/assets/u/Canadian-National-Survey-on-Economic-and-Financial

Toronto Dominion Bank Financial Group Special Report. (2010, May 11). *The case for a lifetime learning approach to financial literacy.* Retrieved from http://www.financialliteracyincanada.com/documents/consultation/TD%20Bank%20Financial%20Group_May%2012.pdf

Waring, M. (1999). *Counting for nothing: What men value and what women are worth.* Toronto, Canada: University of Toronto Press.

CHAPTER 5

UNDERSTANDING AFRICAN AMERICAN WEALTH ATTAINMENT

Implications for Leaders

Andrea N. Johnson

Eliminating wealth disparities within the African American community represents a major goal of those who seek justice-based reforms. In order to design and implement successful innovations for African American wealth attainment, it is important to understand how this population perceives wealth and how these perceptions influence their attributions and actual attainment patterns.

This chapter examines factors that shape African American perceptions of wealth and the possible relationships among their perceptions, attributions, and wealth. Four research questions guide this study: (1) Is family background a predictor of wealth attainment for African Americans? (2) Is religious belief a predictor of wealth attainment for African Americans? (3) Is media influence a predictor of wealth attainment for African Americans? and (4) Is educational attainment a predictor of wealth attainment for African Americans?

Reframing Financial Literacy: Exploring the Value of Social Currency, pp. 79–99

The next section will present research that has been conducted in the area of African American wealth attainment. This section will specifically focus on the differences in the levels of wealth attainment and the vehicles used to attain wealth for African Americans when compared to Whites.

LITERATURE

Wealth Attainment and African Americans

Research has shown that when compared to Whites, African Americans have lower levels of wealth attainment (Oliver & Shapiro, 1995). These differences may be attributed to the ways in which the two races accumulate wealth as well as the differences in spending habits. This section explores some of these differences.

Birnbaum and Weston (1974) found that about 69% of White households own their own home, while less than half of Black households do. Although African Americans are less likely to own their homes than Whites, the majority accumulate their wealth through homeownership. Whites are also more likely to participate in more diversified wealth holdings, which include homeownership, stocks, bonds, mutual funds, and retirement plans (Birnbaum & Weston, 1974). There are also differences in the rate of retirement saving. Saving for retirement was a top priority for 54% of Whites but was a top priority for only 33% of African Americans (Ariel Mutual Funds & Charles Schwab Company, 1999). Allen (2002) investigated the relationships between location, race, and gender and the impact of this relationship on homeownership for unmarried persons. The findings reveal that although black women were less likely than White women to own homes, over two decades, the racial difference declined dramatically in rural areas. This trend was opposite that for women in urban areas.

Bradford (2003) investigated the wealth dynamics of entrepreneurship for Black and White families and found that Black entrepreneurs held a lower fraction of Black family wealth than White entrepreneurs held of White family wealth because Black families have a lower rate of entrepreneurship. Black and White entrepreneurs have more upward and less downward mobility in wealth distribution than Black and White workers, respectively.

Using data from the 1976 and 1978 National Longitudinal Surveys of Young Men and Young Women, Blau and Graham (1990) examined racial differences in the magnitude and composition of wealth and the reasons for them. On average, young Black families held 18% of the wealth of young White families, and they held their wealth in proportionately different forms. Even after controlling for racial differences in income and other demographic factors, as much as three quarters of the wealth gap remained unexplained.

Krivo and Kaufman (2004) found substantial and significant gaps in housing equity for blacks and Hispanics (but not for Asians) compared with Whites, even after controlling for a wide range of location, life-cycle, socioeconomic, family, immigrant, and mortgage characteristics. Blacks and Hispanics also uniformly receive less benefit from mortgage and housing characteristics than do Whites.

Differences also existed in the spending habits of African Americans and Whites. According to data from the Black Investors Survey (Ariel Mutual Funds & Charles Schwab & Company, 1999), the largest expense after necessities for 29% of African Americans was their car payment, followed by education expenses for their children (25%). Approximately one third of Whites (31%), stated that investing was their first expense after necessities, followed by their car payment (25%).

Although research has been conducted into the differences in wealth attainment among African Americans and Whites, few studies have investigated African Americans' perceptions and beliefs about wealth and how wealth building practices are influenced. Research that has explored perceptions of wealth and wealth attainment has been limited. The studies that have been conducted focused on two explanations: structuralist and individualistic. Structuralist explanations of wealth refer to inequalities that exist within social structures within society (e.g., discrimination in the workplace and in society). Individualistic explanations refer to the belief that a person is solely responsible for whether or not s/he attain wealth (Kluegel & Smith, 1982).

For example, Hunt (2004) examined race/ethnicity and beliefs about wealth and poverty. Analyzing data collected from Los Angeles County residents in 2000, the results indicated that ethnic minorities were more likely to simultaneously embrace "structuralist" and "individualistic" explanations than are Whites. Social-class identification and self-reported conservatism both significantly related to beliefs about wealth and poverty, and they did so differently across race/ethnic lines.

Hunt (1996) found that BLACKS and Latinos were more likely than Whites to view both individualistic and structuralist explanations for poverty as important, that respondents' self-explanations had significant effects on poverty beliefs, and the variables that predict beliefs about poverty differ across race/ethnic groups. Other studies have found that beliefs about poverty emphasize structural factors over individualistic factors (Lee, Jones, & Lewis, 1990; Nilson, 1981).

Using data from a national survey, Kluegel and Smith (1982) examined the beliefs Whites held concerning opportunities for Blacks. Whites' perceptions of equality of opportunity, discrimination, "reverse discrimination," and the trend in Black opportunity were also examined. Whites were found to be more likely to perceive widespread reverse discrimination and see a great increase in opportunities for Blacks. Whites in this study also denied structural limits concerning opportunities for Blacks. The researchers also found that Whites' beliefs about Blacks' opportunities are significantly influenced by perceptions of their own opportunities, by stratification ideology explaining opportunity in general, and by feelings of relative deprivation.

More research is needed in the area of understanding African American beliefs and perceptions of wealth, as well as the influence of major institutions such as the family, media, education, and religion on these perceptions. Understanding a person's belief system and perceptions regarding wealth attainment provides insight into overcoming potential barriers that may occur when creating and implementing programs. If a program contradicts a person's personal belief system, it is difficult for him/her to reap the benefits of a program designed to increase his/her wealth.

Familial Factors and Wealth Attainment

This section examines the relationship between family background and wealth, specifically the influence that parental wealth has on the wealth of the children. Ngina and Stafford (1999) examined data from the Panel Study of Income Dynamics (PSID) in order to examine young families' bank account ownership and stock ownership. Only 42.7% of African American parents had bank accounts (86.5% for all others), and only 16.2% of African American parents held stocks (35.5% for all others). These differences may be attributed to beliefs regarding spending habits as well as beliefs about the most important expenses after necessities (Ariel Mutual Funds & Charles Schwab Company, 1999).

Rumberger (1983) investigated the extent to which wealth explained the relationship between family background and adult economic status for White and Black males. The findings revealed that parental wealth influences schooling independent of other social components of family environment. For White males, parental wealth had a direct effect on earnings, even controlling for its effect on schooling. Also, for White males, parental wealth exerted a direct and stronger effect on sons' wealth when compared to Black males, after controlling for effects on schooling and earnings.

Menchik and Jianakaplos (1997) examined the importance of inheritances in explaining the differences in Black and White household wealth.

Using data from the 1976 National Longitudinal Surveys of Mature Men (NLS76) and the 1989 Survey of Consumer Finances (SCF89), the authors found that financial inheritances may account for between 10% and 20% of the average difference in Black-White household wealth.

The relationship between familial factors and wealth attainment among African Americans is important because the family is one of the most important agents of socialization (Schaefer, 2008). Many of our financial behaviors can be traced back to what we have been told by or what we have observed in our family.

Religion and Wealth Attainment

Research has shown that religious beliefs can influence attitudes about wealth and behaviors that can lead to wealth attainment (Mayer & Sharp, 1962). However, studies that examine this relationship do not explore racial differences. They can provide some insight into how African Americans' religious beliefs influence attitudes about wealth attainment. Keister (2003) explored the relationship between religious participation, religious affiliation, and patterns of wealth accumulation of Jews, Protestants, and Catholics. The findings suggest that Jews are wealthier when compared to all other religious groups. Reasons for this include lower fertility rates, a focus on financial success, as well as social connections. The research demonstrates the importance of the family in shaping wealth accumulation, as well as the importance of culture in shaping economic behavior which can ultimately create social inequality.

In their study of 161 fathers and sons in a Midwestern city, Crowley and Ballweg (1971) concluded that Protestant men achieve higher occupational and economic status than their Catholic counterparts. However, Glenn and Hyland (1967) found that Catholics rank above Protestants in most aspects of status. Their research suggests that the rapid advancement of Catholics compared to Protestants can be attributed largely to living in non-Southern communities where earnings, occupations, educational opportunities, and upward mobility are more favorable. The findings from these studies suggest that religion, along with factors such as region, contribute to a person's economic status.

The Media and Beliefs About Poverty and Wealth

The media also continue to influence individual beliefs concerning poverty and wealth. Entman (1989) found that the media make a significant contribution to how people think as well as what they think about.

Bullock, Wyche, and Williams (2001) used content analysis to examine 412 newspaper articles about poverty and welfare published during a 3-month period in 1999. Their research found that although most articles were neutral in tone and portrayed the difficulties facing welfare recipients and the poor in a sympathetic manner, little had been done to shed light on the causes of poverty.

Sotirovic (2001) examined public perceptions of welfare recipients and of welfare programs. The results show that many forms of media, such as television cable news and entertainment shows, play a major role in introducing typical biases in welfare perceptions. These public perceptions of welfare recipients are usually of young, non-White females who benefit from higher federal spending on welfare programs.

Hannah and Cafferty (2006) studied television news shows depicting persons in poverty and found similar results. The news presentations depicted the poor as either primarily Black or primarily White. Individuals who viewed presentations where Whites were primarily depicted as poor felt that not enough money was being spent on poverty programs. They were also more likely to take a flyer about volunteering with a poverty-related charity. However, when participants were shown presentations where more Blacks were poor, no such reaction occurred. Oddly, this pattern of results was found for both White and Black viewers. This finding demonstrates how African Americans may be influenced by the media to react negatively towards others of the same race that are in need. This could prevent some individuals from sharing information regarding wealth attainment with others because they feel those persons are "lazy" or are not truly in need. Although literature exists regarding African Americans and the influence that the media has on self-perception, it does not focus specifically on how those perceptions affect beliefs about wealth or poverty.

Educational Institutions and Wealth Attainment

Limited research has directly linked education and wealth. Although research has shown that individuals who have higher levels of education earn more, discussions are limited in terms of the roles that educational institutions play in promoting financial literacy and wealth attainment. Literature suggests that there is a direct relationship between academic achievement and success and that the success experienced in school can lead to wealth attainment (Mickelson, 1990). Historically, primary and secondary educational institutions have been responsible for teaching students how to add, subtract, divide and work for someone else (Oliver & Shapiro, 1995).

However, research has shown that African American students have been at a disadvantage within education institutions as a result of the teaching methods that are utilized (Love & Krueger, 2005; Mickelson, 1990). Mickelson examined concrete and abstract attitudes toward education among African American students. For African American students, positive attitudes toward education exist when concrete teaching methods are applied instead of abstract methods. Abstract methods are not rooted in life experiences; however, educational credentials are usually awarded based on these abstractions. As a result, education credentials may not be fairly rewarded. The results indicate that race and class, which are large components of the social context of achievement, influence school outcomes.

Similar to the results of Mickelson (1990), research by Kruger (2005) found that the most successful teachers of African American children were those who created a relational and personal environment. In this same study, teachers who taught students with high academic achievement viewed their role as disseminators of knowledge and believed in drill and practice.

The same methods that have been effective when working with African American youth in the school systems should also be incorporated into initiatives that are developed in order to positively influence behaviors that contribute to wealth attainment.

METHODOLOGY

Participants

Data for the purposes of this research were collected from survey and focus groups. Participants were recruited by utilizing convenience and snowball sampling techniques. Potential participants were approached utilizing personal contacts on Facebook (a social networking site), personal e-mail contacts, personal contacts at two churches in Thomasville and High Point, NC, personal contacts in Raleigh, NC, students at North Carolina A&T State University, and participants passing surveys on to others via e-mail or in person. Focus group interviews were conducted in Raleigh, NC, Thomasville, NC, and Greensboro, NC.

Participants in the survey group completed surveys in a variety of settings. Focus group participants were also given a survey to complete at the beginning of the session. The sample size for this research was 130 (N = 44 from the focus group, N = 86 from the survey group).

Descriptive statistics in Table 5.1 provide the characteristics of each group.

Table 5.1. Descriptive Statistics for Survey and Focus Groups

Variable	*Survey Group (Percent)*	*Focus Group (Percent)*
Gender		
Male	20.9	55.3
Female	79.1	44.7
Age		
18-24	37.2	23.7
25-34	24.4	18.4
35-44	24.4	18.4
45-54	11.6	10.5
55 and older	2.3	28.9
Household Income		
Less than 20,000	14.0	21.1
20,000-34,999	30.2	18.4
35,000-49,999	11.6	15.8
50,000-59,999	11.6	2.6
60,000-74,999	12.8	13.2
75,000 and above	18.6	23.7
Religious Preference		
Yes	90.0	97.0
Religious Affiliation		
Baptist	43.0	36.8
Methodist	10.4	36.8
Lutheran	3.5	2.6
Nondenominational	23.2	10.5
Educational Attainment		
High School	14.0	21.1
College (1-3 years)	48.8	36.8
College Graduate	22.1	21.1
Master's Degree	12.8	18.4
Doctoral Degree	2.3	0

Procedure and Analysis

The analysis for this research was carried out in three stages. The first stage consisted of a descriptive analysis of the sociodemographic variables. The second stage interpreted an exploratory model that used logistic regression analyses to assess the predictors of wealth on African American wealth attainment. The third stage further explored the relationship of the predictors of wealth on African American wealth attainment and additional factors that may not have been revealed from survey data. Focus group interviews were utilized in order to accomplish this aim.

In order to gain insight into factors that may possibly influence African American wealth attainment, focus group participants were asked a series of questions regarding their thoughts on wealth attainment as well as what they were taught concerning wealth when they were younger. The grounded theory approach was utilized in order to identify important patterns and themes that emerged as a result of focus group discussions.

Open coding was utilized to organize focus group data. During the process of open coding, data were read first and then categorized into codes that were suggested by the data rather than imposed from the outside. The codes were then clustered into concepts. Once the focus group data were examined, the concepts were organized by themes. Concepts represented the properties and dimensions of a particular theme. The identification of themes and comparisons within each group often required several rounds of transcription analysis. This process continued until the data were saturated or no new properties related to a theme emerged (Cassell & Symon, 2005). The following seven themes surfaced from the focus group data: wealth associations, sources of perceptions and beliefs, pathways to wealth attainment, barriers to wealth attainment, lessons taught, responsibility in building wealth, and opportunities to build wealth.

LOGISTIC REGRESSION ANALYSES

Predictors of Wealth Attainment

In order to explore the six research questions presented, separate logistic regression analyses were performed on the responses of survey and focus group participants to determine the effect of the independent variables on the dependent variables in the sample as well as to detect differences between the survey and focus groups. There was only one relationship that was significant. Table 5.2 shows that the independent variable, educational attainment, was a significant predictor of the dependent variable (owning property/land) for the survey group only in model 1. For every one-unit increase in educational attainment, there was a 1.064 increase in the log-odds of owning property, holding all other independent variables constant.

In model 2, the demographic variables were added; however, educational attainment was no longer a significant predictor of owning property/land. However, household income was a significant predictor of owning property/land. For every one-unit increase in household income, there was a 2.085 increase in the log-odds of owning property, holding all other independent variables constant. In model 3, the mediating variable, individualistic beliefs of wealth attainment, was entered into the model; however, it was not significant. Household income continued to be a significant predictor of owning property/land (see Table 5.2).

QUALITATIVE ANALYSIS

Wealth Associations and Sources of Perceptions and Beliefs

At the beginning of the session, participants were asked what came to mind when they heard the word "wealth." When describing what came to mind, participants replied "money," "White people," "power," and "security." When participants were asked who taught them about wealth, the most frequent responses for all groups included "parents," "grandparents," "teachers," "cousins," "peers," and "church elders."

Pathways to Wealth Attainment

In addition to responding to the question of being taught about wealth, participants also shared some of the things that they were taught concerning how to obtain wealth. Responses included "work," "get an education,"

Table 5.2. Logistic Regression Analysis for Property (Land)

	Model 1		*Model 2*		*Model 3*	
Variables	*β*	*Odds Ratio*	*β*	*Odds Ratio*	*β*	*Odds Ratio*
Education	1.064*	2.898	–.129	.879	.275	1.317
Gender	–3.825	.022	–7.624	.000		
Household Income	2.085*	8.046	4.012*	55.239		
Age	–.077	.926	–1.117	.499		
Individualistic	–3.115	0.44				

$^{*}p < .05$

and "save." One participant indicated that the key to wealth was leaving home to get an education:

> In my home state of Alabama, nobody taught you about being wealthy. You had to get your education and get out of the South; however you got out was left up to you. These cats in the group are much older than I am but my eight brothers and I worked in the field, but we didn't get any money. It was a different time coming up. We were never taught about wealth in middle school, high school; you learned about wealth when you went to college. We didn't learn anything about money because our parents didn't give us any money. Money was what we had on the table. Escaping Alabama was key, and getting an education was pivotal to that because that led to a higher self-esteem that would lead you to a good job.

Barriers to Wealth Attainment

Participants also provided insight into why they felt African Americans were not wealthy. One participant said, "Subconsciously, we get information but won't share it because that person may do more with it than we will. A lot of cultures build each other up, but we haven't reached that point." Another participant stated:

> We work hard enough, but we do not want to keep what we get. We are too busy trying to get the rims on the car; we are about flash and not saving, and we don't want to work together. Can you see three generations of family living in the same house out of necessity to build each other up? The Hispanic family will do that. They will pull each other in and build one another up.

Participants also cited the media as a barrier to wealth attainment noting:

> The media hurts because we see how celebrities live and we try to live like them even though we don't have the money they have. So people will try to wear Beyonce boots or Jay-Z outfits, and you cant afford it. Its not about materialistic things but what you can afford.

Although education was cited in focus groups as a pathway to wealth attainment, some saw educational attainment as a barrier as a result of lack of information about the debt that could be incurred:

> No one tells you how much it's going to cost you to get it (education). You can get those degrees and are $40,000 and $50,000 in debt; now you already have a house payment on your degrees, so how are you going to get a house?

Another participant stated, "In my teenage years we were taught to get a college education, and then it was a master's degree and then another advanced degree. It seems you never catch up to what you need to get that edge."

Lessons Taught

Some participants stated that there were lessons they were taught concerning wealth attainment that had helped them, while others said it hurt them. Some commented that they were taught nothing at all and provided examples of how this hurt them. One participant said, "I remember for my 18th birthday I was given a $2,500 check, and no one told me what to do with it; so I put about $500 in the bank, and I blew the rest." Another person stated, "My mom has a really good mind when it comes to budgeting; she tried to teach me, but she still hurt me because she still bought me what I wanted." Yet another participant remarked, "My grandfather taught me about wealth. He had acres and acres of land, and he built his own house. He had his own farm. All he had was the taxes on the land, so it was debt free."

Responsibility in Building Wealth

Focus group participants indicated that they felt that it was the responsibility of African Americans to teach one another. One participant stated, "We as parents and as youth leaders need to put our fingers on money to help them get to the next step." Another participant said:

> I actually paid someone to come in and speak with my employees when the stock market took a dive. For me as a young Black woman I think it is important because most of my staff is Black and they don't have anyone else to explain their investments to them.

Opportunities to Build Wealth

All age groups felt that the younger generation had a better chance to obtain wealth. They also felt that the younger generation did not appreciate the opportunities currently available because they did not have to struggle for them. Focus group participants 45 years and older stated that it would be the responsibility of the parents to continue teaching their children about wealth. For example, one participant stated, "You need the education and you need to encourage your younger children." Another participant said, "Teach them that it's not about materialistic things, not about stuff."

Although there were patterns and themes that emerged as a result of focus group discussions, there were no variations in responses based on gender. There were similarities between one of the 18-24 year old focus groups and the focus group that consisted primarily of those 35-44 years of age. When asked about the meaning of wealth, both of these groups indicated that wealth not only meant money, but that it also meant whatever made a person happy. Both groups stated that although it was important to save, one should also be able to enjoy some of what one has earned. The majority of participants in the 35-44 years of age focus group were college-educated. These participants pointed out that although they were taught that education was important to wealth attainment, costs had also hindered their wealth attainment.

Their only regret concerning education was that no one talked with them about the debt that they would incur as a result of educational expenses. In addition, none of the focus groups indicated structural explanations, such as discrimination, as a reason that African Americans are not wealthy, but instead focused on individualistic reasons for the lack of wealth, which included not sharing information, laziness, and the pursuit of materialistic things. More specifically, focus group participants felt that some African Americans do not share information because they are fearful other people will excel above them. Others felt that some people do not desire a better life for themselves, while some felt some African Americans live beyond their means by spending money on things that depreciate in value, such as clothing and accessories for cars.

DISCUSSION

Families Are the Predominant Sources of Information for Financial Learning

Qualitative data from focus group discussions name the family as the first source of education regarding wealth. Participants identified family members such as parents, grandparents, and cousins that played an important part in teaching them about wealth. The relationship between familial factors and wealth attainment among African Americans is important because the family is one of the most important agents of socialization (Schaefer, 2008). Many of our financial behaviors can be traced back to what we have been told by or observed in our family. The qualitative findings in this study are similar to those of prior research that examined the relationship between family background and wealth (Menchik & Jianakaplos, 1997; Ngina & Stafford, 1999; Rumberg, 1983).

Religion Shapes Perceptions of Wealth

Along with the family, focus group participants also cited elders in the church as persons who taught them about wealth. Although participants referred to elders in the church, they also noted that speaking about money in church, in general, was also not a part of the church culture. In the age of the "mega church," younger participants stated that some people are not wealthy because they are trying to imitate the lifestyle of the pastor. Although many pastors of "mega" churches are wealthy, many of their congregants are not. Some of the congregants live beyond their means by purchasing items that they cannot afford, such as fancy clothes and cars. This is consistent with prior research findings that religious beliefs and cultures shape attitudes and behaviors that lead to wealth attainment (Crowley & Ballweg, 1971; Glenn & Hyland, 1967; Keister, 2003; Mayer & Sharp, 1962)

The Media as a Pathway to Conspicuous Consumption

Groups also cited the media as a barrier to African American wealth attainment because it promotes instant gratification. Focus group participants emphasized the media's role in promoting African Americans' desire to have the "latest fashions" and the "biggest TV." The spending behavior of African Americans has been referred to as "conspicuous consumption." Conspicuous consumption involves lavish spending on material items, such as cars, clothes, and entertainment (Oliver & Shapiro, 1995). Conspicuous consumption is also used to identify class membership as well as cultural distinctiveness (Lamont & Molnar, 2001).

Educational Attainment as a Barrier to Wealth Attainment

Results from quantitative analyses indicate that the only significant relationship was educational attainment as a predictor of wealth attainment (i.e., owning property/land). This finding from the survey group is consistent with a finding from the subgroup of focus group participants primarily consisting of persons 35-44 years of age. This focus subgroup consisted primarily of college-educated individuals. As described previously, these participants pointed out that although they were taught that education was important to wealth attainment, educational costs had hindered their wealth attainment. Their only regret concerning education was that no one talked with them about the debt that they would incur as a result of educational expenses. They also understood that, in some instances, colleges and universities had not taught them about wealth, contrary to their parents' expectations. These findings are consistent with research regarding the lack of financial education in primary and secondary educational institutions (Oliver & Shapiro, 1995).

Implications for Educators

Research has shown that certain teaching methods are more effective than others when working with African American students (Krueger, 2005; Mickelson, 1990). The same methods that have been effective when working with African American youth in school systems should also be incorporated into financial literacy programs. Effective financial literacy programs should incorporate concrete teaching methods as well as create a personal and relational environment (Mickelson, 1990). Concrete teaching methods are rooted in life experiences. Activities in a financial literacy program should focus on making sure a student is able to relate concepts that they have learned to their personal experiences. In a personal and relational environment, teachers should constantly provide exercises for students in order to reinforce what they have learned (Krueger, 2005).

Limitations of Research

There are limitations of this research that should be noted. One limitation is the possibility that some focus group members may have been reluctant to speak as a result of group dynamics. More reserved participants may have been hesitant to speak as a result of extremely dominant or opinionated members. Others may have felt uncomfortable or had issues of confidentiality because it was a group setting.

The findings of this study are also limited in generalizability because of the small sample size and convenience sampling techniques. Generalizability functions in a very different way in qualitative studies than in quantitative research paradigms. Qualitative generalizations should be made based upon the depth of description and the "fit" of one case with others that are similar in important ways (Geertz, 1975; Janesick, 1994). Therefore, generalizing the findings of this study to other groups should be done with these cautions in mind.

Recommendations for Future Research

Wordings of the survey items in this study may have prompted inconsistencies in the quantitative and qualitative findings. Survey questions were not as specific as focus group questions, and they only measured certain aspects of behaviors that dealt with wealth attainment. Future survey questions need to be reconstructed to ask participants direct questions such as: Did your family teach you about wealth? Did your religion influence your beliefs about wealth attainment and your practices? Do you feel the media influenced your beliefs about wealth and your actual wealth attainment? Since focus group data has provided more insight into the factors that influence wealth attainment, focus group interviews should be utilized to improve future survey questions.

DISCUSSION QUESTIONS

1. When you hear the word wealth, what is the first thing that comes to mind?
2. What has your family taught you about wealth?
3. Does your parent/guardian have a budget? If so, how does s/he use it?
4. Have any of your classes in school taught you about money? What have they taught you?
5. Do you feel that receiving an education will allow you to make more money?
6. Why/why not?
7. If you practice a religion, has it influenced your beliefs about money and wealth? If so, how?

MODEL LESSON

Money Management

Suggested Grade Levels: 7th -12th Grades
Objectives

(a) Students will be able to identify expenses within their respective homes.
(b) Students will be able to distinguish between fixed and variable expenses within their respective homes.

(c) Students will be able to develop a personal budget.

Related Standards

Jump$tart National Standards in K–12 Personal Finance Education

Planning and Money Management

Standard 1: Develop a plan for spending and saving.

Financial Responsibility and Decision Making

Standard 1: Take responsibility for personal financial decisions.

Standard 4: Make financial decisions by systematically considering alternatives and consequences.

Income and Careers

Standard 1: Explore career options.

Standard 3: Describe factors affecting take-home pay

Materials

- Sample budget: (http://www.themint.org//teachers/sample-budget.html)
- Starting salaries sheet: (http://www.themint.org//teens/starting-salaries.html)
- Determining your take home pay (interactive exercise): (http://www.themint.org//teens/determine-your-budget.html)
- Sample pay stub:(http://www.themint.org//teens/decoding-your-paycheck.html)

Procedures

(a) Opening Activities.

1. Go over the sample budget with students. Discuss how budgets are used to help people manage their money as well as negative consequences that occur from not budgeting. Ask students if they know anyone that uses a budget. Also ask if they have ever

discussed budgets with a parent/guardian or other adult. If so, what were they told? If they practice a particular religion, ask what their religious beliefs are regarding money.

2. Discuss the two types of expenses: fixed and variable. Ask students to think of examples of fixed and variable expenses they may have at home. Explain that salaries also play an important part in how one budgets.
3. Share with the students that the amount of one's salary will not be one's actual take home pay. Review a sample pay check stub with students in order to illustrate this point as well as to introduce them to concepts such as gross pay and net pay. Also, share with students that it is helpful if one keeps a log of monthly expenses so that one is aware of his/her personal spending habits. Note the importance of saving money.
4. Ask students if each has a bank account. Discuss with students what should be done if one's expenses exceed one's income. Ask them what types of things influence their spending. Are they influenced by what they see on television, or read in magazines? Or is their spending based on what their friends have? Ask students why they feel people would spend money on things that they cannot afford. Can they provide examples either from television or from personal experiences? Are they aware of what the consequences are when a person overspends?

(b) Developmental Activities

1. Explain to students that they will create their own budget using the sample budget as a guide.
2. Have students select a job that interests them. Recreate the salary sheet by leaving off the salaries so that students choose a job that actually interests them regardless of whether the salary is high or low.
3. Provide the full salary sheet with the salaries no longer hidden. Once students have the salary from their chosen occupation, they calculate their take home pay by using the interactive exercise at http://www.themint.org. (If computers are not available for everyone, have students take turns in front of the rest of the class, using one computer to calculate net pay or calculate the net pay for each job. Or if time is an issue, precalculate net pay for each occupation so that all salaries can be shared whether or not there is time to calculate each individually).

(c) Closing Activities

1. Instruct students to reflect on what they have learned. Encourage responses by asking how they felt about taxes and other deductions that were taken out of their check.
   - Were they aware of the importance of education when determining earning power?
   - Do they have a better appreciation for the income that their parents or other family members bring home?

(d) Summary and Assessment

1. The assessment of what students have learned should be an ongoing process. Teachers should incorporate budgeting activities into their lessons on a regular basis.
2. One possible activity is to assign various amounts of money to students, followed by a blank monthly budget sheet. Students create a plan for how the money will be used based on the amount of money that they were given. This reinforces the importance of staying within their budget and not competing with the perception of what others may have. This activity can be implemented and assessed on an individual basis or students can be divided into groups. In order to assess the activity, students will be given a certain number of points for including their needs (5 points), an amount for savings (5 points), and properly prioritizing their needs over their wants (5 points) in their budget. The number of points assigned will be at the discretion of the teacher. One point will be deducted for every need that is left off of the budget. Students will also lose one point if savings has not been included in the budget. Students that earn the most points will receive an incentive that will be chosen by the teacher. If the activity is done in groups, the groups with the most points will win. This activity can be repeated as many times as the teacher desires in order to give students an opportunity to receive incentives as well as to reinforce lessons learned from the activity.
3. Facilitate a follow-up discussion about what students see in the media regarding money and wealth. Give students an opportunity to reflect on what they have learned. For example, if students are interested in music videos, the teacher can point out that most of the time the cars, houses, and jewelry are rented and do not belong to the performer.

4. Invite guest speakers from local banks, as well as other institutions in the community, to discuss the importance of financial literacy. Students need opportunities to combine the practical skills learned with new perceptions of what wealth actually is and that it actually starts with good financial habits such as budgeting.

REFERENCES

Allen, B. L. (2002). Race and gender inequality in homeownership: Does place matter? *Rural Sociology, 67*(4), 603-621.

Blau, F. D., & Graham, J. W. (1990). Black-White differences in wealth and asset composition. *The Quarterly Journal of Economics, 105*(2), 321-339.

Bradford, W. D. (2003). The wealth dynamics of entrepreneurship for black and white families. *U.S. Review of Income and Wealth, 49*(1), 89–116.

Ariel Mutual Funds & Charles Schwab & Company. (1999). Black investors survey. Retrieved from http://www.arielinvestments.com/content/view/354/1228/

Birnbaum, H., & Weston, R. (1974). Homeownership and the wealth position of black and white Americans. *The Review of Income and Wealth, 20,* 103-118.

Bullock, H. E., Wyche. K. F., & Williams, W. R. (2001) Media images of the poor. *Journal of Social Issues, 57*(2), 229-246.

Cassell, C., & Symon, G. (1995). *Essential guide to qualitative methods in organizational research.* London: SAGE.

Crowley, J. W., & Ballweg, J. A. (1971). Religious preference and worldly success: An empirical test in a Midwestern city. *Sociological Analysis, 32*(2), 71-80.

Entman, R. M. (1989). How the media affect what people think: An information processing approach. *The Journal of Politics, 51*(2), 347-370.

Gertz, C. (1973). *The interpretation of cultures.* New York, NY: Basic Books.

Glenn, N. D., & Hyland, R. (1967). Religious preference and worldly success: Some evidence from national surveys. *American Sociological Review, 32*(1), 73-85.

Hannah, G., & Cafferty, T. (2006). Attribute and responsibility: Framing effects in television news coverage of poverty. *Journal of Applied Social Psychology, 36*(12), 2993–3014.

Hunt, M. O. (1996). The individual, society, or both? A comparison of black, Latino, and white beliefs about the causes of poverty. *Social Forces, 75*(1), 293-322.

Hunt, M. O. (2004). Race/ethnicity and beliefs about wealth and poverty. *Social Science Quarterly, 85*(3), 827–853.

Janesick, V. J. (1994). The dance of qualitative design. In N. K. Denzin & Y. S. Lincoln (Eds.), *Handbook of Qualitative Research* (pp. 209-219). Thousand Oaks, CA: SAGE.

Keister, L. A. (2003). Religion and wealth: The role of religious affiliation and participation in early adult asset accumulation. *Social Forces, 82*(1), 175-207.

Kluegel, J. R., & Smith, E. R. (1982). Beliefs about stratification. *American Sociological Review, 47*(4), 518-532.

Krivo, L. J., & Kaufman, R. L. (2004). Wealth inequality: Racial-ethnic differences in home equity in the United States. *Demography, 41*(3), 585-605.

Lamont, M., & Molnar, V. (2001). How blacks use consumption to shape their collective identity: Evidence from marketing specialists. *Journal of Consumer Culture, 1*(1), 31-45.

Lee, B. A., Jones, S. H., & Lewis, D. W. (1990). Public beliefs about the causes of homelessness, *69(1)*, 253-265.

Love, A., & Krueger, A. C. (2005). Teacher beliefs and student achievement in urban schools serving African American students. *Journal of Education Research, 99*(2), 87-98.

Mayer, A. J., & Sharp, H. (1962). Religious preference and worldly success. *American Sociological Review, 27*(2), 218-227.

Menchik, P. L., & Jianakoplos, N.A. (1997). Black-white wealth inequality: Is inheritance the reason? *Economic Inquiry, 35*, 428-432.

Mickelson, R. A. (1990). The attitude-achievement paradox among black adolescents *Sociology of Education, 63*(1), 44-61.

Ngina S. C., & Stafford, F. P. (1999). Portfolio choices of parents and their children as young adults: Asset accumulation by African American families. *The American Economic Review, 89*(2), 377-380.

Nilson, L. B. (1981). Reconsidering ideological lines: beliefs about poverty in America. *The Sociological Quarterly, 22*(4), 531-548.

Oliver, M., & Shapiro, T. (1995). *Black wealth/white wealth: A new perspective on racial inequality.* New York, NY: Routledge.

Sotirovic, M. (2001). Media use and perceptions of welfare. *Journal of Communication, 51*(4), 750–774.

Rumberger, R. W. (1983). The influence of family background on education, earnings, and wealth. *Social Forces, 61*(3), 755-773.

Schaefer, R. T. (2006) *Sociology: A brief introduction, (6th ed.)*, Boston, MA: McGraw-Hill.

CHAPTER 6

COMPARING UNDERGRADUATE AND GRADUATE STUDENTS' PERCEPTIONS OF FINANCIAL MORALITY

Alan B. Bates and Thomas A. Lucey

In a climate of global economic instability, various explanations for financial havoc occur. Patterns of self-interest and greed underlie these claims, as investment brokers sell financial investments based on speculation and consumers acquire goods and services based on future income and price appreciation. Yet opposite the settings of abstract systemic expertise and financial bliss lies the stark reality of poverty and despair. How appropriate is an environment where these disparities occur, considering various resources that society has to close this financial literacy gap? This situation presents an opportunity for the financial education community to examine the morality aspects of financial education and their relationship to the education of citizens in a largely capitalist global setting.

Literature well publicizes the economic and financial illiteracy of the American populous (e.g., Lucey, 2002; Mandell, 2008, 2009; National Foundation for Credit Counseling, 2008). Yet these measures present a limited interpretation of financial literacy, which concerns acquisition,

Reframing Financial Literacy: Exploring the Value of Social Currency, pp. 101–123

conservation, allocation, and growth of financial resources. They lack a human or moral component that addresses the social consequences of financial decision making (Lucey, 2007).

The early twenty-first century K-12 American education setting tends to emphasize technical and practical aspects of curricula (Lucey & Lorsbach, in press), that relegate emancipatory elements to other education venues. These education settings present knowledge largely as an objective concept and employ standardized testing as a mechanism for sorting out students that resist conformance to accepted norm. Within these contexts, financial education suffers from an emphasis on the technical/practical conception that limits opportunities for exploration of sociohistoric moral connections (Lucey, 2004, 2007, 2008; Lucey & Cooter, 2008) that may prompt critical thinking (Postman & Weingartner, 1969) which challenges the patterns of oppression that occur through existent environments.

Principles associated with narrow financial literacy conceptions are diametrically opposed to broader conceptions that relate to socially just ideals. As illustrated in Figure 6.1, conventional (which are mainly material) views of financial literacy range from concrete to abstract in a material sense. Financial literacy to the disadvantaged concerns a vision of immediacy, in which decisions focus on knowledge of a financial unit in isolation. Those who are economically advantaged view the patterns of economic relationships among various groups of people and interpret how their financial decisions within these contexts may increase their control of financial resources. The underlying principles associated with this framework are merit and reward. By enabling a financially illiterate person to visualize and attain financial goals, that person is able to delay spending, increase investing, and optimize existing systems to accumulate rights to goods and services.

Yet this system supposes that the individual possesses the skills and attributes to acquire an income that produces surplus resources to invest. The system also presumes that the investments chosen are growing at a desired rate or producing needed income. It presumes that employers provide health insurance. In other words, financial betterment comes purely from choices, when these choices relate to elements of fate.

As illustrated in Figure 6.2, the foundational principle within a socially just or moral conception of financial literacy, is that access to financial resources represents an element of fate. People do not choose the contexts from which they derive. They do not choose their families or birth conditions. The decisions and understandings of early generations affect the dissemination of resources and knowledge to later generations. Being born into a family is not a choice. It is a matter that one cannot control. It represents a matter of fate. In this framework, the concept of merit that

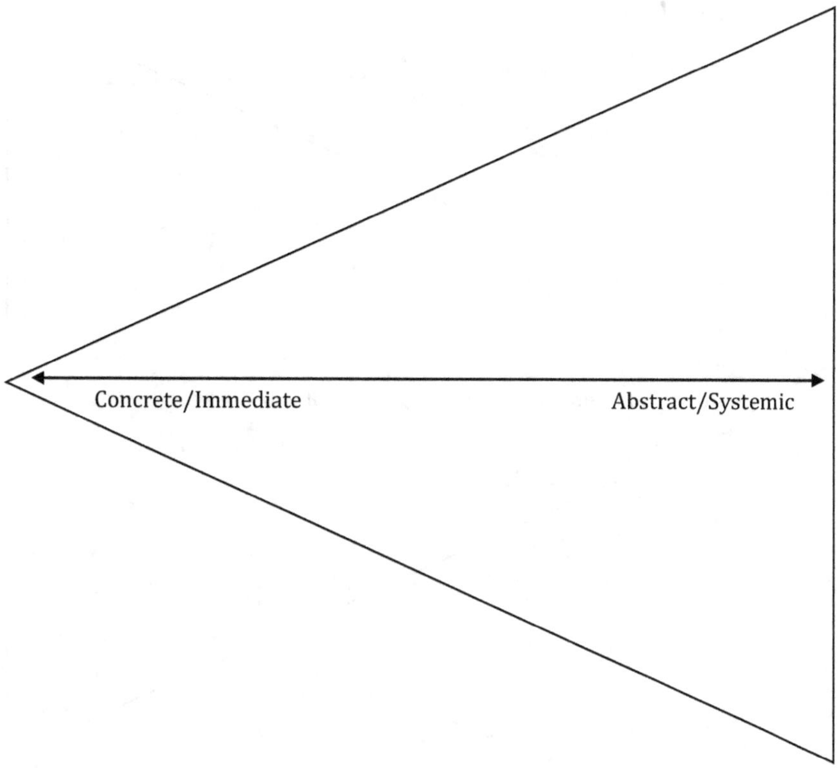

Figure 6.1. Conventional view of financial literacy.

results from decision-making has no place because all decisions derive from uncontrolled origins.

Thus, financially moral or socially-just decision-making requires awareness that access to goods and services are not matters of ownership but stewardship. Financial growth is less important than financial wellness. Interactions should be regarded in the context that no one has control over his or her personal origins; that his or her financial situation is not a matter of choice; and that financial decisions should involve a human-based conception of respect.

This conception of financial decision-making is broader than the systemic framework considered in conventional views. It recognizes that every member of the global community has the potential to make similar patterns of decisions, given like amounts and types of resources. It is much like a card game where one attempts to play his or her cards in a manner consistent with the ranks and suits of the cards received except

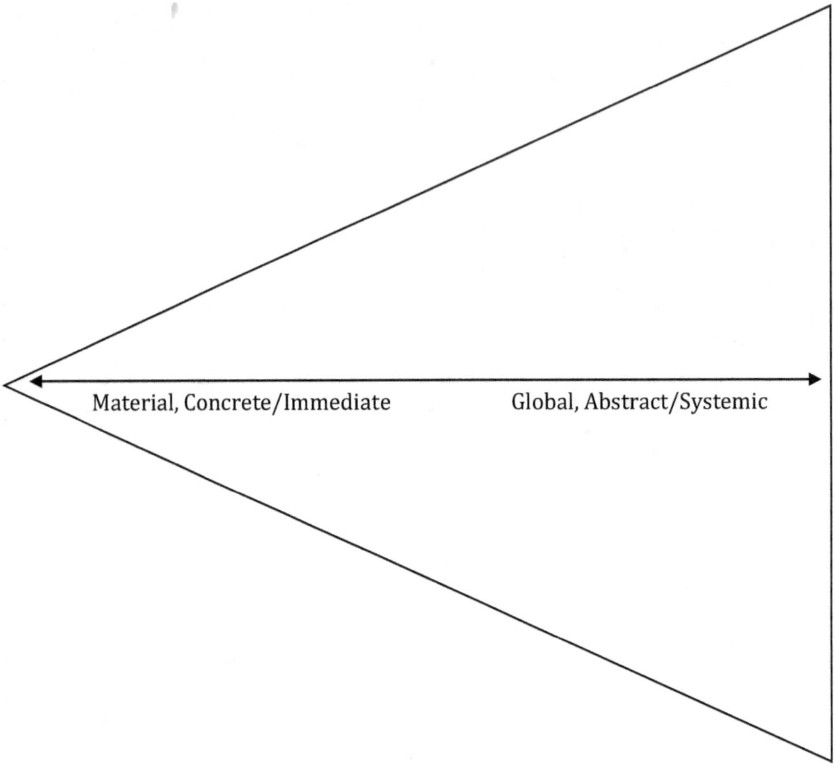

Figure 6.2. Socially just/moral view of financial literacy.

that the nature of the game is not competitive (where one trumps the card of the opposition). The game is respectful, in that players realize that resource access does not represent a matter entirely of individual control and that financial decisions should respect the conditions of others.

One may conceive of financial morality as being more than the simple compliance with one's financial contracts. Financial morality involves a conception of how financial decisions relate to the welfare of others. This differentiation between financial literacy and financial morality extends Nucci's (2001) distinction between social convention and morality.

Understanding how preservice and in-service teachers interpret financial morality has important meanings for K-12 settings, teacher preparation, and moral education. Within K-12 settings, teachers' understandings of content relate to whether and/or how they introduce the subject in their teaching. For example, if teaching about Christopher Columbus, whether or the extent to which a teacher is familiar with critical interpretations of

Columbus's voyage and arrival to the new world and his or her thoughts about the appropriateness of these alternative views determines the extent to which s/he engages students in related classroom conversation.

Empowering candidates to facilitate learning by employing safe environments that develop critical-thinking and open dialogue represents an important part of developing a just learning community. Financial morality challenges financial convention in its recognition that all of humanity benefits from financial practice, not just those who control large amounts of resources. This conception contradicts conventions of capitalism which interpret wealth accumulation as a matter of merit, rather than fate.

College students who plan careers as teachers and educators will have a large responsibility for both teaching content and modeling expectations for future citizenry. Thus, although morality may not represent a subject taught explicitly, the patterns of judgment and treatment of students by teachers provide implicit messages about how children should think and act.

As they enter into early adulthood, college students are very impressionable individuals who wrestle with new autonomous frontiers that challenge their abilities to regulate their social and academic practices. Research shows that moral development continues during the college years (King & Mayhew, 2002; Mayhew & King, 2008). In their extensive review of literature in the area of moral development in college students, King and Mayhew conclude that college students' patterns of moral development that occur throughout college are not due to chronological maturation alone. Development, in any domain, occurs in context, and colleges can be great contexts to encourage moral reasoning. In fact, college courses that include moral content can improve college students' moral reasoning (Mayhew & King, 2008). Courses where moral content is explicit, are more effective in promoting growth in moral reasoning than classes where it is implicit. Furthermore, students who enroll in courses where moral content is explicit reason at higher moral levels as compared to those students enrolled in courses where the content is implicit demonstrating that students enter courses at different levels of moral development (Mayhew & King, 2008). However, recent research shows little or no difference in regards to various majors; rather, the evidence indicates that students in their early years of college are more open to moral education than they are in late years (Livingstone, Derryberry, King, & Vendetti, 2006; Mayhew & King, 2008).

Examining other content areas, research has shown that preservice and in-service teachers vary in regards to their level of knowledge in various areas. Greenhow, Dexter, and Hughes (2008) examined preservice and in-service teachers' ability to integrate technology in the classroom and although both groups were capable, their rationales differed. Preservice teachers' decisions were superficial, noncritical, and did not consider the larger picture. In-service teachers provided more details and considered school and district level influences on their instruction. In a study, that sought to identify the knowledge, skills, and abilities needed by agricultural science teachers, Harlin, Roberts, Dooley, and Murphrey (2007) conducted focus groups with preservice and in-service teachers. They found that the groups identified similar knowledge and skills; however, in-service teachers described broader, more well-rounded skills than did preservice teachers. Other studies have also found differences in regards to preservice and in-service teachers' understanding of early literacy instruction (Mather, Bos, & Babur, 2001) and scientific knowledge (Buaraphan, 2009). In both cases, in-service teachers demonstrate more knowledge, but both studies also conclude that in-service teachers' knowledge in those areas could also be improved.

Research efforts to measure the valuing of financial morality and its components have occurred (e.g., Bates & Lucey, 2008; Lucey, 2004; Lucey & Bates, 2008). Yet these endeavors have employed survey methods that prompted observations of important relationships that needed clarification. This chapter adds to the literature by offering an interpretation of financial morality developed through conversations among various student groups. This chapter describes a study that analyzed responses to five questions asked to preservice teachers and graduate students, most of whom were in-service teachers in a College of Education at a public Midwestern institution for higher learning. It provides an opportunity to continue scholarly dialogue about the nature of financial morality and its relationship to financial literacy.

METHODOLOGY

Participants

Participants consisted of sophomore and junior teacher education majors ($N = 8$) and graduate students from Curriculum & Instruction and Psychology departments ($N = 12$) at a Midwestern institution of higher learning. The Curriculum & Instruction graduate students were all in-service teachers; the psychology students were part of the school psychology program.

Participants were recruited from the researchers' summer courses and were offered extra credit for their participation. Undergraduate students were recruited from a child development course, and the graduate students were recruited from a multicultural education course. Students were offered an alternative extra credit opportunity if they did not want to participate in the focus group; however, all students chose to take part in the focus group.

Procedure

Three focus groups (2 graduate groups and 1 undergraduate group) were conducted at the university in the Department of Curriculum and Instruction conference room. In addition, one undergraduate student participated in an interview by herself. All groups were conducted outside of classroom time and were approximately 30 minutes each. The groups were facilitated by the researcher, who was not the course instructor for those particular students. Focus groups were audio taped, and tapes were transcribed verbatim by an undergraduate research assistant to ensure systematic analysis of the groups' discussions. Each facilitator asked the questions listed below in the same order and asked only clarification questions, if necessary.

Focus Group Questions

Focus group questions were developed by the two researchers to examine participants' conception and application of financial morality. Participants were asked to respond to the following questions:

- What is financial morality?
- What examples of financial morality have you witnessed or experienced?
- How is financial morality similar to or different from conventional morality?
- What would it be like if your future professional environment was financially moral?
- Using the ideas developed in the conversation to support your views, to what extent should financial morality be addressed within your university coursework?

The questions were structured consistently with various levels of Bloom's (1956) taxonomy of cognitive thinking. The sequence was planned to provide participants with an opportunity to consider the concept before extending its meanings to other contexts and making informed judgments about related issues.

Data Analysis

The transcriptions of the taped focus-group discussions were used in the analysis process. The two authors reviewed the participants' responses, comparing and contrasting the responses within and across the three focus groups and the individual interview. The authors attempted to identify patterns across the responses as guided by their professional backgrounds.

FINDINGS

This section conveys the results of the analysis. It presents the outcomes in sequence of the items that were posed to the participants.

What is Financial Morality?

This question was intended to generate ideas about what the participants thought the concept meant. The group offered redundant responses that conveyed their unfamiliarity with the term. The initial responses of both groups indicate that the students did not possess an understanding of financial morality. Students' first inclination was to respond to the question by using vocabulary associated with the term, "morality," without really reflecting on its meaning. For example, "Being moral with your finances," "Using proper ethics in terms of spending or using money," and "The ability to keep money and finances together in a respectable manner without lying, cheating, or deceiving."

The graduate students showed some ability to explore deeper meanings of financial morality as demonstrated by phrases such as "Using your money in ways that will not harm others," and "Saving for the long term instead of short term." These responses indicated an awareness of the relationship of financial decisions to abstract matters, such as other peoples' wellness and future decisions; however, an overarching pattern of abstract relationships did not develop. No comparable phrases were used by the undergraduate group.

What Examples Of Financial Morality Have You Witnessed or Experienced?

This question intended for respondents to build from the conceptions developed in response to the first prompt and provided ways to illustrate the topic. The responses provided by participants for this question further supported the idea that undergraduate students lack an understanding of the term *financial morality*. The undergraduate students' responses focused on the responsibility of others but not their own. They provided examples pertaining to millionaires giving to charities and over-spending by large businesses and the government. They also discussed observing their parents' spending and savings habits. Some undergraduate students gave the examples of getting their first credit card and being financially independent.

Like the undergraduate students, the graduate students provided the example of giving to charities, but their main focus seemed to be on their own responsibilities. For example, they mentioned paying off mortgages, being responsible with their own money and credit cards, and not spending money they did not have. There seemed to be some confusion between morality and responsibility. Graduate students also provided examples that included elements of judgment, such as buying something they could not afford or seeing their students with clothes that they know their students could not afford. Graduate students also mentioned donating to churches, which shows some individual motivation. They also provided examples related to social convention, such as borrowing or lending money. The amount of money did not seem to matter; one particular example involved borrowing and lending money at vending machines. In fact, one can say that the graduate students' other responses could also be related to social convention. For example, not buying something that one cannot afford implies staying within the rules of social convention and may not be amoral issue. Graduate students also commented on the influence of patterns of spending by one's parents or other adults on patterns of financial practice.

How is Financial Morality Similar to or Different From Conventional Morality?

This question prompted students to analyze the concept, comparing it to morality in general. In regards to this question, not many differences occurred between the two groups of students. Both agreed that when money is involved, one's morality can change. One undergraduate student stated, "Morality changes when money is involved. It can be used to persuade and change people. It can corrupt moral individuals." This was corroborated by another student who said, "when money is involved, it can make reasonable and rational people think unreasonably and irrationally}." One example given was the accumulation of credit card debt. Another undergraduate student pointed out that conventional morality is more social and involves knowing how to treat others. However, this student felt that financial morality was an individual act. These statements seem to provide more evidence that these students did not have a strong grasp as to what financial morality is. Another undergraduate student pointed out that both types of morality are important but that financial morality takes more effort in terms of loyalty and correctness.

Graduate students reiterated the belief that general morality should affect financial morality. They thought conventional morals should be guiding principles that affect every decision of life. Yet their interpretations of conventional morals employed absolutist principles. One student said that there should be one set of standards that everyone should live by. This type of statement might indicate the student's perception of morality as a universal concept. Another student distinguished financial and conventional morality by claiming that these moralities possessed different foundational bases, asserting that financial morality should be black or white whereas conventional standards may differ for different people. Another statement that demonstrates the students' confusion about principles of moral theory was evident through the remark that, "morals don't tend to be ideas or behaviors that are intended to help others or make things easier, but when money is involved, it is different." This student seems to be saying that conventional and financial morality influences people in different ways, but the comments may indicate befuddlement over the topic and uncertainty in an attempt to provide a concise interpretation of an involved distinction. Another graduate student pointed out that conventional and financial morality goes hand in hand by saying, "You put your money where your morals are." We tend to spend our money on what is important to us. That is you put your money where your morals are.

What Would It Be Like If Your Future Professional Environment Was Financially Moral?

The purpose of this question was to prompt students to consider a theoretical application of financial morality in a context with which they could easily associate. The undergraduate students seemed to be very idealistic, believing that their future work place would be financially moral and saying that they would not want to work for a place that was not. However, one student said, "Perhaps you would [work there] if you really needed a job." Another undergraduate student said that since he was going to be a teacher, financial morality was not something he needed to think about. He couldn't cheat or raise his salary as one could in a private business. This implies a very individualistic view of financial morality. Another undergraduate student said, "It would be great because it would mean that teachers got paid more compared to other professions." Perhaps then, teachers would have more incentive to perform their best. Other students agreed, saying people, including teachers and other staff in a school setting, should be paid for what they do and that teachers who work with more difficult subjects should be paid more and that those who work harder should be paid more.

Each graduate student was already part of a professional environment, so the question was modified somewhat for them. Graduate students were asked what their current environment would look like if it was financially moral. Although one of the graduate students did mention that teachers should be paid more, as a group, their responses mainly dealt with the school environment as a whole. For example, they mentioned that they would have more classroom supplies and that their students' needs, both educational and general life needs, would be met. One student believed that if administrators handled the district's money as if it were their own money, they would spend it more wisely and in the areas of greatest need. Two graduate students commended their districts for spending money appropriately, to lower class size and improve technology in the classroom, although they were aware that other school districts spent more inappropriately.

To What Extent, Should Financial Morality Be Addressed Within Your University Course Work?

Undergraduate students believed that financial morality was more important than ever, considering the current state of the economy and the recent financially immoral activities that have taken place. They believed all majors should be taught proper workplace ethics; however, they believed it was more important for business majors. Some felt it should be addressed in general education courses and expressed regret for not have taken any business or financial management courses. Other students mentioned, even if they were not business majors, that it was important knowledge because everyone should be able to manage their own personal finances and have knowledge of the stock market. Another student stressed the need for financial morality instruction in many classes, including business and education classes. He felt that many of his peers did not understand the importance of being financially moral.

Graduate students also agreed that financial morality should be addressed in their coursework. One student pointed that none of the respondents had any conception of financial morality. This absence of awareness indicates the lack of attention to this area in school and community settings. They also agreed that, unless you take a business or finance course, you basically have to figure it out on your own. They stated that there should be an opportunity for everyone to think about how they spend their money. One graduate student did not see the connection of financial morality to practice, stating, "What does it matter to us about financial morality in the sense of teaching first graders?" That student thought that if one was pursuing a degree in administration, perhaps it would be helpful. Another graduate student said she was concerned because she saw students who were not given as many opportunities to succeed as they would have in a just system with more equal distribution of wealth.

One graduate student felt that perhaps financial morality would be better addressed at the high school level because that is when many students are getting jobs and are more likely to spend their money on material goods. But another saw the need primarily for college students, especially because they are often given credit cards by various companies. Practicality was another issue addressed in graduate students' responses. Examples include, "It would help understand the socio-economic background of our students," or "We could use it in our everyday lives not just our professional careers." Another student pointed out that their peers did not know much about financial items such as 401K or IRAs. Another pointed out that, as teachers, they could and should be advocates for their students, or at least try to be. Graduate students' responses seemed to be more focused and examined the big picture, where undergraduate students were more worried about getting a job and being compensated for the effort they put into their jobs.

DISCUSSION

The results indicate the presence of disparities in interpretations of financial morality between undergraduate and graduate students. While both types experienced initial challenges conceiving the concept, undergraduates appeared particularly handcuffed by the term and developed their interpretations by brainstorming through the interview. Similar to findings of other studies that compare preservice and in-service teachers (Greenhow, Dexter, & Hughes, 2008; Harlin, Roberts, Dooley, & Murphrey, 2007), the in-service teachers in our study seemed to consider the larger picture and base their responses on their many experiences. As both groups applied and interpreted the concept, patterns of differences occurred in their responses. This section, relates these patterns to literature, presents limitations to findings, and offers direction for further study.

Two Continua

The responses to two prompts indicate that the two groups appeared somewhat opposite in their views of responsibilities and applications related to financial morality. With regard to examples of financial morality, undergraduates referenced the responsibilities of others, while graduates associated them with expectations for themselves. Yet, in relating the concept of financial morality to their view of future practice, undergraduates considered their own connections, while graduates extended the concept to others. Mandell's (2009) findings indicate that financial literacy may increase among college students as they progress through college; however, King and Mayhew (2002) provide evidence that moral development does not occur in this linear progression. This situation relates to the nature of financial knowledge and nature of moral knowledge that are depicted through Figure 6.1 and Figure 6.2.

Financial literacy should include patterns of knowledge that relate to mathematical associations. At a basic level, financial literacy represents the simple addition and subtraction of income and expenses in relation to a budget or spending plan. This conception may be easily represented through visualizations of coin and currency. In a more sophisticated vein, financial literacy involves the exponential consequences of interest earned or paid on money borrowed or lent/invested. Visualizing these amounts requires knowledge of numbers and their relationships because the amount of coins and currency may be too voluminous to depict. Over long periods of time, the interest accumulation builds in a curvilinear fashion, not a straight-line. The ability to accurately view or conceptualize the long-term outcomes of interest-related transactions and others associated with high finance benefits those who may realize them and shape their behaviors advantageously.

Morality represents a metaphysical concept that involves multiple dimensions because of its abstract nature. While human beings represent the core element of this concept, their patterns of thinking and action and the shaping of these thoughts/actions by various contextual influences result in a myriad of influential and consequential combinations. Moral respect does not represent a process of counting the number of times a good behavior has occurred, but one of valuing others for their contexts as they are. Valuing others solely for their benefit to oneself represents an immoral process because the benefit may not represent a mutually supportive process. Thus, contrary to ideals of financial literacy, which take advantage of the abstract nature of a material concept, financial morality works with the abstract nature of human essence to ensure respectful living conditions.

Environment represents an important factor of considering how the differences between undergraduate and graduate students may have developed. Despite King and Mayhew's (2002) findings of moral development among college students, college campuses also represent settings that advocate ideals of consumerism that challenge moral ideals. The conception of students as consumers (Fallows, 2005) and interpretations of college settings as "entrepreneurships" (Fischman & Hass, 2010) suggest that higher education is more of an industrial sweatshop than an intellectual mecca. Another study indicates that higher education may be conceptualized in a hybrid traditional-entrepreneurial mode (Haas & Fischman, 2010).

On campuses, cafeterias expose students to brand name restaurants, and athletic departments solicit corporate sponsorships. Molnar, Boninger, Wilkinson, and Fogarty's (2010) identification and description of seven school-based marketing strategies (funding and incentive programs, exclusive agreements, appropriation of space, sponsorship of programs and activities, sponsorship of education materials, and electronic marketing) in K-12 settings contains striking parallels to many college campuses. In contrived settings that prepare students for life decisions, college students develop consumerist-based habits of mind that challenge their abilities to apply the social justice considerations that may be presented in their academic coursework. The findings on the differences between undergraduate and graduate students' financial moral perceptions are depicted in Figure 6.3. The two axes relate to (a) the self-other continuum of responses found in Bates and Lucey's work (2008) with online survey responses of undergraduate students and (b) an individual-community continuum that depicts the emphasis on professional applications. The diametrically opposed positions of graduates and undergraduates illustrates how the interaction between their various environments and development prompts their different perspectives of financial morality and related issues.

While these differences may be attributed to the fact that graduate students have more real life and work experience and therefore are more likely to think about the effects of how money is used, they also challenge conventional wisdom that college students are more socially concerned than other age groups.

Information Sources

Both undergraduate and graduate students mentioned the importance of taking more business courses at the university level but did not

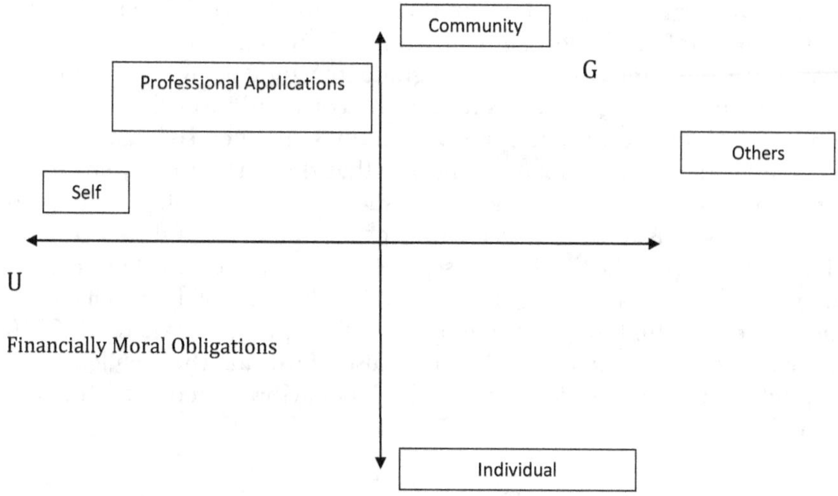

Figure 6.3. Financial moral obligations.

mention the importance of philosophy courses, in which morality is commonly covered. The issue of financial morality appears to these students to be more of a financial issue rather than a moral one. Since participants came mostly from education backgrounds, very few of them had taken philosophy courses; thus, they did not have the foundation on which to build. It is also possible that because the sample involved students from an institution that did not emphasize philosophy or ethics or require community engagement as part of its curricula, the participants had not been prepared to consider these issues as a matter of practice. Interviewing students enrolled in programs at higher education institutions that have these traits might produce different results. Future research related to the subject institution and others like it should study philosophy students, both at the undergraduate and graduate level, to examine how they might apply their philosophy background to the area of finance.

Participants did not make any reference to child development, which indicates they did not see any relevant connection between financial morality and child development. Yet literature (e.g., Holst, 1999) documents young children's need for financial education to decrease their vulnerability to the calls of consumerism. Nucci (2001) also provides a framework for moral education K-12; thus, the relevance of teaching financial morality to young children represents a developmentally appropriate consideration.

The undergraduate students in this study were currently enrolled in a child and adolescent development course in which moral development was discussed, and many of the graduate students were working as teachers in grades K-12. Considering the consumerist environment that undergraduates occupy, the study's findings are not surprising. However, most of the participants indicated that the earliest children should be introduced to financial morality issues is high school, with most of them saying it is most important to expose students at the college level. These findings indicate that preservice and in-service teachers are not familiar with research that describes the relevance of financial education in early childhood settings (e.g., Elliot, Jung, & Friedline, 2010; Johnson & Sherraden, 2007). They also illustrate the challenges in extending knowledge of cognitive and behavioral theory to financial thinking and practice.

Limitations

Although the focus of analysis was on the difference between undergraduate and graduate students, the undergraduate students were all underclassmen (freshman and sophomores), so perhaps the differences between the two groups were not an issue of undergraduate versus graduate level but one due to their status as underclassmen. Also, analysis compared the two groups as they represent preservice and in-service teachers; however, the graduate student group included some school psychology students, and it is unclear as to what their school experiences were. Future studies should include juniors and seniors to interpret how patterns of understanding extend to upperclassmen.

Taylor and Overbey's (1999) finding of different financial behaviors and dispositions between young adults who were in college or out of college indicates that a college attendance may relate to attitudes and practice about finances. Future studies should include samples of adults who do not attend college to determine if their views of financial morality and/or financial literacy differ greatly from those who attend college.

Finally, this study and previous studies are based on survey and interview data. Observational research should be conducted to confirm or refute whether lived behaviors are consistent with attitudes expressed.

CONCLUSIONS

This study found that both undergraduate and graduate students lack a strong conceptual understanding of financial morality. However, graduate students were more capable of explaining the concept and relating it to their own lives. Their life experiences seem to provide a context in which they could better apply the concept, whereas undergraduate students displayed a more individualistic view of financial morality.

These findings are important to financial education for many reasons. First, it shows that college students, both graduate and undergraduate, need more exposure to financial literacy and morality topics. College students are not learning enough about these concepts at the college level; therefore, financial education should begin early in one's education and continue through the college years. Second, since experiences seem to play a role in forming ones' views of financial morality, it is imperative to involve students at all educational levels in real-life experiences that deal with these financial issues. For example, involving students in community service or research projects that critically examine the conditions under which consumer products are manufactured, the bases on which marketing decisions are made, or the environmental impact of consumer decisions could provide experiential opportunities to internalize the relevance of "routine" financial decision-making. And finally, most of the participants in this study were current and/or future educators, so this fact really stresses the need for educating our teachers on financial issues and the importance for these issues to the education of students at all levels.

In this time of global economic instability, there is an increased need to recognize and contemplate issues associated with matters of financial overindulgences that prevent awareness and action with regard to the welfare of others. It is especially important for educators and researchers to seek opportunities to learn more about financial morality and its effects on teaching and learning of children, adolescents, and young adults. If a responsibility of education involves the development of a respectful citizenry, then educators should consider the relevance of financial morality to promoting socially-just settings where all people are respected. To ignore the human or moral component of financial literacy is to value money and inanimate objects more than people. There can be no value in that.

DISCUSSION QUESTIONS

1. To what extent may financial decisions involve moral elements? Why do people not realize there is more to financial morality than just being responsible with money?
2. If teachers and other professionals were to consider the origins of certain products they use, where they were made, the conditions under which they were made, and so on, would they stop using or

buying these items, thus living in accordance with their own financial morals?

3. Why may people automatically put "financial morality" and the word "business" together?
4. If students struggle with abstract concepts (such as financial morality), are they less likely to become financially moral? How does one effectively teach that concept?
5. Would students become more frugal, thrifty, and more economically sound if they were taught financial morality at a young age? Why/why not?

MODEL LESSON

Needs vs. Wants: "Considering the Moral Angles"[1]

Suggested Grade Level: Adaptable for Grades K-12

Objectives:

(a) The student will distinguish between a "need" and a "want" by classifying different items into each category.
(b) The student will recognize both individual and community "needs" and "wants" exist.
(c) The student will explain the difference between a need and a want by presenting his/her own needs vs. wants chart to classmates.
(d) The student will categorize his needs and wants from a community perspective.
(e) The student will write sentences of paragraphs about why it is important to save money for community's benefit.

Related Standards

Jump$tart National Standards in K–12 Personal Finance Education

Financial Responsibility and Decision Making

Standard 4: Make financial decisions by systematically considering alternatives and consequences.

Planning and Money Management

Standard 1: Develop a plan for spending and saving.

Materials:

- Laminated pictures of various needs and wants – pictures of food, clothing, shelter, water, plasma television, luxury car, etc. – clear pictorial examples/non-examples so that students can distinguish between needs and wants.
- Laminated pictures of a sharing community gathering (to represent "need") and a person in isolation listening to an i-pod (to represent "want")
- Lined paper
- Pencils
- Desk space to complete the activities
- A copy of the following article (available online) for reference in planning the assessment: Lucey, T. A., & Grant, M. M. (2010). Using technology to prepare critically thinking global citizens. *Social Studies Research and Practice, 5*(3), 119-138.

Procedures:

(a) Opening Activities

1. To introduce the lesson, the teacher discusses the lesson's key economic terms (e.g., needs and wants; vocabulary may differ depending on age level of students). The students predict what those terms mean in relation to personal finance. The teacher discusses with the students how important it is to distinguish between different items (wants vs. needs), as well as to consider the cost of the item, where it was made, how it was produced, etc. Should we consider these issues when we buy these different items? Why/why not?
2. The teacher will then explain that individuals may make decisions that may harm or hurt others and that communities work together to ensure the benefits of all members. He or she may use the example of formation of class rules at the beginning of the school year. Each person had ideas for rules, yet a process was used to reconcile differences and develop a mutually agreeable list.

(b) Developmental Activities

1. The students are handed the different pictures of the house, cloud, and the various pictures of needs and wants. The stu-

dents sort/classify each picture in their set of pictures into one of the two categories. After a few minutes, the students may switch pictures with a peer and classify a totally new set of pictures. (Older students do not have to be given laminated pictures--just the words would be sufficient.)

2. The teacher gives a 10 minute warning for students to finish classifying the pictures/words and begin writing short summary sentences or a fully-developed paragraph. The sentences or paragraph should include the students' personal definitions of a need and a want, why people feel they need certain things, why people feel it is important to save money, and how people can save money.

(c) Concluding Activities:

1. To finish the lesson, the class members share their sentences or paragraph; the teacher may make a chart of individual needs and wants on the Smart Board or black board and another chart of mutually agreed upon needs and wants. Students can examine their answers. It is important for the children to realize the differences between needs and wants and why people have troubles reconciling their different interpretations of them.
2. The teacher should inquire about the different ways that the children earn/receive money and the influences on their spending and saving decisions. (Discuss allowances, personal budgets, etc.)
3. The teacher assigns a research project in which students seek news reports about various outlets for consumer goods (e.g., Target, Walmart, Gordmans, Kruger, or Walgreens). How may the findings of their research affect their decisions of whether or not to purchase goods at these outlets?
4. The teacher facilitates the lesson activity described in Lucey and Grant (2010) that relates corporate polluters to the income levels of neighboring populations. What are the conditions that prompt people to live in these areas? Where might these people shop? What influenced the decisions of these people to live in these contexts? What are the moral issues that relate to the conditions that these people live under?
5. The teacher begins a classroom conversation about how often students examine the manufacturing conditions that produce commonly purchased consumer goods. Given what we know about the settings related to product manufacturing and con-

sumer use how might we or our parents amend our buying of certain products? What other actions might we take to better this environment? Do our actions matter if these items are needs or wants? Conduct a simulation of a community hearing about the actions of a corporation that pursues unfair labor practices.

(d) Summary and Assessment:

1. A teacher could assess this assignment in multiple ways. One way is to create anecdotal records; as the children are discussing the needs and wants with one another, the teacher may monitor and make various notes about the concepts discussed and the different vocabulary used.
2. The teacher may also develop checklists that (1) document whether students can correctly determine food, shelter, clothing, and emotional needs and wants (2) disclose more sophisticated items.
3. Another way is to create a rubric that would be distributed to students at the beginning of the activity. The students would be assessed based upon their performance during the activity and the form and content of their sentences/paragraph. A sample rubric is provided below.

NOTE

1. Lesson developed by Rachel Kinkelar.

REFERENCES

Bates, A. B., & Lucey, T. A. (2008, November). *Comparing teacher education and finance majors' perceptions of financial morality.* Paper presented at the annual meeting of the Association of Moral Education, Notre Dame, IN.

Bloom, B. S. (Ed.), Englehart, M. D., Furst, E. J., Hill, W. H., & Krathwohl, D. R. (1956). *Taxonomy of educational objectives: The classification of educational goals. Handbook I: Cognitive domain*. New York, Toronto: Longman, Green.

Buaraphan, K. (2009). Preservice and inservice science teachers' responses and reasoning about the nature of science. *Educational Research and Review, 4*(11), 561-581.

Elliot, W., Jung, H., & Friedline, T. (2010). Math achievement and children's savings: Implications for child development accounts. *Journal of Family and Economic Issues*. online first. Retrieved from http://springerlink.com/content/65321r0275479131/?p=75a9d1aa5bfc4548981a485b615fd8a4&pi=5

Fallows, J. (2005). College admissions: A substitute for quality? In R. H. Hersh & J. Merrow (Eds.). *Declining by degrees: Higher education at risk* (pp. 39-46). New York, NY: Palgrave MacMillan.

Fischman, G. E., & Hass, E. (2010). Framing higher education. Nostalgia, entrepreneurship, consumerism, and redemption. In J. A. Sandlin & P. McLaren (Eds.). *Critical pedagogies of consumption. Living and learning in the shadow of the "Shopocalypse"* (pp. 108-121). New York, NY: Routledge.

Greenhow, C., Dexter, S., & Hughes, J.E. (2008). Teacher knowledge about technology integration: An examination of inservice and preservice teachers' instructional decision-making. *Science Education International, 19*(1), 9-25.

Harlin, J. F., Roberts, T. G., Dooley, K. E., & Murphrey, T. P. (2007). Knowledge, skills and abilities for agricultural science teachers: A focus group approach. *Journal of Agricultural Education, 48*(1), 86-96.

Haas, E., & Fischman, G. (2010). Nostalgia, entrepreneurship, and redemption: Understanding prototypes in higher education. *American Educational Research Journal, 47*(3), 532-562.

Holst, C. B. (1999). Buying more can give children less. *Young Children, 54*(5), 19-23.

Johnson, E., & Sherraden, M. S. (2007). From financial literacy to financial capability among youth. *Journal of Sociology and Social Welfare, 34*(3), 119-145.

King, P. M., & Mayhew, J. M. (2002). Moral judgment development in higher education: Insights from the defining issues test. *Journal of Moral Education, 31*(3), 247-270.

Livingstone, G., Derryberry, W. P., King, A., & Vendetti, M. (2006). Moral developmental consistency? Investigating differences and relationships among academic majors. *Ethics & Behavior, 16*(3), 265-287.

Lucey, T. A. (2002). *The personal financial literacy of fourth grade students* (Unpublished master's thesis). Memphis, TN: The University of Memphis.

Lucey, T. A. (2004). *Assessing character and technology as components of a financial education curriculum for grades K-4: A multicultural interpretation* (Unpublished doctoral dissertation). The University of Memphis, Memphis, TN.

Lucey, T. A. (2007). The art of relating moral education to financial education: An equity imperative. *Social Studies Research and Practice, 2*(3), 484-498.

Lucey, T. A. (2008). Economics, religion, spirituality, and education: Encouraging understandings of the dimensions. In T. A. Lucey & K. S. Cooter (Eds.), *Financial literacy for children and youth* (pp. 559-577). Athens, GA: Digitaltextbooks.

Lucey, T. A., & Bates, A. B. (2008, July). *Comparing teacher education and finance majors' agreement with financial morality topics*. Paper presented at the annual meeting of the American Council of Consumer Interests, Orlando, FL.

Lucey, T. A., & Cooter, K. S. (Eds.) (2008). *Financial literacy for children and youth*. Athens, GA: Digitaltextbooks.

Lucey, T. A., & Grant, M. M. (2010). Using technology to prepare critically thinking global citizens. *Social Studies Research and Practice, 5*(3), 119-138.

Lucey, T. A., & Lorsbach, A. (in press). Interpreting dimensions of curriculum. *The Educational Forum*.

Mandell, L. (2008). Financial literacy of high school students. In J. J. Xiao (Ed.), *Handbook of consumer finance research* (pp. 163-207). New York, NY: Springer.

Mandell, L. (2009). *The financial literacy of young American adults. Results of the 2008 National Jump$tart Coalition Survey of High School Seniors and College Students.* Retrieved from http://wwwJumpstart.org

Mather, N., Bos, C., & Babur, N. (2001). Perceptions and knowledge of preservice and inservice teachers about early literacy instruction. *Journal of Learning Disabilities, 34*(5), 472-482.

Mayhew, M. J., & King, P. (2008). How curricular content and pedagogical strategies affect moral reasoning development in college students. *Journal of Moral Education, 37*(1), 17-40.

Molnar, A., Boninger, F., Wilkinson, G., & Fogarty, J. (2010). Schools inundated in a marketing-saturated world. In J. A. Sandlin & P. McLaren (Eds.), *Critical pedagogies of consumption. Living and learning in the shadow of the "Shopocalypse"* (pp. 83-96). New York, NY: Routledge.

National Foundation for Credit Counseling (2008, April 29). *Financial Literacy Survey.* Retrieved from http://www.nfcc.org/2008FinancialLiteracy.pdf

Nucci, L. (2001). *Education in the moral domain.* Cambridge, England: Cambridge University Press.

Postman, N., & Weingartner, C. (1969). *Teaching as a subversive activity.* New York, NY: Dell.

Taylor, D. S., & Overbey, G. (1999). Financial practices and expectations of student and non-student consumers. *Journal of Family and Consumer Sciences, 91*(4), 39-41.

CHAPTER 7

MORAL RESPONSIBILITY AND LEADERSHIP

How Managers Deal With Practical Moral Conflicts

Jennifer Loew

Recent economic and social developments like the global financial crisis and a growing number of cases of corporate crime (Corporate Crime Reporter, 2010) have evoked a sense of insecurity in our societies and mistrust in our economic and financial systems. Public reactions that concern this problem include an increased sensitivity for social and moral conundrums because in times of permanent changes followed by uncertainty people are inclined to search for basic values that express a desire for security and stability (Priddat, 1994). In these times, complaints about a so-called *Moral Degeneracy* and an increasing opportunism in the economic context are very popular (Aufderheide & Backhaus, 2004; Jones, 1991; Kerber, 1991; Priddat, 2007). Several studies (see Ariely, 2010) that focus on decision making in economically relevant situations have shown that as soon as market norms compete with social or moral norms, the latter ones become irrelevant for peoples' decisions and actions. However, from an ethical point of view, one should question if such strategic behavior is also

Reframing Financial Literacy: Exploring the Value of Social Currency, pp. 125–147

demanded in a normative sense—if so, this tendency would represent an inherent failure in human thinking.

People with high decision-making power in leading positions, especially managers, should decide and act in both economically responsible and morally responsible ways (Ulrich & Thielemann, 1992). Hence, managers are often faced with the suggestion that they should assume more responsibility for their decisions and actions as well as be more open to social and moral concerns (Priddat, 1994; Retzmann, 1997). The underlying basis for this assertion is that managers have a special kind of decision-making power that can affect the lives and well-being of others. Thus, their decisions and acts can produce enormous social consequences, "particularly in the realms of health, safety and welfare of consumers, employees and the community" (Klebe-Trevino, 1986, p. 601). Consequently, it is not a big surprise that modern management concepts, such as the concept of corporate social responsibility (CSR), focus their attention on ethical issues. One may interpret a growing number of research and publications in business and management ethics as a sign of the general rise in public ethical sensitivity (Kerber, 1991; Priddat, 2007; Retzmann, 1997).

However, the challenges that concern manager's moral reasoning and moral responsibility are actually greater than in the past (Aufderheide & Backhaus, 2004; Kerber, 1991; Ulrich & Thielemann, 1992). Moral conflicts are constituent parts of everyday managerial life, not least because managers are involved in complex relationships with different stakeholders (e.g., employees, costumers, peers and superiors, suppliers, etc.); hence, managers are faced with different and often conflicting norms, interests and requirements (Waters, Bird, & Chant, 1986).

This chapter addresses a central element of a German dissertation project, currently being conducted by this chapter's author. The endeavor generally aims at gaining insights into how corporate managers do justice to that normative claim (to be more responsible) and assume *moral*[1] responsibility, especially when dealing with practical moral conflicts. Although research in the moral psychological domain has revealed many insights into how people deal with morally relevant situations, there are still too many ambiguities and inconsistencies. Hence, there is a need for a better understanding, especially of the cognitive processing of moral conflicts in order to develop precise practical recommendations for moral education in economic contexts.

The central intent of this chapter is to outline the theoretical framework of the mentioned research project, which, in turn, is based on an integration of existing theories and empirical findings in order to overcome a single-sided perspective and to generate a well-grounded foundation for the empirical study. For this purpose, the next section of this chapter draws upon existing empirical findings that concern managers' moral decision-making and consequential implications for the adopted research approach of the project; it then presents some deliberations that regard the central relevance of the responsibility concept. Kohlberg and Candee's (1984) model of the relationship of moral judgment to moral action is then introduced, followed by theoretical and practical suggestions with regard to business education.

MANAGERS' MORAL DECISION MAKING: SOME PAST EMPIRICAL FINDINGS

In general, empirical studies that concern managers' moral decision-making focus on the identification of central determinants of ethical decision-making behavior in order to explain and predict the decision-making process. In summary, the moral decision-making process of managers is influenced by several organizational-situational and individual factors, which interact in multiple ways.[2] Typically, reviewed factors in the category of individual factors are age, gender, nationality, religion, cognitive moral development, and so on. Overall, findings for tested personal variables that are quite ambiguous, and many studies found no significant correlations. On this account, Ford and Richardson (1994) conclude, "personal attributes are related to an individual's ethical beliefs and decision-making behavior in some studies but not in others" (p. 210).

A similar but yet more precise picture appears regarding the organizational-situational factors, such as an organization's culture and climate, codes of ethics, peers, rewards, and sanctions, etc. Within this category, contradictory results have also be found, although some significant correlations have been detected (e.g., the importance of a person's peer group and a perceived ethical climate on his/her ethical behavior or the influence of codes of ethics and rewards and sanctions on promoting one's ethical behavior) (Loe et al., 2000). The great difficulty with the studies addressed here is that they are hardly comparable because, in each case, different factors and questions were taken into account and different research methods were used. Consequently, they provide no concrete answers, and further research in this domain is required to gain a better understanding of individual moral decision making.

Nevertheless, there are two noteworthy empirical outcomes related to the category of organizational-situational factors that are of peculiar interest, especially in association with the responsibility concept. The first research outcome shows that the level of moral reasoning depends on the kind of moral issue involved and its characteristics, such as the magnitude of consequences, social consensus, probability of effect, temporal immediacy, proximity, and concentration of effect (Jones, 1991). This means, for example, that the higher the suspected magnitude of consequences of a morally relevant decision/action is, the higher the level of moral reasoning used in making judgments (Jones, 1991).

The second research outcome provides evidence that the level of moral reasoning is not only dependent on the moral issue, but also on the context in which the dilemma occurs. Specifically, Weber (1990, 1996) found that the stage of moral reasoning in a real-life business dilemma is lower than in a hypothetical dilemma such as Kohlberg's famous Heinz Dilemma. The assumed explanation for this finding is that the economic context has a restrictive influence on moral decision making. The aforementioned findings from Ariely (2010) as well as other research investigating the so-called *moral segmentation*[3] problem (e.g. Beck et al., 1996; Beck, Bienengräber, Mitulla, & Parche-Kawik, 2001) seem to confirm this conclusion.

All these findings reviewed above are consistent with other already well-known findings that concern the moral judgment process, but which are not explicitly located in the economic context. These findings confirm the general conclusion that moral decision-making depends mainly on the actual situation and the corresponding context (Beck et al., 1996, 2001; Bienengräber, 2002; Higgins, Power, & Kohlberg, 1984; Minnameier, 2010a, 2010b; Oser & Althof, 1992). Therefore, they provide few new insights and no concrete answers. For example, they do not explain which factors are more relevant than others in significantly influencing the decision-making process. Furthermore, the real reason for this situation- and/or issue-dependence in moral judgments is still unknown. What influences moral thinking in such a way that persons judge at different levels? This chapter introduces a possible solution involving the concept of moral responsibility. It argues that the situation- or issue-dependence of moral judgments and actions can be explained as an effect of different attributions of responsibility in different situations.

IMPLICATIONS FOR THE ADOPTED RESEARCH APPROACH

Based on the preceding brief literature review of empirical studies of manager's moral decision making, the research project currently being conducted by the author of this chapter aims to analyze the influence of personal attributions of (moral) responsibility on the decision-making process within the context of real-life moral conflicts. In other words, it examines how judgments of personal (moral) responsibility affect the process of moral decision making, which occurs when a person (e.g., a manager) is faced with a moral conflict and has to decide between two or more alternative actions.

Past studies have failed to focus on this relationship between individual responsibility attribution (resulting in judgments of responsibility) and the ensuing decision. Some studies addressed responsibility in decision-making, but only to find out the circumstances people ascribe more or less responsibility to a potential perpetrator of an immoral or illegal act (Albs, 1998; Hagiwara, 1992; Van der Keilen & Garg, 1994). These studies did not look at how the personal decision-making process and the resulting decision are dependent upon or affected by attribution of individual responsibility. An investigation of this kind would seem to be crucial given the fact that past research has revealed a close relationship between the personal acceptance of responsibility and moral behavior (Blasi, 1980, 1983, 1999; Kohlberg & Candee, 1984, 1999; Latané & Darley, 1976). Furthermore, the theoretical justification of the central importance of the purpose of this study is based on several other factors, which are described in the paragraphs below. After establishing the theoretical foundation of this study, Kohlberg's and Candee's (1984, 1999) model of the relationship of moral judgment to moral action is introduced in order to illustrate the central relevance of responsibility judgments and to provide theoretical guidance. Thus, the chapter's line of reasoning develops from a normative metalevel to a more individualistic action-theoretic level.

One central aspect of the theoretical foundation is that moral conflicts, especially in organizations where people are involved in complex relationships, often imply questions of ascription and allocation of responsibility. For example, there are often conflicts between role responsibility and moral responsibility (Strong & Meyer, 1992; Toffler, 1986). Particularly against the backdrop of globalization and technological advancements, the sphere of human interactions has increased with corresponding effects on various realms, such as social welfare, safety, and environment (Jonas, 1987; Lenk & Maring, 1998). These developments raise new and different ethical issues, and modern economic and business ethics need to take up these issues in order to establish an adequate ethical concept (Jonas, 1987). According to many philosophers, a "basic ethical concept for corporations, at this time, is that of responsibility" (Lenk & Maring 1998, p. 21, author's translation). In this context, Nunner-Winkler and Edelstein (2005) also speak of a change in moral values: "increasingly, man is perceived as being left to himself—responsible for his actions and for their consequences. Kant's maxim never to transgress a negative duty, not even to prevent greater harm, has lost its persuasive power" (pp. 1-2).

Consequently, an "ethics of responsibility takes the place of a pure ethics of conviction" (Nunner-Winkler, 2000, p. 8, author's own translation) or in other words "it [has already become] a question of conviction if one pursues ethics of responsibility" (Zimmerli, 1987, p. 93, author's translation). How this normative category of "responsibility" turns into an individual one needs to be examined, along with the question of how personal attributions of moral responsibility come into play.

Directly linked to the last mentioned aspect is the argument that most research in the moral domain, primarily in the Kohlberg-tradition, concentrates on justice deliberations when analyzing moral decision-making processes (Oser & Althof, 1992). Other possible modes of judging, such as responsibility or care, are considered to be of little importance. In contrast, as demonstrated by Leschke (1995), people do not only judge and decide based upon justice considerations; they also integrate feelings of responsibility and other factors in their decision making. Moreover, many researchers (e.g., Haste, 1993) tend to criticize a unilateral, justice-orientated ethical view, for this is not the only plausible and adequate ethical factor to think about in moral questions, as already mentioned. Therefore, authors such as Carlo (2006) and Nunner-Winkler (1984) advocate an integration of justice and responsibility orientated approaches in order to gain important new insights in moral reasoning and development based on a holistic ethical framework.

In her early work, Carol Gilligan (1982) pointed out the relevance of the two aforementioned moral orientations (i.e., the morality of justice and the morality of responsibility) and related these different orientations to gender, with the morality of justice said to be typical for men and the morality of responsibility or care said to be typical for women. This generalization may no longer be sustainable because several data meta-analyses (e.g., Walker, 1984, 1986) have shown no gender differences in preferring the one or the other moral orientation.

What has been validated is that both moral orientations are used when dealing with moral conflicts, depending on the situation and the type of moral conflict (Carlo, 2006; Derry, 1989; Juujärvi, Myyry, & Pesso, 2010; Oser & Althof, 1992). Based on these normative claims and corresponding empirical findings, it is necessary to focus on both moral perspectives when analyzing moral decision making.

In addition to the rather normative arguments above, there is also a more action-theoretical approach to justifying the present study. One central problem that moral psychology and education have dealt with for a long time is the so-called *moral judgment-moral action gap* (Kohlberg & Candee, 1984; Minnameier, 2010b). This concept refers to the fact that people may frame moral judgments on a relatively high level, but, in fact, do not necessarily act in correspondence with this level (Blasi, 1983, 1984, 1999; Heinrichs, 2005; Kohlberg & Candee, 1984, 1999; Minnameier, 2010a, 2010b; Oser & Althof, 1992; Rest, 1984). Different possible explanations for this problem have been generated (for an overview, see Bergmann, 2002). One such explanation, the lack of moral motivation,[4] receives much attention within the moral scientific community (Homann, 2004; Klemme, 2006; Nunner-Winkler, 1993, 1999, 2005, 2007; Minnameier, 2010b; Patzig, 1996; Wren, 1991). Relating to this, the present study introduces an alternative explanation referring to the concept of responsibility, not least because there are some theoretical and empirical problems with the concept of moral motivation (Homann, 2004; Minnameier, 2010b). The leading thought is that people fail to act on their deontic choice due to a lack of moral responsibility. A more profound possible explanation of this human behavior is given in this chapter after the presentation of Kohlberg and Candee's (1984, 1999) model of the relationship of moral judgment to moral action as a basic frame of reference.

FROM MORAL JUDGMENT TO MORAL ACTION—KOHLBERG'S AND CANDEE'S VIEW

As mentioned above, Kohlberg and Candee (1984, 1999) point out the relevance of responsibility deliberations, assuming that judgments of responsibility serve as mediators between deontic judgments and moral action. This relationship is illustrated in the following well-established model (Figure 7.1), which is explicitly attached to Rest's (1984, 1999) four-component model and the works of Blasi (1983, 1984, 1999).

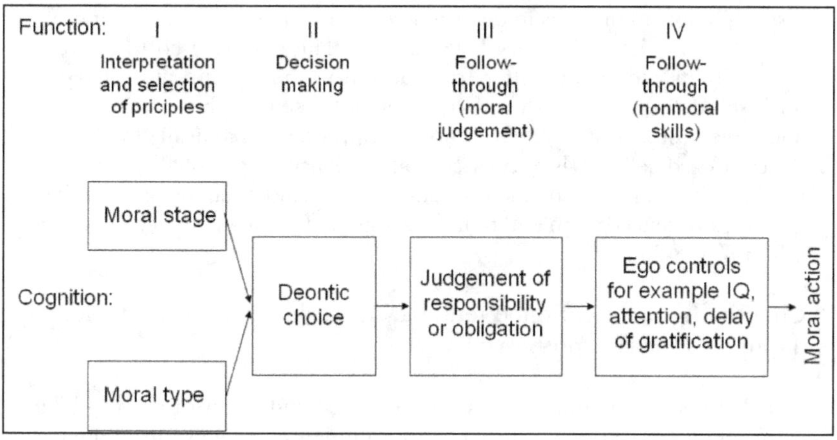

Source: Kohlberg & Candee, 1984, p. 71.

Figure 7.1. Influences on moral actions.

The model describes the formal way in which moral decision-making leads to moral action, based on four psychological functions and their corresponding cognitions. Faced with a moral conflict, in the first step, the individual interprets the situation and selects relevant moral principles according to the cognitive structures of his/her moral stage and moral type. What follows is the deontic choice, a decision about what is right or wrong in this situation, deduced from the selected principles. Then, the responsibility judgment comes into play and serves within this model as a "second-order affirmation of the will to act in terms of that [deontic] judgment.... Responsibility judgments answer not only the question, Why is X right?, but answer, Why me? Why must I do X?" (Kohlberg & Candee, 1984, p. 57) This clearly shows that responsibility judgments have a strong affective component in the form of so-called "*hot cognitions*" (Hoffman, 1991, p. 294) because these cognitions tell that something *should* not only be done but something *must* be done; therefore, they are an important energizing force for moral actions (Wren, 1986).

Other researchers (e.g., Blasi, 1980, 1983, 1984) highlight the apparent motivational character of personal responsibility judgments. In addition, Blasi (1983) relates the concept of responsibility to a theory of the moral self, thus inspiring related work by Kohlberg and Candee (1984, 1999) in this domain. Blasi (1983) summarizes his theoretical self-model in seven propositions. Of these, those relevant to responsibility judgments are briefly outlined below. According to Blasi (1983):

> moral judgments, before leading to action, are at times processed through a second set of rules or criteria, the criteria of responsibility. The function of a responsibility judgment is to determine to what extent that which is morally good is also strictly necessary for oneself.... The criteria used to arrive at responsibility judgments differ from person to person and are related to one's self-definition or to the organization of the self.... The transition from a judgment of responsibility to action is supported dynamically by the tendency toward self-consistency, a central tendency in personality organization.... Following an action inconsistent with one's judgment of responsibility, guilt is experienced as an emotional response to the inconsistency within the self. (pp. 198-204)

Concerning the mentioned tendency toward self-consistency, Kohlberg and Candee (1984) hypothesize:

> that there is a monotonic increase in making a judgment of responsibility consistent with the deontic judgment of rightness as we move from stage to stage. This in turn means that there is a monotonic increase in the proportion of subjects acting "morally" or consistently with their deontic judgment made outside the situation. (pp. 57-58)

Hence, the higher the stage of moral reasoning, the higher the likelihood that one will make a responsibility judgment that, in turn, leads to an action consistent with the deontic choice. Kohlberg and Candee (1984) support their hypothesis by citing two studies, one from Helkama (1979) and one from McNamee (1977), that show this monotonic relationship. Further, Blasi (1983), in line with Kohlberg and Candee (1984, 1999) as well as with Gilligan (1982), points out that a deontic judgment must not always precede a responsibility judgment, and hence it is differentiated between actions based on justice considerations and those based on responsibility (Kohlberg & Candee, 1999). Kohlberg and Candee (1984, 1999) do not agree with Gilligan's (1983) assumption that these are two independent moralities; instead, they see them as possible modes of judging which are dependent on the concrete situation and the kind of moral dilemma involved. Similarly, Higgins, Power, and Kohlberg (1984) distinguish between moral dilemmas of justice and moral dilemmas of responsibility or care. Moreover, they assume that justice dilemmas are those classical hypothetical dilemmas (e.g., the famous Heinz Dilemma[5]) and that everyday real-life dilemmas are mainly related to questions of responsibility (Higgins et al., 1984). This is a possible reason why people score lower in moral judgment competence in practical dilemmas than in hypothetical dilemmas. "This result corresponds to the common sense expectation that classical moral judgment taps highest competence, the moral 'high road,' whereas more real-life practical judgment is more likely to take the 'low road' " (p. 78).[6] Higgins et al. created stages of responsibility judgments as counterpart to stages of deontic reasoning which show qualitatively different judgments at each stage. Unfortunately, they failed to explain the concrete correlation between these two taxonomies.

The motivational relevance of responsibility has been further explored by several empirical studies in the social psychological domain, which have especially engaged in prosocial behavior analyses and focused on the so-called diffusion of responsibility effect (or bystander-effect). For example, Latané and Darley (1976) found that the personal acceptance of responsibility in an emergency situation serves as an important and crucial motivational force for helping behavior, which is a special kind of moral behavior (see also Heckhausen, 1989). Similar to the stages of responsibility described by Higgins et al. (1984), responsibility in this context is qualitatively differentiated in the sense that one may feel responsible for only his/her own concerns or welfare, for the welfare of closely related people like family or friends, or for the welfare of the society as a whole (Dalbert, 1980).

This is the crucial point: These qualitative differences in responsibility judgments are suitable to explain the aforementioned situation-dependence of moral judgments and actions. Depending on what the moral dilemma or situation is, the responsibility judgment varies and leads to a different general moral judgment as well as to a different moral action. For example, if someone scores higher in moral judgment competency in a family dilemma than in a business dilemma, it may be that this person feels more responsible for family concerns than for business concerns; therefore, s/he uses different stages to judge such situations. Nevertheless, for the moment, this remains an assumption and should be empirically validated, which the current research project attempts to do.

As described above, research from the social psychological domain contributes to a profound comprehension of the conditions of personal acceptance of responsibility and the conditions under which persons tend to deny or shift responsibility, which, in turn, may be essential for a better understanding of moral decision-making and moral action. Thus, research on moral decision-making and moral development can benefit from these findings and should aim at integrating thoughts from moral as well as from social psychology (Althof & Garz, 1986; Colby & Damon, 1993).

Based on these theoretical and to some extent on empirically-validated findings as described in literature review above, research in moral decision-making needs to (a) take the differentiation between the two kinds of moral judgments into account and (b) enlarge the focus on individual responsibility attributions that lead to judgments of responsibility in order to better understand individuals' moral decision-making behaviors. On the other hand, some theoretical ambiguities and practical problems affect Kohlberg and Candee's (1984) notion of the relationship between moral judgment and moral action. For instance, these are the supposed linearity of the model and the purely cognitivistic perspective of responsibility (Weyers, 2004), along with other theoretical and empirical inconsistencies (for an overview, see Krebs & Denton, 1999; Minnameier, 2010a; Weyers, 2004). Further research in this domain is urgently required since the existence or nonexistence of such a relationship between moral judgment and moral action has important implications for theory construction and practice. Nevertheless, Kohlberg and Candee's (1984) model can serve as a suitable initial point for further deliberations and investigations because it shows that a lack of personal moral responsibility can potentially explain the inconsistencies between judgment and action.

Beyond the preceding reflections, a focus on responsibility judgments may capture different psychological aspects relevant for moral actions that are usually considered separately when analyzing moral decision-making processes in relationship to moral actions. First, as mentioned previously, responsibility judgments not only have a cognitive component in the sense of an activation of personally obliging norms (Heckhausen, 1989), but also a strong motivational element in the sense of personal concernment (Blasi, 1983; Montada, 1993; Weyers, 2004; Wren, 1986, 1991). Many recent researchers in the moral domain postulate an integration of cognitive and affective aspects (Keller, 2005; Nunner-Winkler, 1993; Weinreich-Haste, 1986) and the focus on responsibility judgments is suitable to integrate these both perspectives. Second, in a responsibility judgment, personal cost-benefit-considerations find expression in the sense that one feels the more responsible the less the personal costs of being responsible are (Hoff, 1995, 1998). Cost-benefit analysis plays an important role within (moral) decision-making processes in general and within the economic context where cost-benefit-considerations belong to the everyday life in particular (Homann, 2004; Leschke, 1995). Last, a responsibility judgment also includes considerations or expectations of concrete action consequences (Hagiwara, 1992), which are known to influence decision making in general and therefore moral decision making in particular (Mischel & Mischel, 1976).

THE MORAL OF THE STORY: AN EXAMPLE

In order to make theory implementable and to highlight diverse problems that existing research in this field has undervalued, a short but very simplified example will be presented in story form. It seems plausible to assume that similar situations occur quite frequently in real life.

Assume that a manager of a company has to decide about a concept, including some morally questionable actions, which could lead to harmful consequences for other people, in order to gain economic advantages. Suppose that this manager has recognized this situation as morally relevant (i.e., s/he recognizes the existence of a moral problem) (Minnameier, 2010b; Rest, 1984). In terms of a deontic judgment, s/he has judged such actions that would have harmful effects for other people as general morally wrong, but s/he decides to proceed. Asked for a reason behind her/his decision, s/he could argue that s/he is not morally responsible for any people because s/he is only responsible for her/his business concern and its performance (i.e., doing a good job and making as much profit as possible). Otherwise, there could be negative consequences for her/his business concern.

In this case, one may explain the obvious judgment-action inconsistency by the denegation of the manager's moral responsibility in favor of her/his role responsibility. The crucial point is that the manager made a responsibility judgment—not a moral judgment, but a judgment referring to his role responsibility. Consequently, two questions need to be addressed: (1) When and under what conditions is a responsibility judgment a sheer rational judgment or a strategy to deny one's moral responsibility? (2) When and under what conditions will it lead to an action based on the deontic choice and therefore express a real moral judgment? Researchers who have not yet dealt with the concept of responsibility in the field of moral decision-making have largely neglected these questions.[7] Responsibility can also be misused in the sense of denying higher moral responsibility (Lempert, 1999),[8] and so research has to differentiate carefully between various kinds of responsibility and their relevance to moral actions. (For an example of a broad definition of the different kinds of responsibility, see Lenk, 1987; Lenk & Maring, 1998.) Moreover, research in this area needs to focus on the role of responsibility attributions within the decision-making process leading to moral judgment and moral action.

CONCLUSION

The purpose of this chapter has been to provide insights into the theoretical framework of a current research project. There are various reasons for further research that concern the relationship between moral judgment and moral action under the focus of responsibility in order to understand the cognitive processing of morally relevant conflict situations. This research is needed to improve theory-building and provide practical suggestions for moral education in economic contexts.

Even though there is a need for more empirical validation in this domain, it can be argued based on the status quo that questions of responsibility are central for people in leading positions in general and therefore should be a topic for management education in particular (Retzmann, 1997). Therefore, managers should be sensitized to those questions as early as possible in order to develop reflexive and responsible moral judgments (MacLagan, 1983; Seeber, 2007). This does not imply that managers should be moralized, but they should be enabled to be aware of different challenges concerning their responsibilities, especially concerning their moral responsibility with regard to the long-term consequences of their decisions and actions for other people. These competencies and values cannot be imposed through indoctrination in the sense of character education (Oser, 2001) but must be encouraged through adequate educational arrangements that promote critical moral thinking, self-reflection, and cooperative discussion (Kohlberg, 1987). Furthermore, corresponding organizational conditions, in the sense of a moral atmosphere, must be created because they have an important influence on individuals' moral judgment as well as moral development (Lempert, 1997).

DISCUSSION QUESTIONS

1. What are several reasons for the increased ethical sensitivity in our society mentioned at the beginning of this chapter?
2. Why are managers especially challenged in fulfilling their ethical responsibilities?
3. How can managers be sensitized to questions of responsibility when dealing with every-day moral conflicts?
4. How do Kohlberg and Candee (1984) describe the relationship of moral judgment to moral action? What role do responsibility judgments play in their view?
5. Why is "responsibility," in the eyes of many philosophers, an adequate ethical principle? Would you agree? What do you think may be some other ethical principles?

MORAL RESPONSIBILITY IN ECONOMICALLY RELEVANT SITUATIONS

Grade Level: 12

Objectives:

(a) Students will be able to generate their own imaginations of *responsibility* and compare them to scientific constructions of responsibility. Students will be able to develop a critical concept of *responsibility* that is based on different perspectives on responsibility.
(b) Students will be able to develop a concept of *morally responsible financial decision-making* and identify financially/economically relevant situations that imply moral questions.
(c) Students will be able to analyze identified situations with regard to questions of morality and responsibility.
(d) Students will be able to (a) discuss, analyze and evaluate a moral conflict, especially concerning questions of responsibility; (b) identify multiple perspectives and multiple possible courses of action; and (c) list pro and contra arguments for each alternative course of action

Related Standards:

Financial Responsibility and decision making
Standard 1: Take responsibility for personal financial decision
Standard 4: Make financial decisions by systematically considering alternatives and consequences

Materials:

- Appropriate excerpts of philosophical literature concerning "responsibility" Example 1:

  Jonas, Hans (1984). *The imperative of responsibility: In search of an ethics for the technological age*. Trans. by Hans Jonas, with the collaboration of David Herr. Chicago: Univ. of Chicago Press.

  Or example 2: Fischer, John Martin and Ravizza, Mark (Eds.) (1993). *Perspectives on moral responsibility.* Ithaca, NY: Cornell Univ. Press.

- Worksheets with a text of the moral dilemma "Ms. Menge" (see below).
- Flipcharts.

Procedures:

(a) a. Opening activities:

1. The teacher introduces the lesson's issue (moral responsibility in economically relevant situations) and explains its relevance in the context of financial education (see lesson objectives).
2. The teacher asks the following question for open discussion: What does "responsibility" generally mean to you? Teacher collects students' ideas on flipcharts or on the board.

(b) b. Developmental activities

1. Students read selected text excerpts (see lesson materials) and identify the relevant core statements. Teacher collects students' statements on flipcharts or on the board.
2. Teacher leads an open discussion on the following questions: Are there differences between your subjective view of responsibility and the one described in the text? If so, what are these differences?

Teacher places the two flipcharts on the subjective and scientific theories about responsibility side by side in order to illustrate the two perspectives and, if necessary, points out the main differences between the subjective theories of responsibility and the scientific ones (e.g., presence/absence of empirical references).

3. The teacher asks the following questions: What does this mean for financial decision making? What constitutes responsible financial decision making? Teacher collects students' ideas on flipcharts or on the board; students reach consensus on a joint definition of responsible financial decision making.
4. The teacher continues open discussion with the following question: In general, What financially/economically relevant situations/dilemmas can you think of that involve moral questions? Teacher collects and records students' exemplary situations/dilemmas and their underlying moral conflicts on flipcharts or on the board.
5. Teacher chooses, with student assistance, two or three of the generated situations and has the class discuss them with respect to responsibility; for example, s/he may ask to designate central questions of responsibility in each situation/dilemma or to identify central role and moral responsibilities of the parties involved. Open discussion is moderated by the teacher.
6. The procedure for dilemma discussions is developed based on the proposed articulation scheme from Retzmann (2007):
   - Teacher presents the dilemma with the aid of work sheets (see exemplary dilemma "Ms. Menge" below).
   - Students analyze the relevant value conflict.
   - The class makes a spontaneous judgment.
   - The class collects arguments.
   - In small groups, the class structures and evaluates all arguments.
   - Students individually arrive at a reasoned judgment and present their judgments to the rest of the class (pp. 42-43).

(c) Closing activities

1. The teacher and class jointly evaluate the dilemma discussion using the following questions: What went well in our discussion and why? What difficulties or challenges did we encounter? What could be done to avoid these problems in the next dilemma discussion?

Summary and assessment

1. For formative assessment, the teacher asks students repeatedly during the lesson to reflect about their learning processes.
2. For summative assessment (nongraded), the teacher asks each student to identify the central insight s/he has gained from the lesson.
3. For summative assessment (graded), each student write an essay about "Moral Challenges in Financial Decisions" or a report about a selected moral conflict in which s/he develops pro and contra arguments.

Exemplary Dilemma: "Ms. Menge"
(following Oser, 2001, pp. 79-81; author's own translation)

At the request of a big electric power company, Ms. Menge (a chemist and climatologist) is currently exploring the climatic effects of a radioactive inert gas (Krypton 85) released during plutonium production in atomic plants owned by this company. Ms. Menge is quite happy about her assignment to this task because the continued existence of the institute for which she works depends on such corporate requests. In addition, Ms. Menge has a strong personal interest in maintaining her current job with the institute because she recently acquired a heavy debt due to a house purchase.

As part of her research, Ms. Menge discovers that Krypton 85 influences climate, changes cloud formation, and the frequency of precipitation. Moreover, it makes nitrous gases and sulfur dioxides more dangerous.

The managers of the electric power company do not want her to publish her results because they are scared of a political discussion about opting out of the nuclear energy program. They want to promote nuclear energy as being generally ecofriendly. The corporation leaders also point out that many jobs will be lost in Ms. Menge's institute if this information is made public. They make an attractive monetary offer that would relieve Ms. Menge from her debts and enable her to lead a carefree life.

If you were in Ms. Menge's shoes, what would you do? What is your problem/dilemma? What are your alternative choices? What values and responsibilities are relevant in this decision-making situation? (e.g., valuing of or responsibility for: human beings and the environment, fellow employees and institute solidarity/survival, personal economic solvency and family welfare) What are the pros/cons of each alternative? Justify your final decision to your classmates.

NOTES

1. "Moral" is italicized because responsibility can have different characteristics—like action responsibility, role responsibility, or moral responsibility (Lenk, 1987; Lenk & Maring 1998), which are admittedly related to each other but must be separated for research purposes because addressing the "one-or-the-other" concept of responsibility in decision-making processes

leads to different decisions and actions based on the particular responsibility judgment.

2. For a broad overview of the empirical literature that concerns ethical decision making, see Ford and Richardson (1994) and Loe, Ferell, and Mansfield (2000).
3. Moral segmentation means that the moral stage used for judging moral dilemmas is—contrary to the research of Kohlberg, who has found that persons tend to use always and in each situation the highest individually available stage (Kohlberg, 1987)—dependent on the domain in which the moral dilemma occurs. In this context, it was ascertained that persons scored higher in extraprofessional domains like family, friends etc., than in the professional domain (Beck et al., 1996, 2001).
4. There has been a long and ongoing debate in moral philosophy between moral internalism and moral externalism concerning the relation of moral judgments, moral motivation and moral actions (Minnameier, 2010b; Wren, 1991). Internalists assume that moral judgments are intrinsically motivating because if a person has judged something to be the right thing to do, this would imply the motivation to act correspondingly. Otherwise this person would be practically irrational. In contrast, externalists state a factual independence of moral judgments and moral motivation, especially based on the observation that people often fail to do what they consider right (Minnameier, 2010b, pp. 58-60). For a further discussion concerning the relevance of responsibility judgments in this context, see Wren (1986).
5. In this dilemma, a husband (i.e., Heiz) is faced with the situation that his wife suffers from a special kind of cancer. In addition, he cannot afford the drug that could help his wife because the druggist charges ten times as much as the drug's production costs. Hence, the husband is confronted with a dilemma, whether he should steal the drug and risk possible arrest or not steal the drug and risk the loss of his wife.
6. Another reason may be that the scoring system used to evaluate one's moral judgment competence according to the stages is only made for deontic reasoning and that responsibility reasoning is not covered by this system in the same way. Thus, the judgments in the language of responsibility are considered to be lower in this scoring system. This is also what Carol Gilligan (1982) has emphasized.
7. First results of the empirical study have reinforced this issue. Responsibility judgments do not always lead to consistency between deontic judgment and action, but can induce exactly the opposite.

   From these first results it can be stated, that there seems to be indeed a correlation betwen deontic judgment, responsibility judgment and action decision in the manner theory suggests: if one feels personally morally responsible to act on his/her values and beliefs of what is morally right/wrong, this can bridge a deontic judgment in a corresponding action decision. Vice versa, an inconsistency between deontic choice and action decision can be explained through strategies of denying higher moral responsibility and by referring to personal concerns/consequences (Loew, 2011).

8. The famous Milgram (1963) experiments also show this relationship. The test administrators delegated their moral responsibility to the investigator and felt only responsible for doing what they had been told – serving out electric shocks (Althof & Garz, 1986). "In the Milgram experiment, for instance, it was found that higher-stage subjects quit shocking the stooge victim because of a judgment of responsibility, asserting that what was going on was their responsibility, not just that of the experimenter, despite the experimenter's assertion that he would take the responsibility for shocking the victim" (Higgins et al., 1984, pp. 74-75).

REFERENCES

Albs, B. (1998). Ein Beitrag zur Messung moralischer Emotionen: Das State-Trait-Schuldgefühle-Ausdrucks inventar. In B. Reichle & M. Schmitt (Eds.), *Verantwortung, Gerechtigkeit und moral. Zum psychologischen verständnis ethischer aspekte im menschlichen verhalten [Leo Montada zum 60. Geburtstag]* (pp. 163-172). Weinheim: Juventa-Verl.

Althof, W., & Garz, D. (1986). Moralische zugänge zum menschen - Zugänge zum moralischen Menschen. Schlussbetrachtungen. In F. Oser, W. Althof & D. Garz, (Eds.), *Moralische zugänge zum menschen - Zugänge zum moralischen menschen. Beiträge zur entstehung moralischer identität* (pp. 327–362). München: Kindt.

Ariely, D. (2010). *Denken hilft zwar, nützt aber nichts. Warum wir immer wieder unvernünftige Entscheidungen treffen*. München: Knaur.

Aufderheide, D., & Backhaus, K. (2004). Ethische verantwortung als führungsaufgabe. In K.-P. Wiedmann, W. Fritz, & B. Abel (Eds.), *Management mit vision und verantwortung. Eine herausforderung an wissenschaft und praxis; Festschrift für Hans Raffée zum 75. Geburtstag* (1st ed., pp. 451-466). Wiesbaden: Gabler.

Beck, K., Brütting, B., Lüdecke-Plümer, S., Minnameier, G., Schirmer, U., & Schmid, S. N. (1996). Zur entwicklung moralischer urteilskompetenz in der kaufmännischen Berufsausbildung - Empirische befunde und praktische probleme. In K. Beck & H. Heid (Eds.), *Lehr-Lern-Prozesse in der kaufmännischen erstausbildung. wissenserwerb, motivierungsgeschehen und handlungskompetenzen*. (Zeitschrift für Berufs- und Wirtschaftspädagogik, Beiheft 13) (pp. 187-206). Stuttgart: Franz Steiner.

Beck, K., Bienengräber, T., Mitulla, C., & Parche-Kawik, K. (2001). Progression, stagnation, regression - Zur entwicklung der moralischen urteilskompetenz während der kaufmännischen berufsausbildung. In K. Beck & V. Krumm (Eds.), *Lehren und lernen in der beruflichen erstausbildung. Grundlagen einer modernen kaufmännischen berufsqualifizierung* (pp. 139-161). Opladen: Leske & Budrich.

Bergmann, R. (2002). Why be moral?: A conceptual model from developmental psychology. *Human Development, 45*, 104-124.

Bienengräber, T. (2002). *Vom egozentrismus zum universalismus: entwicklungsbedingungen moralischer urteilskompetenz*. Wiesbaden: Dt. Univ.-Verlag.

Blasi, A. (1980). Bridging moral cognition and moral action: A critical review of the literature. *Psychological Bulletin, 88*(1), 1-45.

Blasi, A. (1983). Moral cognition and moral action: A theoretical perspective. *Developmental Review, 3*, 178-210.

Blasi, A. (1984). Moral identity: Its role in moral functioning. In W. M. Kurtines & J. L. Gewirtz (Eds.), *Morality, moral behavior, and moral development* (pp. 128-139). New York, NY: Wiley.

Blasi, A. (1999). Moralische kognition und moralisches handeln: Eine theoretische perspektive. In D. Garz, F. Oser, & W. Althof (Eds.), *Moralisches urteil und handeln* (pp. 47-81). Frankfurt am Main: Suhrkamp.

Carlo, G. (2006). Care-based and Altruistically-based morality. In M. Killen & J. G. Smetana (Eds.), *Handbook of moral development* (pp. 551-580). Mahwah, NJ: Erlbaum Associates.

Colby, A., & Damon, W. (1993). Die integration des selbst und der moral in der entwicklung moralischen engagements. In W. Edelstein, G. Nunner-Winkler, & G. Noam (Eds.), *Moral und person* (pp. 203-231). Frankfurt am Main: Suhrkamp.

Corporate Crime Reporter (2010). Retrieved from http://www.corporatecrimereporter.com/index.html

Dalbert, C. (1980). *Verantwortlichkeit und handeln (Berichte aus der arbeitsgruppe "Verantwortung, Gerechtigkeit, Moral", 5)*. Trier

Derry, R. (1989). An empirical study of moral reasoning among managers. *Journal of Business Ethics, 8*, 855-862.

Ford, R. C., & Richardson, W. D. (1994). Ethical decision-making: A review of the empirical literature. *Journal of Business Ethics, 13*, 205-221.

Gerstenmaier, J., & Mandl, H. (1995). Wissenserwerb unter konstruktivistischer Perspektive. *Zeitschrift für Pädagogik, 41*, 867-888.

Gilligan, C. (1982). *In a different voice: Psychological theory and women's development*. Cambridge, MA: Harvard University Press.

Hagiwara, S. (1992). The concept of responsibility and determinants of responsibility judgment in the Japanese context. *International Journal of Psychology, 27*(2), 143-156.

Haste, H. (1993). Die Moral, das selbst und der soziokulturelle kontext. In W. Edelstein., G. Nunner-Winkler, & G. Noam (Eds.), *Moral und person* (pp. 385-413). Frankfurt am Main: Suhrkamp.

Heckhausen, H. (1989). *Motivation und handeln* (2nd ed.) Berlin: Springer

Heinrichs, K. (2005). *Urteilen und handeln. Ein prozessmodell und seine moralpsychologische spezifizierung*. Frankfurt am Main: Lang

Helkama, K. (1979). *The development of the attribution of responsibility: A critical survey of empirical research and a theoretical outline (Research Reports. Department of Social Psychology)*. Unpublished manuscript. University of Helsinki.

Higgins, A., Power, C., & Kohlberg, L. (1984). The relationship of moral atmosphere to judgments of responsibility. In W. M. Kurtines & J. L. Gewirtz (Eds.), *Morality, moral behavior, and moral development* (pp. 74-108). New York, NY: Wiley.

Hoff, E. -H (1995). Berufliche verantwortung. In E. -H. Hoff & L. Lappe (Eds.), *Verantwortung im arbeitsleben* (pp. 46–64). Heidelberg: Asanger.

Hoff, E. -H (1998). Verantwortungsbewußtsein und industirearbeit im zeichen der umweltkrise. In G. Blickle (Ed.), *Ethik in organisationen. Konzepte, befunde, praxisbeispiele* (pp. 71–94). Göttingen: Verl. für Angewandte Psychologie.

Hoffman, M. L. (1991). Empathy, social cognition, and moral action. In W. M. Kurtines & J. Gewirtz (Eds.), *Handbook of moral behavior and development. Vol. 1: Theory* (pp. 275-301). Hillsdale NJ: Erlbaum.

Homann, K. (2004). Braucht die wirtschaftsethik eine "moralische motivation"? In V. Arnold (Ed.), *Wirtschaftsethische perspektiven VII – Methodische grundsatzfragen, unternehmensethik, verteilungsfragen, gentechnik und fragen der medizinischen ethik* (pp. 33-60). Berlin: Duncker & Humboldt.

Jonas, H. (1987). Warum die technik ein gegenstand für die Ethik ist: Fünf gründe. In H. Lenk & G. Ropohl (Eds.), *Technik und ethik* (pp. 81–91). Stuttgart: Reclam.

Jones, T. M. (1991). Ethical decision-making by individuals in organizations: An issue-contingent model. *The Academy of Management Review, 16*(2), 366-395.

Juujärvi, S., Myyry, L., & Pesso, K. (2010). Does care reasoning make a difference?: Relations between care, justice and dispositional empathy. *Journal of Moral Education, 39*(4), 469-489.

Keller, M. (2005). Moralentwicklung und moralische sozialisation. In D. Horster & J. Oelkers (Eds.), *Pädagogik und ethik* (pp. 149-172). Wiesbaden: VS Verlag für Sozialwissenschaften.

Kerber S. J. W. (1991). Zum ethos von führungskräften. Ergebnisse einer empirischen Untersuchung. In H. Steinmann & A. Löhr (Eds.), *Unternehmensethik* (2nd ed., pp. 303–313). Stuttgart: Schäffer-Poeschel.

Klebe Trevino, L. (1986). Ethical decision-making in organizations: A person-situation interactionist model. *The Academy of Management Review, 11*(3), 601-617.

Klemme, H. F. (2006). Praktische gründe und moralische motivation. Eine deontologische Perspektive. In H. F. Klemme, M. Kühn & D. Schönecker (Eds.), *Moralische motivation. Kant und die alternativen* (pp. 113-154). Hamburg: Meiner.

Kohlberg, L. (1987). Moralische entwicklung und demokratische erziehung. In G. Lind & J. Raschert (Eds.), *Moralische urteilsfähigkeit. Eine auseinandersetzung mit Lawrence Kohlberg über moral, erziehung und demokratie* (pp. 25-43). Weinheim. Basel: Beltz.

Kohlberg, L., & Candee, D. (1984). The relationship of moral judgment to moral action. In W. M. Kurtines & J. L. Gewirtz (Eds.), *Morality, moral behavior, and moral development* (pp. 52-73). New York, NY: Wiley.

Kohlberg, L., & Candee, D. (1999). Die beziehung zwischen moralischem urteilen und moralischem handeln. In D. Garz, F. Oser & W. Althof (Eds.), *Moralisches urteil und handeln* (pp. 13-46). Frankfurt am Main: Suhrkamp.

Krebs, D. L., & Denton, K. (1999). Die beziehungen zwischen der struktur des moralischen urteilens und dem moralischen handeln. In D. Garz, F. Oser & W. Althof (Eds.), *Moralisches urteil und handeln* (pp. 220-263). Frankfurt am Main: Suhrkamp.

Latané, B., & Darley, J. M. (1976). *Help in a crisis: Bystander response to an emergency.* Morristown. NJ: General Learning Press

Lempert, W. (1997). Moralische entwicklung im beruf und ethische erziehung in der berufsbildung - Empirische befunde und pädagogische konsequenzen. In H. Geißler (Ed.), *Unternehmensethik, managementverantwortung und weiterbildung* (pp. 268–282). Neuwied. Kriftel. Berlin: Luchterhand (Grundlagen der Weiterbildung).

Lempert, W. (1999). Verantwortlichkeit als erziehungsziel? In G. Pollak & H. Heid (Eds.), *Erziehungswissenschaft und pädagogik zwischen kritischer reflexion und dienstleistung. Festschrift zum 65. Geburtstag von Helmut Heid* (pp. 319–335). Weinheim: Dt. Studien-Verlag.

Lenk, H. (1987). Über verantwortungsbegriffe und das verantwortungsproblem in der technik. In H. Lenk & G. Ropohl (Eds.), *Technik und ethik* (pp. 112-148). Stuttgart: Reclam.

Lenk, H., & Maring, M. (1998). Das moralphilosophische fundament einer ethik für organisationen - korporative und individuelle verantwortung. In G. Blickle (Ed.), *Ethik in organisationen. konzepte, befunde, praxisbeispiele* (pp. 21-38). Göttingen: Verl. für Angewandte Psychologie.

Leschke, M. (1995). Zur ökonomischen analyse moralkonformen handelns. *Analyse und Kritik, 17*(2), 209-231.

Loe, T. W., Ferell, L., & Mansfield, P. (2000). A review of empirical studies assessing ethical decision-making in business. *Journal of Business Ethics, 25*(3), 185-204.

Loew, J. (2011, October). *Moral judgments of responsibility and their influence on moral decision making in the economic context.* Presentation at the annual conference of the Association for Moral Education (AME) in Nanjing, China.

Maclagan, P. W. (1983). The concept of responsibility: Some implications for organizational behaviour and development. *Journal of Management Studies, 20*(4), 411-423.

McNamee, S. (1977). Moral behavior, moral development and motivation. *Journal of Moral Education,* 7(1), 27-32.

Milgram, S. (1963). Behavioral study of obedience. *Journal of Abnormal and Social Psychology, 67(4),* 371-378.

Minnameier, G. (2010a). Entwicklung moralischen denkens aus einer neo-Kohlbergschen perspektive. In B. Latzko & T. Malti (Eds.), *Moralische entwicklung und erziehung in kindheit und adoleszenz* (pp. 47-67). Göttingen u.a.: Hogrefe.

Minnameier, G. (2010b). The problem of moral motivation and the happy victimizer phenomenon: Killing two birds with one stone. In B. Latzko & T. Malti (Eds.), *Children's moral emotions and moral cognition: Developmental and educational perspectives. New Directions for Child and Adolescent Development, 129* (pp. 55-75). San Francisco, CA: Jossey-Bass.

Mischel, W., & Mischel H. N. (1976). A cognitive social-learning approach to morality and self-regulation. In T. Lickona (Ed.), *Moral development and behavior. Theory, research, and social issues* (pp. 84-107). New York, NY: Holt, Rinehart and Winston.

Montada, L. (1993). Understanding oughts by assessing moral reasoning or moral emotions. In G. G. Noam & T. E. Wren (Eds.), *The moral self. Press (Studies in contemporary German social thought)* (pp. 292-309). Cambridge, MA: MIT-

Nunner-Winkler, G. (1984). Two moralities?: A critical discussion of an ethic of care and responsibility versus an ethic of rights and justice. In W. M. Kurtines & J. L. Gewirtz (Eds.), *Morality, moral behavior, and moral development* (pp. 348-364). New York, NY: Wiley.

Nunner-Winkler, G. (1993). Die entwicklung moralischer motivation. In W. Edelstein, G. Nunner-Winkler & G. Noam (Eds.), *Moral und person* (pp. 278-303). Frankfurt am Main: Suhrkamp.

Nunner-Winkler, G. (1999). Moralische motivation und moralische identität. Zur kluft zwischen urteil und handeln. In D. Garz, F. Oser & W. Althof (Eds.), *Moralisches urteil und handeln* (pp. 314-339). Frankfurt am Main: Suhrkamp.

Nunner-Winkler, G. (2000). Wandel in den moralvorstellungen. Ein generationenvergleich. In W. Edelstein & G. Nunner-Winkler (Eds.), *Moral im sozialen kontext* (pp. 299-336). Frankfurt am Main: Suhrkamp.

Nunner-Winkler, G. (2007). Development of moral motivation from childhood to early adulthood. *Journal of Moral Education. 36*(4), 399-414.

Nunner-Winkler, G., & Edelstein, W. (2005). Introduction. In W. Edelstein & G. Nunner-Winkler (Eds.), *Morality in context* (pp. 1-24). Amsterdam, The Netherlands: Elsevier.

Oser, F. (2001). Acht strategien der wert- und moralerziehung. In W. Edelstein, F. Oser & P. Schuster (Eds.), *Moralische erziehung in der schule. Entwicklungspsychologie und pädagogische praxis* (pp. 63-89). Weinheim. Basel: Beltz.

Oser, F., & Althof, W. (1992). *Moralische selbstbestimmung. Modelle der entwicklung und erziehung im wertebereich*. Stuttgart: Klett-Cotta.

Patzig, G. (1996). Moralische motivation. In G. Patzig, D. Birnbacher & W. Ch. Zimmerli (Eds.), *Die rationalität der moral* (pp. 39-55). Bamberg: Verl. Fränkischer Tag.

Priddat, B. P. (1994). *Ökonomische knappheit und moralischer überschuss. Theoretische essays zum verhältnis von ökonomie und ethik.* Hamburg: S und W Steuer- und Wirtschaftsverlag.

Priddat, B. P. (2007). *Moral als indikator und kontext von Ökonomie.* Marburg: Metropolis-Verl. (Ethik und Ökonomie, 3).

Rest, J. R. (1984). The major components of morality. In W. M. Kurtines & J. L. Gewirtz (Eds.), *Morality, moral behavior, and moral development* (pp. 24-40). New York, NY: Wiley.

Rest, J. R. (1999). Die Rolle des moralischen Urteilens im moralischen Handeln. In D. Garz, F. Oser & W. Althof (Eds.), *Moralisches urteil und handeln* (pp. 82-116). Frankfurt am Main: Suhrkamp

Retzmann, T. (1997). Wirtschafts-, unternehmens- und führungsethik - Eine gute gelegenheit zur moralischen bildung von führungskräften? In H. Geißler (Ed.), *Unternehmensethik, managementverantwortung und weiterbildung* (pp. 283-306). Neuwied. Kriftel. Berlin: Luchterhand (Grundlagen der Weiterbildung).

Retzmann, T. (2007). Die dilemmamethode im ökonomieunterricht. *Unterricht Wirtschaft, 2*(2), 41-47.

Seeber, G. (2007). Wirtschaft und moral im fachunterricht. *Unterricht Wirtschaft, 2*(30), 3-4.

Strong, K. C., & Meyer, G. D. (1992). An integrative descriptive model of ethical decision-making. *Journal of Business Ethics, 11*(2), 89-94.

Toffler, B. L. (1986). *Tough choices: Managers talk ethics*. New York. Chichester. Brisbane. Toronto. Singapore: Wiley.

Ulrich, P., & Thielemann, U. (1992). Ethik und erfolg: Unternehmensethische denkmuster von führungskräften - eine empirische Studie. *St. Galler Beiträge zur Wirtschaftsethik: Vol. 6*. Bern: Haupt.

Van der Keilen, M., & Garg, R. (1994). Moral realism in adults' judgements of responsibility. *Journal of Psychology, 128*(2), 149-156.

Waters, J. A., Bird, F., & Chant, P. D. (1986). Everyday moral issues experienced by managers. *Journal of Business Ethics, 5*(5), 373-384.

Walker, L. J. (1984). Sex differences in the development of moral reasoning: A critical review. *Child Development, 55*, 677-691.

Walker, L. J. (1986). Sex differences in the development of moral reasoning: A rejoinder to Baumrind. *Child Development, 57*, 522-526.

Weber, J. (1990). Managers' moral reasoning: Assessing their responses to three moral dilemmas. *Human Relations, 43*(7), 687-702.

Weber, J. (1996). Influences upon managerial moral decision-making: Nature of the harm and magnitude of consequences. *Human Relations, 49*(1), 1-22.

Weinreich-Haste, H. (1986). Moralisches engagement. Die funktion der gefühle im urteilen und handeln. In W. Edelstein & G. Nunner-Winkler (Eds.), *Zur Bestimmung der Moral. Philosophische und sozialwissenschaftliche Beiträge zur Moralforschung* (pp. 377-408). Frankfurt am Main: Suhrkamp

Weyers, S. (2004). *Moral und delinquenz. Moralische entwicklung und sozialisation straffälliger Jugendlicher.* Weinheim. München: Juventa

Wren, T. E. (1986). Moralpsychologie und metaethik: Ein arbeitsbündnis. In W. Edelstein & G. Nunner-Winkler (Eds.), *Zur Bestimmung der Moral. Philosophische und sozialwissenschaftliche Beiträge zur Moralforschung* (pp. 37-54). Frankfurt am Main: Suhrkamp.

Wren, T. E. (1991). *Caring about morality: Philosophical perspectives in moral psychology.* London: Routledge.

Zimmerli, W. C. (1987). Wandelt sich die verantwortung mit dem technischen Wandel? In H. Lenk & G. Ropohl (Eds.), *Technik und Ethik* (pp. 92-111). Stuttgart: Reclam.

CHAPTER 8

INTERSECTIONS OF IDENTITY AND IDEOLOGY IN LEARNING ABOUT FINANCIAL CAPABILITY

Valerie Farnsworth

Cartesian dichotomies continue to structure Western ideologies and "Discourses" (Gee, 1999). This chapter will argue that Discourses about the meaning of financially capability in the United Kingdom are structured in relation to a rational/emotional dichotomy. This position establishes financial decisions as rational, not emotional (and, by implication, not moral) decisions. These dichotomies permit positions such as what has been presented by Flanders (2010), an economist writing for BBC's online blog:

> It may be Tony Blair's great legacy to British politics that we've spent the past few days debating whether the government's budget cuts are fair, not whether they will smother Britain's economic recovery. (para. 1)

The final message of the blog states that debates over what is "fair" are "almost impossible to pin down." The author implies in her blog that, given the messiness of debates over equity, the best the government can do is make rational and appropriate decisions based on sound financial practice for the economy. Concerns for what is "fair" are viewed as letting

Reframing Financial Literacy: Exploring the Value of Social Currency, pp. 149–169

emotions take over, and hence they "smother Britain's economic recovery." (Flanders, 2010, para. 1)

Interviews conducted by a team of researchers at the University of Manchester, who inquired into the ways that young people in the United Kingdom learn about finance, also reflected this Discourse. Students' talk about personal financial management practices, ideals, and expectations was found to be similar to the comments made by Flanders (2010) in that they drew from similar dichotomies.

The Discourse, which the following analysis will present, effectively perpetuates an ideology of individualism and sets up rational decisions as distinct from (and even corrupted by) emotional and moral considerations. Another well-established dichotomy which sets public and private domains as distinct and separate also supports an emphasis on individual financial choices and rational decision making. As such, these mutually supportive dichotomies of emotional/rational and public/private structure financial capability education so as to subvert discussions and actions that are initiated in the name of the public good and social justice.

This chapter focuses on the ways particular ideologies and Discourses are substantiated, sustained, and circulated, but also challenged and resisted in financial capability education. It is proposed that the propagation of these dichotomies in financial capability education (e.g., one is either emotional or rational, and decisions are private not public matters) is not only problematic from a social justice perspective, but also a mythical one. It is also proposed that a more dialectical view is needed in order to realize the inter-dependencies of the "public" and the "private" and between the "rational" and the "emotional."

This chapter is developed through an analysis of interviews conducted with United Kingdom students aged 16-19, who completed a financial capability course as one of their options in postcompulsory schooling. From these interviews, in which students talked about what they learned from the course about finance, particular meanings of finance were implied. A Discourse analysis of how students talked about personal finance identifies consumer-oriented cultural models or storylines (Gee, 1999) about financial capability that are consequently framed in terms of private and rational decisions/choices with regards to one's finances. Particularly notable are instances in which the public and the emotional storylines were marginalized or discounted as not indicative of financial capability. The analysis highlights implied dichotomies between public and private and between rational and emotional in order to then critically examine the social and ideological functions that these dichotomies play.

The analysis utilizes Fairclough's (2001) definition of ideology such that "ideologies are representations of aspects of the world which can be shown to contribute to establishing, maintaining and changing social relations of power, domination and exploitation" (p. 9). A critical perspective is applied in the analysis of Discourse using tools from Gee (1999), such as concepts of "cultural models" and "Discourses." These conceptual tools, described below, enable an analyst to identify social and cultural constructs that help to structure (or mediate) social practices and social relations, including financial practices and decisions. The domination and uncritical acceptance of particular norms, beliefs, and practices is of particular concern because these serve to oppress, marginalize, or exploit certain groups of people, while maintaining advantages for other groups. Examining Discourse practices in order to explore issues of power and control necessarily considers the subtleties of social relations and practices, but these subtleties are nonetheless powerful in their impact on individual beliefs and identities (van Dijk, 1997).

The Financial Capability Research Project

The research data presented in this chapter come from a longitudinal study that included interviews with students, aged 16-19, who completed a financial capability course as one of their options in postcompulsory schooling. The sample for this analysis included 30 students from 11 different institutions across the United Kingdom who participated in two or more interviews, 10 and 22 months after course completion. This sample represents a subgroup of the 222 students interviewed over the course of the 3-year project conducted from 2004-2007 (66 in Cohort 1, 101 in Cohort 2 and 55 in Cohort 3) which aimed to capture the diversity of the students who took the course (e.g., by social class, ethnicity, and gender).

Focusing on the ways students narrate their learning and their identification with personal finance, this chapter explores the ideologies that are able to co-exist in an individual's narrative. It argues that the presence of rational and emotional considerations in students' sense-making of their learning about financial capability may disrupt dominant dichotomous representations of the world. In our analysis, the narrative refers to the story of students' learning as they progressed through the finance courses. For most students, this was a 1 year "certificate" course only; while for some, it was a 2-year "diploma" course. All the students referenced in this analysis participated in at least two interviews, which allowed capture of their learning narratives over time, regardless of the program in which they enrolled. The "Year 1, 2, or 3" referred to in the analysis denotes the year of the research project during which the interview was conducted.

Theoretically, the intersections of the emotional and the rational, as well as the individual and the social, are understood with the help of sociocultural theory. From this theoretical perspective, the ways in which social context and ideology mediate individual meaning-making may be recognized. This mediation is observable in the ways individual students presented themselves and the learning they described. In the interviews, students expressed "cultural models" of personal finance which make up the "figured worlds" (Holland, Lachicotte, Skinner, & Cain, 2001) of personal finance for these students. As argued by Holland et al., cultural models, or what they call "figured worlds," "carry disposition, social identification, and even personification just as surely as they carry meaning" (p. 271). In other words, cultural models or storylines about social phenomena evoke particular subject positions in relation to personal financial management practices and decisions (Gee, 1999). These subject-positions and cultural models were expressed by the students through their interactions with the research interviewer. The analytic process employed by the researcher involves looking across these subject positions and cultural models for similarities, differences, intersections and relations. For example, a cultural model of financial decisions as rational and in opposition to emotional decision-making may conflict with a subject position in which the student places himself/herself as an emotional (and perhaps moral) decision maker. The analysis uncovers instances of the perpetuation of these dichotomies as well as resistance to these.

Most of the analysis focuses on cultural models signaled in the Discourse event of the interview. However, Gee's (1999) notion of Discourses has also been influential in the analysis as a guiding concept for how the students chose to present themselves as particular kinds of individuals. To explain the concept of a "Discourse," Gee uses the example of someone wanting to be recognized as a street-smart kid, pointing out ways that a kid will draw on multiple ways of thinking, acting, feeling, and interacting to be seen as street-smart. A Discourse is therefore a particular combination of resources people can use to enact an identity. For this analysis, "ideologies" are abstracted from the analysis of a Discourse as the set of cultural models inform the Discourses expressed by students in the research interviews. This account of ideologies as a set of cultural models is justified based on van Dijk's (1997) notion of ideologies as socially-shared but also individually-situated in the sociocognitive sense belief systems that define social groups (Van Dij, 1997). Because students' daily financial practices in this study were not observed, the perspective on how students present themselves as financially capable people (i.e., their financial Discourse) is based purely on interview data. Importantly, however, the ways in which students talk about personal finance reveal ways that they have decided to engage with a Discourse about what it means to be financially capable. In other words, it is how the students choose to present themselves as financially capable individuals, and hence is suggestive of the financial practices with which they will engage.

Analysis of Financial Capability Discourses

This section contains a description of the analysis of the ways that young people in the United Kingdom talked about their developing financial capabilities. Students talked about choices and financial decisions in two main ways: (1) as working within a set of constraints, such as debt and limited funds, or (2) as working to "come above" constraints, such as debt, by investing or saving money. This cultural model of finance was termed the "constraints/affordances" cultural model. A dominant Discourse that was identified, which drew on these cultural models, was that of the "financially aware consumer." A "debt averse" Discourse or identity was also sometimes combined with this Discourse of the aware consumer. These Discourses also drew upon a cultural model of personal finance that presented financial capability as being knowledgeable about financial products and "the fine print."

An excerpt from Rana's[1] interview in Year 1 is presented here to illustrate these overall findings. Rana expressed notions of both constraints and affordances when reflecting on the financial capabilities course:

> [The] Financial Studies [course] has helped me think okay '[these are] the available options' when I, you know, start earning my money. Whereas before, the only thing to think about was if you don't control your spending you're going into debt, and there's a lot of loans and mortgages. But this is actually showing that there are so many other options if you have money saved up or what you can do while you're earning.

Rana presents her identity as someone knowledgeable about different options or financial products; hence, she represents for us the "financially aware consumer" Discourse. Although she refers to a cultural model of personal finance in terms of constraints (e.g., controlling spending), she rejects this by saying that is what she used to think. She is one of the minority of students in the sample who combined the consumer aware Discourse with what may be called an "entrepreneur" Discourse, in which students made references (in their identity presentations) to making investments and taking risks in order to "make money make money."

Financial Capability as Rational, not Emotional

The constraints/affordances cultural model of personal finance appears to support a Discourse of financial practices in moral terms, as "should do" activities. Whether students in the study talked about financial practices within their day-to-day life or for the future, their practices were typically framed in terms of things a person does to avoid debt or stay within their financial means. This view portrays personal financial management as a matter of recognizing and living within certain *constraints*.

For example, Ahmed mentioned credit card debt a few times. In his Year 2 interview, he said:

> Obviously, I know what kind of debt you can get into with credit cards and stuff like that, so obviously you know what I mean. We've been taught like to read, you know, thoroughly and all that before we actually, you know, make our decisions. And obviously to read, it doesn't cost us, so obviously I know what to do to come above it.

A rational/emotional dichotomy also structured these students' Discourses and identities as financially capable individuals. Ahmed's comment above implies that anyone who can read should be able to come out of debt or avoid it by making informed decisions (having read up on the options). The specific cultural model or storyline expressed here (and across the data sample) is a belief that the financially capable person is consumer aware and able to make considered decisions, not impulsive ones. A notable moralistic tone to Ahmed's discussion exists, but it is a Discourse that also refers to rationality, signalled by the reference to reading to become informed. Students in the course expressed their growing rational financial sensibilities, sometimes referring to using "common sense" but mostly detailing practices that they now considered sensible, such as writing out their weekly budgets rather than keeping track in their head. Avoiding debt was another common "sensible" financial practice, as Ahmed commented:

> I try to avoid borrowing, get loans and things, but if it has to be done [I] just need [to be] sensible about it. Make sure you can pay it back.

At the same time, Ahmed betrays the blanket assumption that finance is entirely rational by referring to feelings. Evoking a constraints cultural model of finance, he stated:

> My parents don't like [debt] either. You don't want to get black listed; you don't want to get in debt; you don't want to get bankrupt, stuff like that. Know what I mean? Go for it, [but] if you can't afford [anything], you can't. If you want something, you save and save to get it. That's the way we feel.

In his Year 2 interview, Ahmed expressed a view of personal finance framed in terms of affordances but also included a reference to "luck" when he remarked:

> "We've obviously learned outcomes of the debt, but we've also learned getting, you know, your money … and then if you're lucky, then you make money on top and pay that off.

Most students implied financial choices and decisions should be sensible and rational. However, these decisions have an implied moral sensibility in that there is an implied right and wrong way to be financially capable. For example, Rana explained how the financial capability course had impacted her:

> At the moment, it hasn't [informed my financial practices], but it is helping in that I'm thinking about/for the future … what I actually want to do, and how I am going to control my budget, and what I am going to use my money for. For planning purposes, it has helped because, obviously, I'm not in that position right now to even have a house…. I'm quite well supported from my parents, so it's not really a worry. But, obviously, I have thought about it, and the course did help me to consider the options I would have and stuff *and which one would be the most appropriate [action] to take*" (italics emphasis by researcher).

Rana expressed the cultural model of financial capability as a matter of controlling behavior and making appropriate decisions. Her reference to "appropriate," falls within the "should I" Discourse of morality in which a right versus a wrong behavior is implied. The moralistic tone expressed in this cultural model of personal finance is problematic to the extent that it (a) supports the domination and uncritical acceptance of particular norms, beliefs, and practices and (b) limits and structures possibilities for financial decision making and action. The boundaries for appropriate action are constructed to include rationality but exclude emotionality and other considerations that may fall outside of rationality, such as beliefs about fairness and social justice. This exclusion of considerations for fairness and social justice from individual financial decision making is supported by another dichotomy implied in students' Discourse—the division between public and private domains.

Financial Capability as Private Not Public

As a matter of rational choice, not social consciousness, personal finance was largely relegated to the private sphere within the students' Discourse. Financial capability was expressed as private, not only by referring to personal choices and decisions (that are rational, of course), but also by integrating the home and family into their narratives.

For example, Helen talked about how she could advise others, such as her brother, as a result of the course, describing it as "nagging" (a gendered term) her brother:

> Well, actually, [I've] just been nagging my brother. He's just [got] a job now, and I've actually been nagging him and telling him stuff that I've [learned] in the lesson [about what] to do with his money.... He's getting quite a lot, and he doesn't know what to do with it. He wants to save it, but he doesn't know how to save it. And he doesn't know where to go. And my mum and dad are having trouble with their insurances as well, so I've told them about that as well.

Helen also talked about what she has gained from the course with reference to being able to "contribute" to a conversation about these issues with her parents:

> Yeah, 'cause otherwise I would have just sat there and listened to them, but now I can contribute and tell them that ... they need such things; go and see these people; or [go] shop around and get the best interest and stuff like that.

Similarly referencing the family, Ayesha explained how she now knows:

> what they are talking about and you know what ARPs mean properly—all their terms and conditions. Normally, you are confused, so you think about the product. But now it's just ... if you go with your mum or your dad, you can tell them so you don't have to wait in a big queue at customer service to explain it to them.

Talking to others about what they knew and learned was part of the students' learning; it seemed to provide motivation for learning (e.g., even if they were too young to use the knowledge about mortgages, they were able to inform others who could use it). This ability to share practical knowledge reassured students that they had learned something useful.

Student views of financial capability emphasized financial decisions as personal ones. Analyses of interviews found finance to be relegated to the "private" sphere with students seeing financial issues as a private (i.e., industry or business) matter, not, by contrast, a social concern. One student interview, that of Ahmed from Year 2 of the study, provides an example of a student depicting financial practices as a matter of business, limited to the private sphere. In the following interview excerpt, the student is giving his perspective on credit cards and the danger of not making card payments:

> And if you don't know anything [about credit card debt], that's your problem. You're supposed to find out, and then what happens is your debt

> increases … and then all [the credit card company] can do is get the money off you like that. That just ruins [your] life, which is not their fault because it's business, isn't it?

By claiming "it's just business" the student expresses his belief that there is no shared responsibility for an individual going into debt. Moreover, this Discourse leaves little space for discussing debt as a public matter.

A Look at Learning: Myths and Contradictions

Although the constraints and affordances cultural model problematically bounds financial practices and decisions to rational, personal, and private matters, it is also recognized that it was this personalizing of the knowledge domain and field of finance that initially engaged the students in learning about this topic. In making sense of the course curriculum, students shared their own meaning-making of finance topics, which revealed possible intersections of the public and the private. For example, on the one hand, the course emphasized the personal by encouraging the students to make decisions "appropriate" to their circumstances. One student, Christie, interpreted this as meaning she should consider her own behavioral tendencies. She reflected on the course as follows:

> It's probably made me more realistic. I just know that I will have to manage my finances carefully because I do like to spend. I'm not going to get a credit card because after reading [some of those newspaper clips provided by the teacher], … it's changed my ideas.

In the quote above, Christie refers to the news media, hence the public sphere. Interestingly, the media makes the private experiences of others public, which is one of the resources that this student has drawn upon in her learning about debt and finance. Thus, public and private are interconnected in this interview response.

Students spread learned cultural models about personal finance through talking about finance with others. In becoming consumer-aware and knowledgeable, through personal reflection on their own circumstances and experiences with finance as well as through consideration of personal hopes and plans for the future, students evolved into semi-advisors to family and friends. In this way, students shared their knowledge, spread their cultural models, and hence entered the public sphere by constructing socially-shared knowledge. Thus, although their learning began as a personal journey, it often became a public one. These examples betray an arguably dialectic relationship between the public and private, which shall be argued further in the discussion section of this chapter.

Another way to view the dichotomy between public and private being challenged is in the intersecting of home, family, and/or cultural values with the financial values expressed through the school curriculum. That is, many students referred to their families, in addition to referencing the course, when they offered their views or knowledge of finance. In a course on financial capability that includes personal finance topics, matters of the home are inevitably going to enter into class discussions. This may be initially experienced by students as a contradiction, given that school knowledge is often considered to be something relevant only in school, not in "real" life. Sociocultural historical activity theory considers such contradictions to be opportunities for "expansive learning" (Engeström, 2001), which suggests that this course can play a unique role in supporting students' learning-learning that is a matter of negotiating meaning and self-identity (e.g., negotiating home-cultural values and school-finance values). In making the informed decision to save her money through her mother rather than through a bank, Salima reformulated the dominant financial practice of saving money through banks in a unique way:

> Yes, I actually save a lot of money now. I do a lot of saving. I don't have an account. I have actually saved money with my mother. I give it to her, and she saves it for me now. I think it's a bit safer than an account because [with a bank] I could go and take the money out, but with my mum, she just won't give it [back to] me.

Thus, although most students expressed their intentions to enter into the formal financial system, this particular student negotiated it in other ways.

Ayesha also worked through her understanding of financial capability and appropriate decision-making by considering not only what she learned in the course but also what she recalled about her relatives' experience with financial investments:

> My aunty bought stocks and shares because someone told her they'd double within a year, but they actually went down. What she invested went down nearly a half, and she thought, "When I get back my capital, I'll withdraw out of it." ... I would just [use] savings accounts or bonds or something, but it depends on what kind of bonds they are.

Ayesha implies that her aunt's experience has made her cautious and less trustworthy of claims made about stocks being good investments and refers to other products she knows about as safer options she would consider. Ayesha is rejecting the notion that financial decisions are purely rational, and in doing so, she constructs her own knowledge and identity with regards to personal finance. Such personal knowledge construction can contribute to empowerment (Farnsworth et al., 2011), but it can be constrained by dominant ideologies that mythically limit personal finance to rational decision making.

What is deemed to be "irrational" is arguably culturally determined, and it is important to recognize cultural differences in views on finance (see for example, Lucey's (2005) interpretation of bias in the Jump$tart survey). A strict delineation of financial capability in terms of rational choices marginalizes alternative cultural views on personal finance, leaving little room for cultural diversity. Moreover, privileging the individual aspects of personal finance underacknowledges the ways that financial knowledge and practices are cultural. This enables a lack of further questioning of financial social justice along cultural lines of argument (such as failing to consider ways that systems of finance may favor certain cultural groups and cultural practices over others). To illustrate this oversight, David, in year 2, negotiates his opinion on debt, which he presents as a matter of personal preference:

> Well, I'd rather not borrow, but I don't think borrowing's a bad thing as long as it's a reasonable amount that you can afford easily to pay back. Because then it allows you to get things you want without having to wait for them, as long as it's paid back. But I don't think you should get into an over-sized amount of debt which you can't afford to pay back anyway.

His comment diverges somewhat from the dominant Discourse of avoiding debt as a blanket "should do" statement—he expressed here a belief that a "reasonable amount" of debt is not "a bad thing." This is related to his sociocultural background. That is, David told us about his experience of investing in property with his father which suggests that his family is financially stable. He can afford then to weigh his options and consider the potential affordances of money and even debt.

Discussion

Dichotomous thinking structures the ideologies of financial capability Discourses. Additionally, emotional and public concerns are integral to learning, despite the curricular focus on finance as private and rational decisions. The analysis suggests that the public/private and rational/emotional dichotomies are alive and well, with finance being a matter of rational and private decisions and choices. However, students resist as well as appropriate these cultural models as they construct particular identities of themselves, expressed as a Discourse of someone who is financially capable. Students have shown the fissures in the social fabric of the ideologies that maintain a split between the public and the private and the emotional and the rational. Importantly, some of these fissures have become apparent through the students' learning processes. However, breaking down these dichotomies requires new conceptualizations of public and private as being dialectical. In other words, the ways in which the private implicates and is implicated by the public need to be made explicit in financial capability curriculum. Similarly, rational and emotional spheres can be viewed as dialectical—as interdependent ways of being and making decisions, even financial decisions.

Students' sense-making of financial capability drew upon a range of rational and emotional considerations, as well as cultural and public forms of knowledge and beliefs/norms. Taking a sociocultural view of learning, this study found that students' learning through the financial capability course entailed a process of internalizing the sensibilities of rational, consumer-aware financial decision-making to become common sense.

Given that critical theory is about challenging the taken-for-granted status quo, this chapter has identified the assumed split between public and private and between rational and emotional as problematic. This split was not necessarily clear cut in the ways these students made sense of finance. However, the dominant ideological split risks sidelining important discussions about finance that need to be had—ones that consider the public or socially shared responsibilities of finance as well as the emotional or irrational aspects of finance.

In a critical analysis, it also needs to be asked what function these Discourses have in society. Based on this research, the response to this line of inquiry is that they help to ensure that young people will and are prepared to enter the financial system. Although these students will now enter the system with consumer knowledge and an awareness of the "fine print" among other good things, they will also be prepared to perpetuate a Discourse of finance based on the dichotomies of public/private and rational/emotional. These dichotomies help to sustain practices that avoid messy emotions, moral decisions, and social justice considerations.

The problem of ideological divisions can also be considered on a personal level to the extent that the Discourse limits the bounds for financial decisions as financial, which may leave out the bigger picture which involves social justice and moral questions and considerations. For example, this student who presents the decision of going to a university as a simple matter of whether you "prefer" a loan or not has left out of the big picture issues, such as earning potential and the possibility of critical learning/thinking that may be part of a university education. When David explained why he plans to do an apprenticeship with an accountancy firm rather than go to university, he said:

> Then it's just your preference really. If you do the training there, you're getting paid a wage as well, but if you go to University, you're getting debts ... from student loan. So it's really preference, yes.

Another point raised through this study is that the financial capability course is not the only shaper of students' Discourse on financial capability. The media, society, and family (public *and* private Discourses) also influence this Discourse. As Christie comments in the second year interview, the course helped her, but some things she does are things she would have already believed or done prior to the course:

> It's helped me learn how to budget better, just how to set it all out. I mean I budgeted before, but it was just all in my head, you know. I just thought, "I've got so much for this, so much for this." But I write everything down now. So it has helped me do that. But I mean my attitude to money hasn't changed. I've always been careful with it.

The students who participated in this research remind us that personal finance is personal, as well as cultural, and it is this duality that financial capability education ideally embraces.

Conclusion

The analysis of interview data in this study does not provide a clear answer to the question, "What should a financial capability curriculum entail?" However, it does make it evident that teaching young people about financial capability is not simply about imparting technical knowledge on the choices and products available. One implication of this finding is that financial capability is not simply about being informed and knowledgeable, for it also invokes social and cultural ways of being, thinking, and feeling. The split between the rational and the emotional is a myth that allows for the pretence that these are not also moral choices and decisions. Moreover, the split between public and private, where finance is relegated to the private sphere, detracts from public and social implications of financial decisions and the finance system itself. As Apple (1995) notes, the predominance of management systems and cost-effective decision making are not neutral. His argument is that since "efficiency, bureaucratic management, economic models applied to everything—these are ethical constructs. Adopting them involves moral and political choices" (p. xv). Hence, the curriculum framework proposed by Lucey (2007), which "interweaves morality into the areas of financial education" (p. 493), may be a more fruitful approach to financial capability education.

Finally, this analysis suggests that an important area for further development in financial capability education is the development of pedagogic strategies that build upon the ways of learning illuminated through students' personal narratives and cultural histories. This undertaking involves recognizing the emotional and sociocultural aspects of learning and students' sense-making about finance. The financial capability course's focus on the personal and making finance a useful subject provides an opportunity for learning. One way to take this further is to not stop at developing young people who are consumer-aware, but to aim at supporting them in becoming consumer- informed and socially-conscious by making the public aspects of financial capability apparent as an integral part of the course curriculum. In building on the personal, emotional, and even sociocultural aspects of finance, it is important to not get lost in the private at the expense of wider moral and societal issues relating to finance. This makes knowledge of economic systems an essential part of financial capability education, as Davies (2006) has previously argued. Thus, it is no easy task to find a balance between rational versus emotional, public versus private, and shared versus individualized approaches to finance when developing financial capability education.

DISCUSSION QUESTIONS

1. How are your personal financial choices influenced by public Discourses on finance?
2. What are some financial decisions that are simultaneously rational and emotional? Private and public?
3. What is lost or not accounted for in a definition of financial capability that is confined to rational decision making of individuals?
4. How do individual choices influence wider financial practices and Discourses? What are some examples?
5. What are some other ways to conceive of financial capability that do not rely on dichotomous thinking? How might financial capability be defined in ways that account for the personal, public, cultural, moral and emotional aspects of financial practices and decisions?

MODEL LESSON

Financial Practice Beyond the Individual

Suggested Grade Levels: 9th-12th Grades

Objectives:

1. To develop students' thinking about issues of public responsibility in private decision making.
2. To illustrate the various ways individual choices are influenced by public Discourses and advice/choices of others.
3. To foster critical readings of financial product offers and advertisements.

Related Standards:

Jump$tart National Standards in K–12 Personal Finance Education

Financial Responsibility and Decision Making

Standard 2: Find and evaluate financial information from a variety of sources.

Standard 4: Make financial decisions by systematically considering alternatives and consequences.

Standard 5: Develop communication strategies for discussing financial issues.

Credit and Debt

Standard 1: Identify the costs and benefits of various types of credit

Saving and Investing

Standard 1: Discuss how saving contributes to financial well-being.

Standard 2: Explain how investing builds wealth and helps meet financial goals.

Standard 3: Evaluate investment alternatives.

Materials:

- Handout 1: A table of 6 different financial products (such as a savings account, loan. or bond) with their key features as described in brochures that the teacher has collected. List each product in Column 1. Columns 2 and 3 represent pros and cons for each product that the teacher has identified. Products that have been found to be fraudulent or subject to legal action should be included in the sample if possible, which may include schemes offered by different types of businesses (e.g., credit-card debt reduction schemes). Ideally, research on the history of the product would include a personal account of the damage the product or scheme has had on an individual's finances. If no account is available, one of the "products" should be the loans provided by "loan sharks," and the continued existence of such practices should be noted (supported by evidence and examples if available). One resource is the United States Department of Justice website: http://www.justice.gov/criminal/fraud/internet/.
- Handout 2: A short scenario that illustrates the case study to be used in the Developmental Activity, provided on a sheet of paper for students. There should be space on the paper for students to make notes on the two scenario descriptions. The first scenario should briefly say that Jane has purchased a product (type and details of the product should be determined by the teacher based on prior knowledge of the students and current products available in their locality). For the purposes of the activity, a diagram may be included in order to represent two trajectories for the life of the product (e.g., two divergent arrows). Title the arrow going upwards toward the top right corner of the page "Jane tells friends he/she got a product that she thinks is good" and title the arrow going downwards toward the bottom right corner of the page "Jane returns the product to the provider because she thinks it is a bad product." Include space for students to write near each of the arrows as they continue their investigation of the case.

Procedures:

(a) Opening Activities:

1. Presented and explain a range of financial products, such as types of loans, savings, and investment schemes.

2. Present pros and cons of each scheme (approximately six different products) using a table format, as described with respect to Handout 1 in the Materials section above.
3. The life of each "product" should be noted (e.g., whether it was available for a short or long time and if it is still available). The aim is to be able to pose the following questions to students for discussion and to prompt thinking with regards to the Developmental Activity:

   Why do "bad" products continue to be offered and available to customers?

   How does someone determine whether a product is "bad" or "good?"

(b) Developmental Activities:

1. Read through the written case study provided on Handout 2.
2. Ask students to map out two possible scenarios for the life of the product given one initial event in which Jane tells her friends about the new product she bought and how good it is. Further elaboration may be needed to explain that these friends then tell other friends. Students should hypothesize what could happen with this product in terms of how long it will be available to customers. The second scenario, related to the downwards arrow, should begin with the event in which Jane returns the product to the provider. Again, students should hypothesize what could happen with this product in terms of how long it will be available.

(c) Closing Activities:

1. Conduct a whole class discussion in which the students brainstorm together all the different ways that people make decisions. This should bring up a range of factors and influences, including the advice of friends. These ideas should be written on a blackboard/whiteboard by the teacher who facilitates this discussion.
2. If ideas are stilted, another activity may be used in which groups of 4-6 students are given brochures from banks about different products, such as savings accounts, loans, and bonds. Students then role play by imagining themselves in a position to purchase or sign up for the product described in the brochure, and they list things that they would do or want to find out in order to help them

make a decision. Among this list of things they consider before deciding should be related decisions and implications of their decision to purchase or acquire the product or not. They should discuss how they would determine whether the product was "good" or "bad." Groups should be allotted approximately 10 minutes for this discussion. Each group should elect a note-taker who reports back to the class on the group's decision and how the group came to it.

3. Note-takers from each group report back on the issues their respective groups discussed to add to the list of factors and influences that inform decision-making about product purchase. Depending on the number of groups, the reporting back activity should take approximately 20 to 30 minutes.

(d) Summary and Assessment:

From engagement in these activities, students should be able to consider the ways in which public and private matters intersect. This means both that public Discourses influence private decisions and that private decisions of individuals influence public Discourses and practices. In particular, students will gain insight into how markets and capitalism work through consumer choice, but also how consumer choice is not a straightforward matter.

The assessment of learning from these activities, framed as an activity that continues their learning on these issues, asks students to analyze an advertisement or brochure that they identify in a magazine or newspaper or that from a local bank. The following questions should guide their analysis:

Q1: What assumptions about the customer are implied or explicitly stated in the language used in the brochure or advertisement?

The students should be advised to begin this analysis by focusing on each phrase or sentence and considering any assumptions made in those phrases or sentences about the reader and/or the customer who is being offered the product. In order to focus further, students can then be guided to respond specifically to the following question:

Q2: What is being assumed or implied in the brochure or advertisement about how the customer should/could make his/her decision about whether to buy the product?

Finally, students should reflect on and address the following question:

Q3: What factors or concerns are not being assumed or implied as relevant to decision-making but that you know can be relevant or important?

The assessment should be submitted by students in the form of an essay of approximately 1,500 words. Scoring should be based on the comprehensiveness and clarity of the responses to each of the three questions. A minimum pass should require the student to have answered at least Q1, with assumptions noted about the customer clearly justified with examples from the brochure text. Q2 engages the student in deeper analysis of these assumptions and scoring should be based on the quality of this analysis, judged by the justification of the claims and the student's use of issues discussed in the course lesson. Sufficient response to Q1 and Q2 qualify for an above-pass score, depending on the quality of the writing and analysis. However, the highest score should be reserved for those who engage also with Q3, which requires a more critical response than the other question prompts.

Hand Out 1 Mock Up

Product	Pros	Cons
Product 1 • Key feature 1 • Key feature 2 ...	• Pro 1 • Pro 2 ... •	• Con 1 • Con 2 ...
Product 2 • Key feature 1 • Key feature 2 ...	• Pro 1 • Pro 2 ... •	• Con 1 • Con 2 ...
Product 3 • Key feature 1 • Key feature 2 ...	• Pro 1 • Pro 2 ...	• Con 1 • Con 2 ...
Product 4 • Key feature 1 • Key feature 2 ...	• Pro 1 • Pro 2 ...	• Con 1 • Con 2 ...
Product 5 • Key feature 1 • Key feature 2...	• Pro 1 • Pro 2 ...	• Con 1 • Con 2 ...
Product 6 • Key feature 1 • Key feature 2 ...	• Pro 1 • Pro 2 ...	• Con 1 • Con 2 ...

Handout 2 Mock Up

Case study scenario: [Teacher to add in paragraph or two.]

Fill in the possible trajectories for the product:

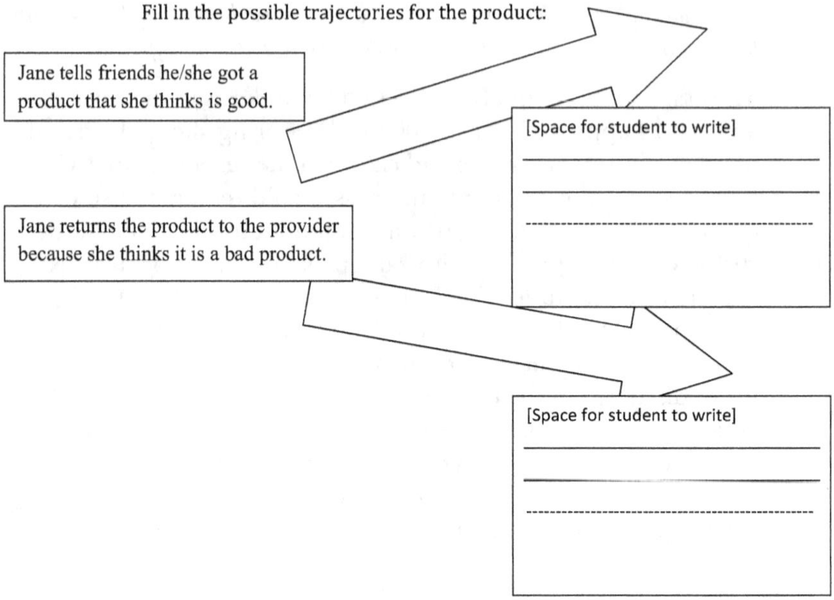

NOTE

1. All names are pseudonyms.

REFERENCES

Apple, M.W. (1995). *Education and power* (2nd ed.). London: Routledge.

Davies, P. (2006). Educating citizens for changing economies. *Journal of Curriculum Studies, 38*(1), 15-30.

Engeström, Y. (2001). Expansive learning at work: Toward an activity theoretical reconceptualisation. *Journal of education and work, 14*(1), 133–156.

Fairclough, N. (2001). *Language and power* (2nd revised ed.). London: Longman.

Farnsworth, V., Davis, P., Kalambouka, A., Ralph, S., Shi, X., & Farrell, P. (2011). Students' production of curricular knowledge: Perspectives on empowerment in financial capability education. *Education Citizenship and Social Justice, 6*(2).

Flanders, S. (2010). Fairness and the recovery: Two verdicts for Mr. Osborne. *BBC Online.* Retrieved from http://www.bbc.co.uk/blogs/thereporters/stephanieflanders/2010/10/fairness_and_the_recovery_two.html

Gee, J. P. (1999). *An introduction to Discourse analysis: Theory and method.* London: Routledge.

Holland, D., Lachicotte, W., Jr., Skinner, D., & Cain, C. (2001). *Identity and agency in cultural worlds*. Boston, MA: Harvard University Press.
Lucey, T. A. (2005) Assessing the reliability and validity of the Jump$tart Survey of Financial Literacy. *Journal of Family and Economic Issues, 26*(2), 283-294.
Lucey, T. A. (2007). The art of relating moral education to financial education: An equity imperative. *Social Studies Research and Practice, 2*(3), 484-498.
van Dijk, T. A. (Ed.). (1997). *Discourse as structure and process*. London: SAGE.

SECTION 2

EDUCATIONAL ISSUES

CHAPTER 9

A SENSE OF VALUES

Developing Financial Capability in Scottish School Curricula

Cathy Fagan

Two issues greatly impact the development of financial capability in young people in Scotland. The first is teachers' own levels of financial literacy and their abilities to develop realistic and relevant contexts for learning. The second is the global financial crisis that has exposed questionable values frameworks in our financial institutions while providing an impetus for reflection and debate in our schools on aspects of financial morality. This chapter seeks to outline an historical basis for Scotland's unique approach to education, demonstrating values bases from within which Scottish policy makers and educators construct curricula. There is particular emphasis on financial education and some examples are provided of useful contexts for students' development of and reflection upon values in financial matters.

The Scottish Education Context

Although situated within the U.K. context for most monetary and fiscal matters, Scotland often has its own unique way of dealing with issues that

Reframing Financial Literacy: Exploring the Value of Social Currency, pp. 173–187

have direct relevance for the Scottish people. There is historic and contemporary evidence of Scotland applying values with high degrees of common sense, for the Enlightenment philosopher who proposed the theory of "common sense"[1] was a Scot named Thomas Reid (Broadie, 2000). The most northerly part of the United Kingdom, Scotland is a small country that proudly retains its own national identity and is generally held to have a global impact that is disproportionate to its relatively small population (Herman, 2003). Currently, the population is just under 6 million, representing approximately one tenth of the population of the United Kingdom. Although constitutionally part of the United Kingdom, with its citizens residing within the confines of a unitary state and governed by the Westminster Parliament, Scotland often claims that it is a special case (Friel & Fagan, 1998). The Scottish education system has a very long history. The University of Glasgow, for example, which was founded in 1451, is the second oldest university in Scotland and the fourth oldest in the English-speaking world. There is historical evidence of widespread pre-reformation schools (i.e., before 1560), and the Protestant Reformation that swept across Europe from the early sixteenth century brought with it ideas of a national system of education (MacCulloch, 2003). Indeed, by the time that the Scottish Parliament was united with that of England in 1707, there were already many schools teaching a traditional curriculum of reading, writing, and arithmetic under the auspices of the Church of Scotland, with the intention of providing all citizens with access to the moral guidance of the Bible. Thus the "lad o pairts," "the poor but able scholar of iconic significance in Scottish history" was able to work and obtain an education in the Parish School alongside the sons of the "laird"[2] (Friel & Fagan, 1998, p. 18). From these early days of educational history in Scotland, there has been a democratic, collectivist approach to education for all citizens in the interests of the common good. Despite the union of the Crowns and Parliaments in forming the United Kingdom, Scotland retains a consciousness of what can be described as national values supported by the fact that jurisdiction over three major institutions remains in the control of the Scottish people. These institutions are (1) the established church, that is, the Presbyterian Church of Scotland; (2) the legal system, which has more in common with other European legal systems than with that of England; and (3) the education system, which has a fondly-held, excellent, and at times somewhat embroidered reputation that is seen as a "badge" of Scottish identity.

Despite the Act of Union in 1707, Scottish education retained responsibility for its own organization and management, but in practice, while maintaining a greater proportion of publicly funded education than in England, it followed most of the socially- and politically-driven policy imperatives that emerged in the U.K. as a whole. However, although policies were broadly similar, the Scottish interpretation often represented a softer approach to some of the more strident pronouncements of Westminster. Two brief examples are the Labour Party-driven adoption of comprehensive education in the 1960s and the Conservative Party drive for neoliberal policies in the 1980s. In the first example, Labour governments sought to minimize the rigid class divides in English education by moving to comprehensive education for all, which caused great consternation among providers of private education in independent schools. In England, the comprehensive system was eventually only partially introduced, with a variety of different kinds of schooling remaining. In Scotland, where there were many fewer independent schools to begin with, most state-run schools became comprehensive without too much trouble, for comprehensive education was replacing an older system that required reform.

The second example refers to the period of the 1980s when Mrs. Margaret Thatcher was Prime Minister at the beginning of a long period of Conservative politics in the United Kingdom. Efforts were made to reduce big government, to renationalize state-owned industry and utilities, and to instil the principles of free market capitalism into the country's psyche. Education was also changed in line with the neoliberal policies of the Conservative government (relating, for example, to parental consumer choice, school boards, or self-governing status), but these changes were less marked in Scotland, suggesting some greater degree of caution with regards to embracing "New Right" ideology (Humes, 1995). Essentially, the Scots are British citizens, but in educational matters they strive to do their own thing. In 1997, Tony Blair's New Labour government came to power, and soon afterwards, in 1999, a devolved Scottish Parliament was established, almost 300 years after the Act of Union had abolished its predecessor. There was now even greater scope for Scotland to pursue its own agendas in education.

A New Curriculum

Dealing with money, social arithmetic, and personal finance are among the historical guises of financial education in curricula in Scotland. In the last decade, new curriculum documents for developing education for financial capability have been produced for primary and secondary schools, and more recently resources and teacher support for financial education have resulted from new curricular initiatives. The new Scottish Parliament quickly instigated reviews of education, including a national debate in which everyone could participate, in order to identify ways to take forward education policy. One of the outcomes of the debate was a resolve to change the curriculum in Scotland in order to reduce the amount of state accountability and to give teachers more professional responsibility. The result was a new curriculum initiative, A Curriculum for Excellence (SEED LTS, SQA, HMIE, 2004).

A Curriculum for Excellence is, in fact, an attempt to introduce a values-based curriculum to Scottish school education. It is significant that this is being stressed as an underlying principle of the new curriculum. The values selected to underpin the new curriculum are listed as wisdom, justice, compassion, and integrity—the words that are inscribed on the ceremonial mace of the Scottish Parliament and chosen because they are said to represent defining vales of Scottish society.

> One of the prime purposes of education is to make our young people aware of the values on which Scottish society is based and so help them to establish their own stances on matters of social justice and personal and collective responsibility. Young people therefore need to learn about and develop these values. The curriculum is an important means through which this personal development should be encouraged. (SEED et al., 2004, p. 1)

The four phrases that sum up the intentions of A Curriculum for Excellence are that young people should become (a) successful learners, (b) confident individuals, (c) responsible citizens, and (d) effective contributors. These have been adopted and are referred to as the capacities[3] that the new curriculum seeks to instil and develop in the years of school-based education.

Aspects of the values involved could be made much more specific to assist (a) the groups writing the requirements of the curriculum so that they keep in mind their value-driven purposes and (b) teachers in making ethical and values-based decisions about the details/specifics of the curriculum. In practice, the capacities as they are outlined have very few explicit mentions of values-based requirements, although arguably they could all be located within values considerations (e.g., confident individuals with secure values and beliefs; and responsible citizens able to develop informed, ethical views of complex issues). Young people will be faced with, and have to learn to make, ethical decisions about how they will conduct themselves and how they will prepare for their futures as productive and respected members of society. A Curriculum for Excellence is at the forefront of curriculum development and is ahead of many other countries in searching for more ethical ways of designing curricula. It now seems apparent to professional educators and the designers of curricula in Scotland that performance measurement of teaching and learning is not a sound basis for curriculum design or development, especially when it is taken to be the only basis for measuring and judging students' attainments. Checking off lists and comparing targets is seen to be technicist-oriented and lacking in ethical perspectives on human development. The challenge for curriculum designers is to empower teachers as professional educators to interpret the four capacities that are central to the new curriculum and use them to devise relevant contexts for learning at a time when many in the teaching profession (especially the newer members) have become used to high levels of prescription and accountability. The need for continuing professional development to support all teachers is paramount and there is a coherent strategy for this development of teachers at every stage of their professional careers.

Developments in Financial Education

Within arrangements for the new curriculum in Scotland, there has been considerable development in thinking about how to instill financial capability in all young people. The new curriculum provides teachers and learners with scope to address all areas in a more cohesive and interconnected manner, and financial capability can be linked to a myriad of curricular aspects. The aim is to provide learners with opportunities to develop knowledge and skill in financial understanding, competence, responsibility and enterprise to link with the four core capacities. A range of exciting and contemporary resources has been developed by curriculum bodies in Scotland, some of this in partnership with the banking community, to provide teachers with relevant contexts for developing financial capability and literacy at all stages of school-based learning. Teachers are expected to select what is appropriate for their classes and use the resources to meet the needs of their own groups of students. There seem to be no explicit mentions of values in these resources other than use of the phrase "value for money" and an implicit level of support for the state of acquiring 'a sense of values' about the worth of goods or services. One of the resources is the excellent *On the Money* (http://www.ltscotland.org.uk/onthemoney/index.asp) which uses entertaining pieces of literature, contributed by well-known Scottish authors, to convey issues in financial education. There is a suggestion in this material that there may be value judgements to be made in connection with financial matters and that young people should be challenged to address such issues. Financial education as described here seems to be in line with other factors that contributed to the four capacities of the new curriculum by stating the intention of giving consideration to values-based issues. In practice, however, very little support is provided in the form of recommendations or suggestions for teachers and thus much of the practice depends upon teachers' own identification of opportunities to raise values based considerations with their students. Thus teachers are being left with a big responsibility in the current climate of financial and economic shock that is upsetting livelihoods, limiting access to finances, and affecting most people whatever their previous circumstances. There is an opportunity here for teachers to support young people in (a) acquiring necessary financial capability and (b) raising and exploring issues of responsibility and concern for the common good—both of which contribute to a wealthier but also morally healthier society. This is what the new curriculum advocates. However, central to the success of financial education is teachers' own financial capability; their awareness of the impact of social, cultural, and political influences in the world of finance; and their ability to select and make use of resources that allow opportunities for cross-curricular learning, particularly as all teachers have responsibility for delivering all of the curriculum and not just their specialist subjects. As always in the Scottish curricular context, teachers bear the responsibility for delivering more than performance-based or technicist-oriented pedagogy, and they must take on the related challenges of examining and updating their own understanding of value-related issues across the curriculum and of encouraging critical enquiry in their students' habits of study.

Examples of Values Contexts for Financial Education

The currency used in the United Kingdom is the pound sterling (£), which is the world's oldest currency still in use (Rendell, 2007). In 1971, the U.K. currency was changed from the historic £.s.d. (pounds, shillings, and pence) to the current decimal system of pounds and pence. One Pound Sterling contains 100 pence (£1 = 100p). Prior to the change there had been 20 shillings in one pound and 12 pennies in one shilling and thus 240 pennies in one pound. The related arithmetic was therefore complex and one of the many advantages anticipated in moving to a decimal currency system was the expected ease of monetary calculations consistent with other decimalized measures in the International System of metric units. A lot of planning and organization went into preparing everyone in the U.K. for the change of monetary system, and there were concerns about how the population, and older people in particular, would manage to make the transition from using old money to using decimal money. The old ways were deeply ingrained. There was no easy conversion method, and lots of algorithms and handy hints for working out equivalences were suggested to the general public in the widespread advertising campaign that was used in the run up to the transition. In fact, the event passed without incident. Like the Year 2K computer scare almost 30 years later, decimalization happened in the U.K. currency with unexpected ease and the predicted mass panic and chaos did not come to pass. People were able to use equivalence markers to guide them in getting accustomed to the new pence that replaced shillings and old pennies. The coins used for 10p were the same size and value as those of the old two-shilling piece (2/- in old notation), so these were unchanged apart from the inscriptions; and old 2/- coins were still in circulation for a time. This provided a useful point of comparison. Moving to the new coinage proved straightforward. What was not so easy to achieve in the early days of decimalization was the quick and ready sense of the value of the coinage. The population's sense of the values of the nation's currency and coinage was temporarily blurred. There was also a feeling that shopkeepers had used the excuse of the change of currency and the uncertainty about equivalences to raise prices. Because there was no direct correspondence in amounts of money (of course, everyone rounded up), there was a general sense of inflation in prices. The U.K. economy of the time was experiencing quite high inflation anyway, with just below an 8% yearly average for 1970 increasing to 9% for 1971 and falling back to below 8% for 1972. It would be difficult to gauge the inflationary impact of decimalization amidst other factors, but there certainly was a bump that may well have been the result of the decimalization effect. This episode in U.K. financial history provides an interesting snapshot of a situation where the relationship between the monetary value of coinage and currency and the value associated with the marketable worth of goods and services is brought into sharp focus. There is, of course, a third sense of value that surrounds such episodes that is rarely commented upon or even noticed and that is the ethical connotations of eroding people's trust in and dependence upon the forces of the market and on whether business is behaving honestly. A new challenge has arisen in our time that again tests the resolve and forbearance of the U.K. people, but this time it is set within a global context and so is affecting ordinary people all over the world. The global financial crisis that erupted in 2009 has exposed questionable values frameworks in our financial institutions that will take many years to rectify, yet it provides an opportunity and impetus for reflection and debate in our schools on aspects of financial morality and responsibility.

There has been a change of national government in the U.K. since the start of the financial crisis and an indecisive election result in May 2010 has prompted the formation of a coalition government in Westminster. Among the many measures being introduced to attempt to deal with deficits and get the economy moving again are large cuts in public spending and an increase in the rate of Value Added Tax (VAT). VAT is a tax on purchases made in the European Union (Directgov, 2010) for which each member state sets its own rate. In the United Kingdom, the rate has been 17.5% but is now increased to 20% in order to increase treasury revenue. Every organization that sells goods or services in the U.K. that is eligible to be taxed through VAT has had to re-price in order to comply with the new rate. There have been reports of price rises that are larger than can be accounted for by a 2.5% tax increase, prompting concerns that some sellers are attempting to increase profits by stealth and by hiding behind the statutory change. Sections of the population old enough to remember the currency changes of decimalization in 1971 are recognizing some similar trends and contributing comments on whether this represents unethical behavior in the market. Unscrupulous behavior can unfold unchallenged and sometimes unnoticed if members of the public are not sufficiently aware of, or capable of being critical of, unethical practices. Sensitivity to values and a sense of values are necessary in order to identify and hopefully challenge unprincipled financial operating. As in many values-laden matters, the responsibility for alerting and preparing young people in Scotland falls to educators. Even those parents well-equipped to impart sound values and moral sensitivity to their children expect school education to contribute to students' character formation and their development as principled citizens.

All teachers are expected to pay close attention to the development of students' values and moral behavior associated with issues that young people are likely to encounter both in their working and social lives and in preparing for their futures as economically responsible citizens. As financial matters can potentially be areas of moral conflict, students need to be values literate. They need to be able to (a) question (for example, the honesty or safety of operation of their environment) and (b) recognize and challenge such matters from a secure understanding of their own identities and beliefs. It is important that students recognize the pressures under which organizations and individuals operate in our complex economic world in order to compete, survive, and be aware of ethical dimensions in their dealings with their employees, their customers, and their competitors. Stephen Bigger (2000) suggests that the building blocks for dealing with business ethics can be established in the characters of young people during school education and that this can support them in their lives and future careers by enabling them to exert positive influence on policy and strategy in their places of work and other life contexts.

In many ways Scottish education is looking forward and attempting to enhance the professional autonomy and scope for creative and critical thinking in all teachers. There is currently, however, a need in Scotland for teachers, teacher educators and curriculum designers to consider this period of financial turmoil as an opportunity for meeting the challenges that face all of society, both locally and globally, with renewed openness and integrity. Locating financial capability within the wider learning contexts of the new curriculum in Scotland links it to the development of learners as responsible, moral citizens who are capable of contributing confidently and effectively to society and the common good.

DISCUSSION QUESTIONS

1. The author explains that Scotland provides its teachers with instructional resources, but does not impose pedagogical methods or styles. What are the possible benefits of this amount of professional autonomy for teachers? What are the disadvantages?
2. The author uses some examples from the historical and philosophical development of education in Scotland to explain aspects of the current system. What are the principles upon which the system is founded? How does your own background shape your views on such principles?
3. "*Value*" is a term that appears throughout the chapter and the Scottish curriculum claims to be values-based. Why is it important to consider the value systems that underpin curricula?
4. The author mentions the phrase "a sense of values" when referring to familiarity with the worth of the money and assets needed in financial transactions. There is also mention of values in human relationships. Are these the same values? Is there a disconnection between financial dealings and human values following the financial crises of recent times?
5. The four curricular capacities of the new Scottish curriculum are the development of: successful learners; confident individuals; responsible citizens; and effective contributors. To what extent are these complete or reasonable aims for education? How can financial education contribute to the development of these aims?
6. The Scottish system makes minimal use of performance-based tests, checklists, and other technical assessment tools. Instead there is an emphasis on formative assessment that supports and informs learning with some summative assessment used against agreed criteria for recording purposes. How might this approach to assessment support learners and encourage deep learning? How does a values-based approach to financial education fit with formative assessment methods?

MODEL LESSON

Economies and the Common Good[4]

Suggested Grade Level: 9th Grade

Objective(s):

(a) The student will define "economy."
(b) The student will define the "common good."
(c) The student will define different kinds of economies.
(d) The student will compare and contrast how different economies address the "common good."
(e) The student will describe the underlying values of each type of economy.
(f) The student will take a value position and support it through logic and evidence.
(g) The student will listen to other positions and be able to critically interpret them.
(h) The student will demonstrate a critical understanding and tolerance of values within different types of economies in a short essay.

Related Standards:

Illinois State Standards

STATE GOAL 15: Understand economic systems, with an emphasis on the United States.

Standard: 15.A.4a: Explain how national economies vary in the extent that government and private markets help allocate goods, services, and resources.

Materials:

- Paper
- Post-it notes
- Markers

Procedures:

(a) Opening Activities

1. Give each student four post-it notes, two of one color and two of another (e.g., two red and two blue) and a marker.
2. Invite students to write down an idea that comes to mind when they hear the term "economy" on each of the post-it notes of one color.
3. When the students finish writing down their ideas, have them display these ideas on the chalkboard/whiteboard. Sample terms include: profit, resource, trade, good, service, oil, unemployment, government control)
4. Once everyone has posted their ideas, facilitate students' categorization of ideas. Ask students to group ideas that seem to go together and to come up with a verbal label for each group.
5. Then shuffle the post-it notes and invite students to organize the ideas using different categories than used previously.
6. Repeat these steps with the post-it notes of the second color, but this time ask the students to develop ideas about the term "common good."
7. Once the students have done this, the teacher provides formal definitions of "economy," the different types of economies, and "common" good" and leads discussion that compares these definitions with how students construed an economy and interpreted the "common good."

(b) Developmental Activities

1. Organize the class into four groups, each representing a different type of economy:

    - Traditional: Consists largely of subsistence agriculture. These are often referred to as "underdeveloped." In these economies, every person has a purpose or role. Produced goods tend to be functional or purposeful.
    - Mixed: Includes both public and privately run businesses. It is essentially a cross between a market and controlled economy. There are many forms of mixed economies, as determined by the emphasis on state involvement.
    - Market: The prices of goods depend on the available supply of goods and demand from users. There is very little governmental control of prices. The economy consists of private businesses that experience little governmental regulation. Businesses are largely private enterprises.

- Control/planned: The government is highly involved in its regulation of the economy. It manages and controls industry and makes all decisions that concern resource distribution. Businesses may be state-owned, private businesses controlled by the state, or both.

2. Provide each group with an opportunity to research and discuss the traits, strengths and weaknesses of its type. As part of their research, they should consider the following topics;

    - What is the underlying ideal that guides this type of economy? Is the goal to survive? To produce goods?
    - How does this type of economy view the common citizen? As an essential community member? As a production tool?
    - What current, familiar examples exist of this economy type?
    - What standards of living occur within this economy?
    - What is the longevity of this economy? How long have historical examples of this economy tended to last? Do they tend to proceed or follow any other economy types?
    - How does this economy approach the common good? What are the arguments for and against this strategy?

3. To demonstrate the outcomes of its research, each group will develop and perform a skit. The skit should use one of the following prompts, should include each group member, and should address each of the six points listed above.

    - Recreate what life may have been like in one of the studied examples.
    - Pretend that you are national leaders who are developing government economic policy.
    - Develop a "television documentary" about your economy. Include interviews with national leaders and the common man.

4. Provide note-taking sheets that guide observers through the aforementioned six research requirements to document characteristics of each presented economy,
5. Facilitate a whole-class conversation about the economies depicted in the four skits, asking the following questions.

    - Which "economy" do you believe offers the most freedom for its citizens?

- What are citizens in this economy free to do? What constraints are citizens free from in this economy?
- Are there elements that need to be controlled in this economy, but are not?
- In which "economy" do you believe citizens experience the least freedom?
- Which "economy" best provides an opportunity for everyone in the society to succeed? What are the elements of that economy that promote the success of all?
- How well do you think each economy focuses on the "common good?" What conditions promote that focus?
- What are your impressions of the four economy types after viewing skits depicting each type? To what extent did the skits confirm or contradict your ideas about the four economy types?

(c) Closing Activities

1. Using the four skit groups described above, instruct the members of each group to discuss among themselves (a) the values reflected in their assigned economy and (b) the positives and negatives of their assigned economy. The members of each group should select one spokesperson for a panel discussion, held in front of the entire class of students. The spokespersons serve as advocates for their respective economies, responding to questions as they adhere to the following rules:

    - Hand-raising is not permitted.
    - All opinions are valued
    - Speakers may not be interrupted.
    - Speakers should wait at least one second after the previous speaker has finished before expressing his or her thought.
    - Observers may not talk or give support to their spokespersons.
    - Observers may replace their spokesperson by tapping on shoulder and switching places. The former spokesperson should be quiet after switch.
    - A spokesperson who cannot follow the rules for conversation should switch with another community member.

2. The following questions may be used by the teacher, as moderator of the panel discussion, to prompt conversation during the panel discussion.

- What values are associated with each type of economy?
- Which economy provides the best system for deciding what to produce, how to produce, and for whom to produce? Which economy best promotes the "common good?"

(d) Summary and Assessment

1. After the lesson, the students write a 1-2 page essay that describes their feelings about the four economies and the values that are inherent within them. Each student should also make a judgment about what economy s/he would like to be a part of. This essay should include (a) the general/global definitions of "economy" and "common good" that were discussed in class and (b) consideration of how different economies have different values and address (or do not address) the "common good." Students should include their guided notes with the submitted essay.
2. The teacher will grade this essay based on accuracy of information and on students' understanding and tolerance of the different viewpoints and values reflected within different economic systems.

NOTES

1. Background to Thomas Reid's theory of common sense can be found at http://plato.stanford.edu/entries/reid/
2. *lad o pairts* (pronounced lad-a-payrts) is an old Scottish phrase for a youth, particularly one from a humble background, who is considered talented or promising. *Laird* is old Scottish for landowner.
3. Explanations of the significance of the four capacities of A Curriculum for Excellence may be found at http://www.ltscotland.org.uk/understandingthecurriculum/whatiscurriculumforexcellence/index.asp
4. Lesson developed by Cathy Fagan, Kelsy Kaatz, and Thomas A. Lucey

REFERENCES

Bigger, S. (2000). Vocational Education and SMSC. In R. Best (Ed.), *Education for spiritual, moral, social and cultural development* (pp. 130-142). London: Continuum.

Broadie, A. (2000). *Why Scottish philosophy matters.* Edinburgh, England: The Saltire Society.

Directgov. (2010). VAT basics for Consumers, HM Revenue and Customs, http://www.direct.gov.uk/en/MoneyTaxAndBenefits/Taxes/BeginnersGuideToTax/VAT/DG_190918

Friel, V., & Fagan, C. (1998). Citizenship: A challenge to teacher education, *Children's Social and Economic Education, 3*(1), 19-27.

Herman, A. (2003). *The Scottish enlightenment: The Scots' invention of the modern world*, London: Fourth Estate.

Humes, W. M. (1995, Spring). The significance of Michael Forsyth in Scottish education, *Scottish Affairs, 11*, 112-130.

MacCulloch, D. (2003). *The Reformation: A history.* New York, NY: Penguin.

Rendell, A. (2007). Economic terms explained. *The BBC News Channel.* Retrieved from http://news.bbc.co.uk/1/hi/programmes/bbc_parliament/7090665.stm

SEED, LTS, SQA, HMIE. (2004). *A curriculum for excellence: The curriculum review group*. The Scottish Executive Education Department, Learning and Teaching Scotland, Scottish Qualifications Authority, Her Majesty's Inspectorate of Education. Retrieved from http://www.scotland.gov.uk/Publications/2004/11/20178/45862

CHAPTER 10

THE EFFICACY OF FINANCIAL EDUCATION IN THE EARLY GRADES

Results From a Statewide Program

Weiwei Chen and Julia A. Heath

Financial literacy represents a new rock star in the field of educational reform. The financial community has touted it as a panacea for the country's low savings rates, credit delinquencies—indeed, the entire financial crisis. Even before the crisis, financial institutions funneled a lot of resources into providing financial education to both youth and adults. The financial services industry and nonprofits have increased their curriculum offerings; school administrators and school boards implemented standards and mandatory courses with financial literacy components; churches and community nonprofits increased the provision of financial education in their outreach.

Research on financial literacy does not offer the clear-cut solutions that these efforts would imply. In the effort to draw straight lines from program to outcome (especially long-term outcome), the pencil can often leave the paper. Research has focused on financial education of adults and youths; on the level of knowledge and the degree to which knowledge

Reframing Financial Literacy: Exploring the Value of Social Currency, pp. 189–207

increased after financial education (i.e., value-added effects); the effects (on both knowledge-level and value-added) of particular financial literacy curricula, and the effects of teacher training. Many issues are confounded, and many results are contradictory. To a large extent, these empirical contradictions are due to inadequate study design and attempts to compare results across different groups and/or disparate treatments.

This chapter addresses some of the sources of confounding results in the research on financial literacy. It also focuses on some of the environmental factors that affect the efficacy of financial education with elementary and middle school students. While most other studies have excluded school- and community-level data from their analyses, the current study examines those environmental factors that improve student outcomes associated with a financial education program in the state of Tennessee.

PREVIOUS RESEARCH

Research conducted in the area of the financial literacy of youths generally falls into three main categories: determinants of financial knowledge; the effects of financial instruction on the level of financial knowledge; and the effects of financial instruction on the *change* in the level of financial knowledge.

Determinants of financial knowledge. While most research evaluated the impact of financial education, two oft-cited studies simply analyzed the factors that determined the level of financial understanding among student groups. Valentine and Khayum (2005) analyzed the effect of selected demographic and economic socialization factors on the results of a financial literacy quiz administered to high school students in Indiana. Overall knowledge of financial literacy was not affected by urban/rural residence; however, working at a part-time job, having a savings account, and being in a middle income family all were positively associated with financial knowledge. At the college level, Chen and Volpe (2002) found that female students knew significantly less about financial literacy than their male counterparts, even after controlling for major, work experience, and class rank.

Both of these studies focused on identifying those factors that explained a given level of financial knowledge (albeit of two different populations), establishing explanations for "baseline" knowledge. Students in these analyses were not exposed to any formal financial education instruction.

Effects of financial instruction on the level of financial knowledge. Most research in this area has attempted to address the impact of financial instruction on student outcomes. Mandell (2008) reported that high school students who took a semester course in personal finance did not score better on the Jump$tart survey than those who did not take such a course. Peng, Bartholomae, Fox, and Cravener (2007) found no significant effect of financial education on investment knowledge among high school students (but did find a significant effect among college students). By contrast, Walstad, Rebeck, and MacDonald (2010) demonstrated a significant, positive effect for financial literacy instruction on student knowledge, compared to a control group. While not an explicit analysis of a specific curriculum, Swinton, DeBerry, Scafidi, and Woodard (2007) discovered a significant, positive relationship between teacher training and student outcomes on an end-of-course test in economics in Georgia.

Effects of financial instruction on the change in the level of financial knowledge. The majority of research on financial literacy has examined the effect of financial education on value added—the change in students' knowledge as a result of the instruction. Varcoe, Martin, Devitto, and Go (2005) found positive effects from instruction in all areas of financial literacy among teenagers. Harter and Harter (2009) found significant improvements in test scores of financial knowledge as a result of students being taught *Financial Fitness for Life* (*FFFL*) in eastern Kentucky. Likewise, the Walstad et al. (2010) study found significant value-added as a result of a particular financial literacy curriculum. Others have studied both immediate and longer-term effects. For example, Danes, Huddleston-Casas, and Boyce (1999) found that financial education significantly improved both the immediate and 3-month, postinstructional knowledge and savings rates among teens.

Many of these past studies are difficult to interpret, however, because they rely on data that were not generated in a consistent manner. In some, a consistent curriculum is not used. In others, teacher training is not controlled for; in still others, the testing instruments were not shown to be reliable and/or valid. In addition, with few exceptions (e.g., Harter & Harter, 2009; Sherraden, Johnson, Guo, & Elliott, 2010), the focus of the efficacy of financial education has been on high school or college students. If financial education is similar to every other content area in education, it relies on foundational knowledge acquired in the early grades to be truly effective. Given this rather obvious parallel, the dearth of research on financial education in the early grades is puzzling. As McCormick (2009) notes, financial education in the elementary grades has not received sufficient attention and represents a significant gap in our understanding.

Accordingly, the current study adds to the literature in several ways. The focus of this analysis is on upper elementary and middle school students, populations that have not received much attention in previous analyses. The analysis includes "environmental" factors that have been previously ignored in considering the effectiveness of financial education. These factors include teacher, school, and neighborhood characteristics that may significantly affect the efficacy of financial education instruction. Following the exhortations of Walstad et al. (2010), the current study (1) provided consistent curriculum content to all students (within appropriate grade bands—described below); (2) provided consistent teacher training on the curriculum content; (3) used validated and reliable assessment instruments; (4) collected data both pre- and posttest; and (5) employed appropriate statistical methodology.

PROGRAM BACKGROUND

The data for this analysis come from a statewide financial literacy program, Smart Tennessee, instituted in 2006. The Smart Tennessee program trains teachers in grades K-8 on financial literacy using the *FFFL* curriculum developed by the Council for Economic Education. The original funding for the program was a public/private partnership between the state of Tennessee and the largest statewide bank, First Tennessee. The state funding was a result of an amendment to the appropriations bill. First Tennessee committed to funding three years of the program. The second year of the program (2007-08), the state again funded the program through an amendment to the appropriations bill, and the funding from First Tennessee continued through its multiyear commitment. In the third year of the program (2008-09), the state budget precluded any appropriation. However, the state's Department of Financial Institutions provided funding to maintain the program. In the fourth year (2009-10), First Tennessee provided another year of funding, and the state provided money from the TARP funds that came to the state.

It was in the fourth year of the program that the state treasurer's office became involved, both in terms of helping to direct the stimulus money to the program and in terms of laying the foundation for a more permanent source of funding. In the 2009-10 session, the treasurer's office was instrumental in getting legislation passed, the Financial Literacy Program Act of 2010, establishing a financial literacy commission. The purpose of the commission is to raise funds, develop, manage and implement programs relating to financial literacy of elementary school students and their parents. The scope of the commission also includes promoting college savings as part of the financial literacy effort. The Treasurer's office oversees the state's 529 plan (a college savings plan), and while a positive outcome of this commission would be an increase in participation in that plan, the commission's objectives are much broader—to increase college savings and attendance overall. The commission's membership draws from the financial institutions community and includes a teacher and parent representative as well.

In the first year of the program (2006-07), funding was not actually received until mid-way through the academic year. As a result, only a limited number of schools were recruited, most from the Memphis City School district (although a few schools from Nashville also participated). In subsequent years, schools from all across the state were recruited, varying from 50 to75 schools per year.

The teachers who participate do not self-select into the program. Participation in the Smart Tennessee program is a decision that is made by either the school or the district, and the appropriate teachers are instructed to attend the training sessions. The *FFFL* curriculum is divided into four grade bands: K-2, 3-5, 6-8, and 9-12. The original plan for Smart Tennessee was to train teachers in all four grade bands. However, during this same time frame, Tennessee adopted a requirement that all students take a one-semester course in personal finance in high school in order to graduate. Therefore, Smart Tennessee focused on training K-8 teachers, who would be providing elementary and middle school students the foundation to prepare them for that high school course. All teachers received curriculum instruction in the same way: workshops were of the same duration, covered the same material, and were taught by the same facilitator.

The assessment instruments used in this study were developed by Walstad and Rebeck (2005a, 2005b) and consisted of 40 (elementary school) or 50 (middle school) multiple-choice questions arranged in the themes covered in the *FFFL* curriculum. The elementary curriculum has four themes—education/earning an income; savings; being a smart consumer and borrowing; and managing money. The middle school curriculum has these same themes with the addition of the economic way of thinking. The instruments have a high degree of reliability and validity (Walstad et al., 2010). The majority of teacher training occurred in the fall semesters. The facilitator traveled to various parts of the state to conduct the training. Teachers were trained in separate workshops according to grade level. All teacher training was conducted by the same person using the same curriculum (the appropriate grade level of *FFFL*), and all training sessions were of approximately the same length. After the training, teachers administered the assessment instrument to their classes to establish a baseline level of student knowledge before they taught the curriculum. After they taught the curriculum, teachers administered the same assessment as a posttest. Teachers were not informed of their students' pretest scores before they taught the curriculum. Both the pretest and posttest instruments were mailed by the teachers to an independent educational research unit at the University of Memphis, which compiled the information into the data set used for this chapter.

MULTIYEAR ASSESSMENT RESULTS

Program effectiveness was measured in very broad terms by two factors. First, the researchers ascertained the difference in pre- and postscores for both upper elementary and middle school students. The second measure was the pre- and postdifferences in the percentage of students who achieved a minimal level of financial education proficiency, which was defined as correctly responding to 70% of the assessment items. These results for 3 years of the program are presented in Table 10.1.

As stated in Table 10.2, the first year of the program (2006-07) involved recruitment of only a limited number of schools, given the timing of program funding. Therefore, the results from this year were not as robust as in subsequent years. The results for elementary students (excluding 2006-07) indicated an improvement pre to post of over 40%. For middle school students, the improvement was slightly smaller—between 35% and 40%. The most dramatic difference comes in the change in proficiency. For elementary students (in 2007-08 and 2008-09), the proportion of students who achieved proficiency pre to post increased by approximately 40 percentage points. Again, for middle school students, the gain was slightly lower. All of these differences were statistically significant.

DETERMINANTS OF FINANCIAL EDUCATION EFFICACY

While the aggregate assessment results suggest that the Smart Tennessee program is successful in increasing students' financial knowledge, further analysis is necessary to determine the environmental factors that influence program efficacy. To that end, additional data were collected in 2008-09, the year used in the remainder of this study.

Table 10.1. Smart Tennessee Pre- and Postassessment Results

	2006-07			*2007-08*			*2008-09*		
	Pre	*Post*	*% Chg.*	*Pre*	*Post*	*Chg.*	*Pre*	*Post*	*% Chg.*
					Elementary				
# correct/40	15.65	23.62	50.90	16.86	24.89	47.60	18.01	25.50	41.60
% at 70% proficiency	2.03	34.77	32.74	11.64	52.93	41.29	7.60	46.44	38.84
					Middle				
# correct/50	18.27	20.91	14.40	19.31	27.09	40.30	21.81	29.48	35.20
% at 70% proficiency	0.40	2.13	1.73	5.30	44.50	39.20	4.91	37.34	32.43

DATA AND METHODOLOGY

The only student-level data available to the researchers were the students' pre- and posttest scores and the students' middle school or upper elementary school status. Accordingly, the focus of this analysis was on those "environmental" factors that influence student gain in financial knowledge. The dependent variable was the efficacy of financial education, as measured by the difference in post- and prescores as a percentage of the potential or full marks score. That is, efficacy was equal to $\frac{post-pre}{perfect\ score}$. For upper elementary students, a perfect score was a 40, and for middle school students, it was a 50. Measuring the efficacy of financial education in this way precluded the bias inherent in variability in the prescores. Using a percentage gain measure $\left(\frac{post-pre}{pre}\right)$ or a percentage gain relative to potential gain measure $\left(\frac{post-pre}{full\ marks-pre}\right)$ would bias the efficacy measure in favor of low and high pre-scores respectively.

Therefore, the linear model is

$$Efficacy = f(S_i, T_i, C_i, N_i),$$

where S_i, T_i, C_i, and N_i denote vectors of student, teacher, school, and neighborhood characteristics respectively.

Student-level variable. As stated above, other than the assessment score, the only student-level data available indicated whether the student was a middle school student (Midsch) or not. This variable took on a value of 1 if the student was in grades 6, 7 or 8, not if a student attended a middle school. The reason for this distinction was that some schools in the sample had combinations of elementary and middle school grades, making the coding of this variable by school (rather than by student) meaningless.

Teacher-level variables. Along with the postassessment instruments, teachers also submitted a survey instrument. From that instrument, six variables reflected various teacher characteristics. A dummy (MA) indicated whether the teacher had a degree more advanced than a bachelor's. How many years of teaching experience the teacher had (Yrsteach), as well as the square of that variable (Yrsteach2), were also measured. The inclusion of the squared term accounts for any possible nonlinearities in teaching experience. A class size variable (Classize) was also included. Because teacher enthusiasm might be variable given that teachers did not self-select into the program, program efficacy could be affected by teacher "buy-in." Therefore, the analysis included two dummy variables to proxy teacher commitment to the program and the curriculum. One variable (Enjoy) indicated teachers' agreement (or strong agreement) with the statement, "My students enjoyed the curriculum." The other variable (Benefit) indicated teachers' agreement (or strong agreement) with the statement, "My students will benefit from this curriculum."

School-level variables. Several variables were included to reflect the learning environment and to ascertain those school factors that may influence the efficacy of financial education. Two variables reflected the size of the school: the number of grades served in the school (Grade) and the number of students in the school (Student). A large, yet homogeneous (in terms of limited number of grades) school may present a different learning environment than a smaller, more heterogeneous one. Variables that represented the percentage of the students in the school who were economically disadvantaged (Econdisadv)—on free or reduced lunch—and who were White—were also included. Finally, variables that measured the schools' average TCAP scores (the state's achievement test) for math, science, reading/language arts, and social studies (Math, Science, Readlang, and Socialsci, respectively) were included. These measures could indicate whether overall school achievement affected financial education efficacy, and/or indicate if the efficacy of financial education varied by specific content focus of the school.

Neighborhood-level variables. A school in an urban area (Urban) was denoted by a dummy variable. Variables for the percentage of the surrounding neighborhood that was native English-speaking and the percentage of the surrounding neighborhood that had at least a high school degree were included. Both were included in an attempt to capture any external factors that might represent a limit on the efficacy of financial education initiatives within the school environment.

The original sample size was 1,116. After eliminating observations with missing values for pre and post assessments and incomplete student ID numbers, the data set had 917 observations.

RESULTS

Means and descriptions of variables are included in Table 10.2. The average score on the pretest was 44.2%, and for the posttest, 61.2% correct, making the average improvement 17 percentage points. The slight difference in the percentages in Table 10.2 compared to those in Table 10.1 for the same year is due to some deleted observations that resulted from a lack of teacher data. If a teacher did not return a survey, his/her students could be included in the broad assessment analysis presented in Table

10.1, but had to be excluded from the regression analysis shown in Table 10.2.

Again, control data were not available for the year used in this analysis, 2008-09. However, in the first year of the program, 2006-07, a control group was used to determine the efficacy of the program. The control and treatment groups consisted of matched pairs of schools. Schools were matched using: number of students; percentage of economically disadvantaged students; percentage of White, African American, and Hispanic students; averaged percentage of students at proficient and advanced level in reading and math for all students; and average percentage of students at proficient and advanced level in reading and math by targeted grade level. Fourth and seventh grade students from these matched schools were used. The control group was administered the test once--at the same time that the treatment groups took the posttest. Therefore, the pre and post scores are the same for this group. The results of the control/treatment comparison are shown in Table 10.3.

For elementary school, the control pre-test mean was significantly higher than that of the treatment group, while there was no significant difference in pretest scores between the two groups of middle school students. Looking at posttest scores, the treatment groups for both elementary and middle school had significantly higher scores than did the control groups, a finding that suggests significant program effectiveness, particularly at the elementary level since the control group had higher scores on the pretest. While resource constraints did not permit continued collection of control group data, the current analysis is somewhat strengthened by previous findings of program effectiveness. However, without current control data, the observed differences could be partially attributed to factors other than financial education. With that note of caution, the ordinary least squares results (using robust standard errors) are presented in Table 10.4.

Student-level effects. The variable for differentiating between middle and upper elementary school students was not significant, suggesting that the gains in financial knowledge were not dependent upon whether the student was in middle or elementary school.

Teacher-level effects. Both the number of years of teaching experience and its square were significant in explaining the difference in financial knowledge, suggesting that seasoned, midcareer teachers were the most effective at imparting financial education. In addition, the teachers' level of education was significant. Students whose teachers had at least a master's degree had greater gains in financial knowledge than those whose teachers had a bachelor's degree. The larger the class size, the smaller was the effect of financial education. The two variables included to measure teacher commitment to teaching the curriculum indicated mixed results. While the variable that indicated students enjoyed the curriculum (from

Table 10.2. Means and Descriptions of Variables (Standard Deviations in Parentheses)

Variable	*Mean (Std. Dev.)*	*Description*
Preperc	0.442 (0.15)	Percentage correct on pretest
Postperc	0.612 (0.21)	Percentage correct on posttest
Difperc	0.17 (0.185)	The difference between the percentage of correct answers on post- and pretest
MA	0.556 (0.50)	Dummy variable = 1 if teacher had a degree higher than a bachelor's; = 0 otherwise
Yrsteach	15.07 (9.36)	Years of teaching experience
Yrsteach2	314.70 (332.77)	Square of years of teaching experience
Enjoy	0.60 (0.49)	Dummy variable = 1 if teacher agreed or strongly agreed with statement, "My students enjoyed the curriculum"; = 0 otherwise
Benefit	0.78 (0.42)	Dummy variable = 1 if teacher agreed or strongly agreed with statement, "My student will benefit from the curriculum"; = 0 otherwise
Classize	19.91 (5.62)	Size of class student is in
Midsch	0.51 (0.50)	Dummy variable = 1 if student is in grades 6, 7, or 8; = 0 otherwise
White	75.40 (31.43)	Proportion of students in school who are White
Ecodisadv	58.22 (22.97)	Proportion of students in school who are on free or reduced lunch
Studnts	525.35 (254.97)	Number of students in school
Gradserv	7.43 (3.17)	Number of different grade levels in school
Math	51.27 (7.32)	School's average math TCAP score
Readlang	51.52 (7.10)	School's average reading/language arts TCAP score
Socialsci	50.90 (7.55)	School's average social science TCAP score
Science	50.95 (7.91)	School's average science TCAP score
Urban	0.55 (0.50)	Dummy variable = 1 if school is in an urban area; = 0 otherwise
Perchs	74.04 (12.06)	Proportion of those in school Census tract with at least a high school degree
English	96.28 (3.39)	Proportion of those in school Census tract whose primary language is English

Table 10.3. Comparison of Number of Correct Answers on Pretest and Posttest for Treatment and Control Groups

	Pretest Means (SD)			*Posttest Means (SD)*		
	Control	*Treatment*		*Control*	*Treatment*	*t*
Elementary	16.28 (5.98) $N = 678$	14.70 (5.14) $N = 725$	5.20*	16.28 (5.98) $N = 678$	22.43 (8.24) $N = 566$	–14.77*
Middle	15.88 (4.66) $N = 17$	18.12 (5.70) $N = 141$	1.55	15.88 (4.66) $N = 17$	21.09 (5.96) $N = 138$	–3.47*

Table 10.4. OLS Results—Dep. Var. Difperc

Variable	*Coefficient*	*Std. Error*
Student-Level Variable		
Midsch	–0.018	0.013
Teacher-level Variables		
MA	0.029*	0.014
Yrsteach	0.012**	0.003
Yrsteach2	–0.0003**	0.000
Enjoy	+0.030	0.017
Benefit	+0.321**	0.032
Classize	–0.007**	0.001
School level variables		
White	+0.002**	0.001
Ecodisadv	+0.002*	0.001
Studnts	–0.00004	0.00004
Gradserv	–0.014**	0.003
Math	–0.015**	0.003
Readlang	+0.008	0.004
Socialsci	+0.031**	0.004
Science	–0.022**	0.005
Neighborhood/District-level Variables		
Urban	+0.104**	0.015
Perchs	+0.0012	0.001
English	+0.013**	0.002
Constant	–1.733 (0.241)	

$R^2 = 0.297$; $F(18,898) = 18.91$; Prob > $F = 0.000$

the teacher's perspective) was not significant, the variable that measured the extent to which teachers believed their students would benefit from the instruction was significant.

School-level effects. With the exception of the number of students in the school and the average TCAP scores for reading/language arts, all the school-level variables were significant in explaining the change in students' financial understanding. The greater the schools' proportions of white and economically disadvantaged students, the greater the gains from financial education. Since economically disadvantaged students could have more to potentially gain from financial education than students more comfortably situated, the suggestion that financial education is more efficacious the more disadvantaged the school is an important finding.

As the number of grades in schools increased, the size of the gains decreased. This finding suggests that more academically/developmentally homogeneous schools could provide a better environment for financial education. Finally, the school's academic focus, as evidenced by its average TCAP scores by subject area, indicated that student gains in financial education were greater in those schools that had higher scores in the social sciences, while higher math and science scores were negatively associated with student gains. This result may be due to (a) less importance being placed on the financial education curriculum in schools that are academically focused on math and science (apart from the effect of the teacher's perceptions of the benefits) or (b) the curriculum being integrated more fully in schools that are stronger in social science.

Neighborhood-level effects. Two of the three neighborhood variables were significant in explaining the gains in financial cognition. It appears that the greater the percentage of native English-speakers in the surrounding neighborhood, the greater the efficacy of financial education. Because non-English speakers may face hurdles in understanding the financial education basics and the financial services industry in the United States, in addition to general education challenges, this result suggests that particular care should be used by financial education providers to account for these potential differences. The percentage of high school graduates in the neighborhood had no effect on the efficacy of financial education, but gains in financial literacy appear to be greater for students in urban schools, relative to their nonurban counterparts.

CONCLUSIONS

The ascendance of financial education in various forms and modes of delivery carries with it a responsibility to attempt to provide it in the most effective way possible. For those who deliver these programs, foreknowledge of those factors that ameliorate the efficacy of financial education is critical. This analysis focused on those teacher, school, and neighborhood characteristics that influence the extent to which financial education is effective.

The results suggest that financial education efficacy can be enhanced (a) with training teachers who have higher levels of education and/or who are midcareer teachers and (b) by facilitating teachers' "buy in" of the importance of the subject. Further, financial education appears to be more effective in urban schools and in schools that have higher proportions of economically disadvantaged students—a segment that could potentially benefit the most from financial instruction. Schools whose academic focus is in social studies appear to be more effective at delivering financial education, as are schools with a smaller number of grade levels (with teacher characteristics held constant).

The data and analysis leave questions unanswered. An ideal situation would have more student-level demographic data, rather than relying on school- and neighborhood-level characteristics. It would have a control group for the year of analysis, rather than from a prior year. While the results of the control/treatment analysis are suggestive, a more tightly controlled experimental protocol would lend additional evidence on the efficacy of financial education. Finally, the time during which teachers could implement the curriculum once they were trained was variable. Teachers were required to complete the curriculum in their classrooms by the end of the school year, but since they were trained in the fall semester, varying amounts of time had passed between training and program implementation. To the extent that factors other than the financial education itself can explain the results, the variability in timing of implementation may somewhat counteract this study's findings.

In terms of future research, this analysis used the aggregate scores from assessment tests as the measure of overall financial knowledge, but the *FFFL* curriculum allows the assessment scores to be broken down into subgroups by topical coverage (credit, savings, etc.). Additional research is planned to investigate whether students' environmental influences have differential effects, by topic, on the efficacy of financial education.

While this study does not allow one to draw all the definitive lines in the financial education picture, it does provide partial illumination of the background, and it suggests some areas in which future research could be the most instructive. Perhaps, more importantly, it suggests factors that providers of financial education should take into account when designing delivery systems to increase the effectiveness of instruction. In particular, teacher characteristics—their education, their experience, and their commitment to providing financial education—are critical components in program efficacy.

DISCUSSION QUESTIONS

1. How might your experience with financial education in school relate to this study's findings?
2. How do various ways that teachers present information relate to your learning of content? What, if anything, does your response suggest about how teachers should teach personal finance?
3. The study interpreted results of a program implemented in one state. How might the results be fairly compared to findings from similar programs in other states?
4. By yourself, make a list of some reasons why the percentage of economically disadvantaged students in the school is positively associated with student gains in financial knowledge. Use your list and others to develop a class list of reasons. Now, reread the section about classism in Lucey's chapter about financial morality. What are the underlying assumptions of the reasons used to explain the findings of Chen and Heath?
5. Why might students gain less from financial education instruction in a school that earns higher mathematics scores?

MODEL LESSON

Credit Is Based on Trust

(Reprinted With Permission From Council for Economic Education)

Suggested Grade Levels: 3rd-5th Grades

Objectives: At the end of this lesson, the student will be able to:

(a) Define borrower, lender, credit, trust, and trustworthiness/creditworthiness.
(b) Generalize that borrowing and lending are based on trust between the lender and the borrower.
(c) Identify the personal qualities that build trust and creditworthiness.

Related Standards

Jump$tart National Standards in K–12 Personal Finance Education

Standard 9: Personal financial responsibility
Standard 14: Credit history and records
Standard 15: Rights and responsibilities of buyers, sellers, and creditors

Materials: Exercise 1—Jungle Puzzle

Background: Children borrow money and other things from each other every day. Though the "loans" are usually very small, they are a typical part of a young consumer's experiences. Children learn at an early age to trust some people and not others. They form these opinions about others through their experiences and their ability to predict behavior. This same process of generalization and prediction of behavior will assist them as they become adults and participate in credit markets as purchasers of automobiles, homes, and other consumer goods.

Procedures:

(a) Opening Activities:

1. Tell the students that they are ready to being learning a little about lending and borrowing. Refer them to Exercise 1—Jungle Puzzle. Go over the instructions with the students. Have them solve the word puzzles.
2. When the students are finished, allow them to share their answers (*1. Rely; 2. Thinks; 3. Sincere; 4. True; 5. Upright; 6. Trust).* Write the final word, "TRUST" on the board. Discuss the following questions and write the highlighted words on the board under the word "TRUST" as they are covered.

   - If you trust someone, do you expect the person to be **reliable**, meaning that the person does what he or she said? *(Yes).*
   - If you trust someone, do you expect the person to be **sincere**, meaning that the person is honest and tells the truth? *(Yes).*
   - If you trust someone, do you expect the person to be **true**, meaning that the person keeps his or her promise? *(Yes).*
   - If you trust someone, do you expect the person to think twice, meaning make **careful** decisions? *(Yes).*

3. Explain that the words under "TRUST" are characteristics that a "trustworthy" person would have.

(b) Developmental Activities:

1. Ask the students if they have ever lent a friend or family member something. *(Answers will vary)*. Explain that lenders allow people to use money or goods for some period of time. Lenders expect to be repaid.
2. Ask the students if they have ever borrowed money or something from a friend or family member. *(Answers will vary)*. Explain that borrowers use someone else's money or things for some period of time.
3. Read the following short story about a lender and a borrower to the class.

> "Rhonda, remember the $15 I lent you when we went to the amusement part?" Royce asked.
>
> "Yes, I remember, Royce. I'm really sorry I haven't paid you back yet. I've just had so many expenses. I needed new in-line skates because my old ones were too small. The ones I wanted were really expensive, and Mom told me I had to pay half the price for them. I needed the $15 I was going to pay you, or I wouldn't have had enough money for the skates. I have a babysitting job this weekend. I'll be able to pay you on Monday. I'm really sorry," Rhonda replied.
>
> "I know you're sorry, but that doesn't help me. I need that money. My baseball team is playing in a tournament, and each player has to pay a $30 entrance fee. You told me you would pay me last week, so I thought I would have enough money for the fee. Now I don't. What am I supposed to do?"

4. Debrief with the following questions.

- Why is Royce upset with Rhonda? *(He needs the money he lent her, and she didn't repay him as she promised.)*
- Is Rhonda being reliable? Why? *(No. She didn't do what she said she would do.)*
- Is Rhonda being sincere? Why? *(Maybe/Maybe not. She's telling Royce the truth, but she didn't keep her promise to repay.)*
- Is Rhonda being true? Why? *(No. She didn't keep her promise.)*
- Is Rhonda careful? Why? *(No. She didn't think twice about buying the inline skates even though she owed Royce money.)*
- Is Rhonda trustworthy? Why? (*No. She doesn't have the characteristics that make someone trustworthy.*)

5. Explain that when people lend to other people they are giving credit. Usually credit involves lending money, most often for a fee. The money and the fee must be repaid at a future time.
6. Point out that Royce gave Rhonda credit. He lent Rhonda money (in this case, without a fee), and he expected Rhonda to pay him back.
7. Explain that there is an important connection between trust and credit. If you trust someone, you are more willing to give him or her credit. If someone trusts you, he or she is more willing to give you credit.
8. Ask the students whether they would be willing to give Rhonda credit in the future if they were Royce. *(Probably not.)* Why? *(They couldn't trust her to repay.)*

(c) Closing Activities

1. Debrief students about the learning by asking the following questions.

   - What is a borrower? *(Someone who uses money or things that belong to another person with the intention of returning the things or repaying the money.)*
   - What may be an example of something you have borrowed and returned or repaid? *(Answers will vary.)*
   - What is a lender? *(Someone who lends another person money or things and expects to have the money repaid or the item returned.)*
   - What may be an example of a time that you've been a lender? *(Answers will vary.)*
   - What are some characteristics that a trustworthy person would have?. *(Reliable, careful, sincere, true, upright.)*
   - What is credit? *(Lending money to someone, usually for a fee, with the expectation that the money will be repaid in the future.)*
   - Why are lenders more likely to give credit to someone who is trustworthy? *(A reliable, careful, sincere, and upright person is more likely to repay a loan than a person who doesn't have those characteristics.)*

(d) Summary and Assessment

1. Read the following scenario:
   Your friend, Angela, wants to borrow $10. Last week she borrowed your favorite sweatshirt. When she returned it, there was a stain on the sleeve. The last time you lent her money, she didn't repay when she was supposed to.

2. Write a letter to Angela explaining why you aren't willing to lend her money this time. You must use the following terms correctly in your letter: creditworthy, reliable, sincere, and trust. Be sure that you explain what these terms mean so Angela understands. Remember to use correct letter format, grammar, and punctuation.

Exercise 1: Jumble Puzzle

Read each set of clues and think about a word that would fill in the blanks. Below the set of clues are scrambled letters of the word. Unscramble the letters and write them in the boxes. A few letters are given for you.

1. You can count on this person to do what he says he will do. You can ______on this person.

RYLE [R] [ ] [ ] [ ]

2. This person is very careful. This person __________ twice about choices.

HINKTS [T] [ ] [ ] [ ] [ ] [ ]

3. This person means what she says. This person is ______________.

SNICREE [S] [ ] [N] [ ] [ ] [R] [ ]

4. This person is a real friend. This person is a ____________________ friend.

RUET [ ] [ ] [ ] [ ]

5. This person would not lie or steal. This person is ________________.

PUTIRGH [U] [ ] [R] [ ] [G] [ ] [T]

6. This person will not tell your secret to another person. This is a person you can ________.

RTSTU [ ] [ ] [ ] [ ] [ ]

REFERENCES

Chen, H., & Volpe, R. P. (2002). Gender differences in personal financial literacy among college students. *Financial Services Review, 11*, 289-307.

Danes, S. M., Huddleston-Casas, C., & Boyce, L. (1999). Financial planning curriculum for teens: Impact evaluation. *Journal of Financial Counseling and Planning, 10*(1), 26-37.

Harter, C., & Harter, J. F. R. (2009). Assessing the effectiveness of *Financial Fitness for Life* in Eastern Kentucky. *Journal of Applied Economics and Policy, 28*(1), 20-33.

Mandell, L. (2008). Financial education in high schools. In A. Lusardi (Ed.), *Overcoming the saving slump: How to increase the effectiveness of financial education and saving programs* (pp. 257-279). Chicago, IL: University of Chicago Press.

McCormick, M. (2009). The effectiveness of youth financial education: A review of the literature. *Journal of Financial Counseling and Planning, 20*(1), 70-83.

Peng, T., Bartholomae, S., Fox, J., & Cravener, G. (2007). The impact of personal finance education delivered in high school and college courses. *Journal of Family and Economic Issues, 28*(2), 265-284.

Sherraden, M. S., Johnson, L., Guo, B., & Elliott, W. (August 19, 2010). Financial capability in children: Effects of participation in a school-based financial education and savings program. *Journal of Family and Economic Issues.* Retrieved from http://www.springerlink.com/content/h2k5h67685517q77/fulltext.html

Swinton, J., DeBerry, T., Scafidi, B., & Woodard, H. C. (2007). The impact of financial education workshops for teachers on students' economic achievement. *The Journal of Consumer Education, 24*, 63-77.

Valentine, G. P., & Khayum, M. (2005). Financial literacy skills of students in urban and rural high schools. *Delta Pi Epsilon Journal, 47*(1), 1-9.

Varcoe, K. P., Martin, A., Devitto, Z., & Go, C. (2005). Using a financial education curriculum for teens. *Journal of Financial Counseling and Planning, 16*(1), 63-71.

Walstad, W., & Rebeck, K. (2005a). *Financial fitness for life: Middle school test examiner's manual (grades 6-8).* New York, NY: Council for Economic Education.

Walstad, W., & Rebeck, K. (2005b). *Financial fitness for life: Elementary school test examiner's manual (grades 3-5).* New York, NY: Council for Economic Education.

Walstad, W., Rebeck, K., & MacDonald, R. (2010). The effects of financial education on the Financial knowledge of high school students. *The Journal of Consumer Affairs, 44*, 336-357.

CHAPTER 11

USING TECHNOLOGY TO DEVELOP A BROAD UNDERSTANDING OF FINANCIAL LITERACY AMONG K-12 STUDENTS

Jeffrey J. Sanson and Phillip J. VanFossen

In January 2011 the 10 billionth app was downloaded from the Apple iTunes App Store. An app (application) is a software program designed for mobile device (smartphones, iPods, and tablets) operating systems. This event was remarkable in both the number of programs that consumers had downloaded, but also the relatively short time in which it occurred.

Coupled with this sign of the times is the reality that the financial world and the methods by which people manage their financial lives have evolved as well, due to the changes in technology. It is not uncommon for individuals to rarely visit a bank or other financial institution given that many transactions can be handled in the comfort of home with an Internet connection. Some financial services are even available to smart phone users. These users can track deposits and expenses, transfer funds, and deposit checks with the click of camera phone and the uploading of the image to the financial institution. For economic and financial educators, it

Reframing Financial Literacy: Exploring the Value of Social Currency, pp. 209–233

seems only natural to consider how to integrate technology applications into existing instruction.

This chapter examines the rationale for and integration of digital instructional technology in economic and financial education at the elementary and secondary level. It will provide an overview of the use of technology in economic and financial education, and it will also summarize and analyze the limited research that has been conducted on the impact of technology on students' learning in personal finance. In conclusion, it recommends classroom activities that effectively integrate technology to enhance financial literacy instruction.

Economic Literacy and Financial Literacy

Financial education stakeholders have not reached a common understanding of what it means to be financially literate (McCormick, 2009; Remund, 2010). Even the term "financial literacy" is debated as a goal of financial education (Hung, Parker, & Yoong, 2009). More recently, the term "financial capability" has been highlighted as a key goal in personal finance instruction (E. Johnson & Sherraden, 2007, p. 122; Lusardi, 2011). For this chapter, the authors work from the definitions of economic and financial literacy as defined by organizations and institutions that have historically been advocates and supporters of financial education for youth in K-12 school settings.

For over 50 years, The Council for Economic Education (CEE) (formerly the Joint Council on Economic Education and the National Council on Economic Education) has promoted economic literacy among youth. In 1997, the CEE published the *Voluntary National Content Standards in Economics* (National Council on Economic Education, National Association of Economic Educators, & Foundation for Teaching Economics, 1997) which have "informed education practices" (Council for Economic Education, 2010, p. vii) of what an economically literate K-12 student should know and be able to do with the knowledge. The Council originally developed these standards in 1997 to address gaps and inaccuracies in economic content found in social studies content standards (VanFossen, 1999b).

In the mid-1990s, the Jump$tart Coalition for Personal Financial Literacy, a coalition of corporations, nonprofit organizations, government agencies, and educational institutions with an interest in financial literacy for youth (pre-K through college), formed to advocate for an increase and improvement in financial education. The Jump$tart standards provide financial educators with content standards of key concepts and skills that the financially literate student should have mastered by the time he or she graduated from high school (JumpStart Coalition for Personal Financial Literacy, 2007).

Curriculum and content standards from other national organizations such as the National Council for the Social Studies [NCSS], the National Business Educators Association [NBEA], and the National Association of Teacher Educators for Family and Consumer Sciences [NATEFACS] include content strands and competencies in their standards that support the integration of economics and personal finance in these subjects.

The U.S. Federal Government represents another major influence in financial education efforts. In response to growing concerns of financial distress spurred by the 2009 financial crisis, the U.S. Departments of Treasury and Education defined what constitutes a financial and economic literacy education program. This definition supplied to the agencies was given as a guide for "any ongoing effort to educate, inform, and help the population, or specific segments of the population, in financial and economic literacy matters. Programs should have clear, measurable objectives and goals" (Hung, Mihaly, & Yoong, 2010, pp. 7-8).

Instructional Technology

Similar to financial literacy, "instructional technology" has many definitions (Roblyer, 2006). For purposes of this chapter, we have chosen to focus on the use of digital technologies otherwise known as computer aided instruction (CAI). As with financial and economic education, there are also standards to support the integration of technology in instruction. In 1998, The International Society for Technology created the National Education Technology Standards (NETS) to guide the integration of technology in instruction (Roblyer, 2000). Today, these standards have been expanded to include frameworks for teachers (NETS-T) and administrators (NETS-A) as well as student (NETS-S) expectations. These standards are a nationally recognized set of guidelines for technology use and have been adapted by many disciplines and educational organizations (International Society for Technology in Education, 2007, 2008, 2009).

The rationale for increased financial literacy has been discussed at great length (see Bernanke, 2010; Bucks, Kennickell, Mach, & Moore, 2009; Duke, 2010; Greenspan, 2003; Mandell, 2008). With the need for financial literacy education clearly identified, efforts and focus on effective methods of instruction have increased. Some authors (Braunstein & Welch, 2002; Lusardi, Mitchell, & Curto, 2010; Mandell & Klein, 2009) have questioned the effectiveness of current methods of teaching personal finance. If existing financial education efforts are apparently lacking, then enhancements or supplements should be considered (Cole &

Shastry, 2009). Technology integration offers a potential solution to improve and enhance instructional outcomes.

Rationale for Technology Integration

Technologically enhanced instructional strategies have the potential to increase student motivation and engagement in learning. In the best cases, technology applied in pedagogically appropriate manner also has the potential to enhance student learning and improve outcomes (Hammond & Manfra, 2009; Harris, Mishra, & Koehler, 2009; Roblyer, 2006; Sosin, 1997). According to Lucey (2007), pedagogical content knowledge is critical for effective teaching of personal finance. Consequently, for technology integration in economic and personal finance instruction to be effective, the teacher also needs technological pedagogical content knowledge (TPACK) (Harris et al., 2009). Yet, while the literature includes some broad discussions of TPACK for social studies educators (Hammond & Manfra, 2009; Wilson & Wright, 2010), there are fewer (Lee, 2008; Swan, Hofer, Swan, & Mazur, 2010) that specifically mention or address TPCK in economics or personal finance.

Swan et al. (2010) describe a website, Econocast, that the authors developed to scaffold and support secondary teachers' integration of podcasts in economics instruction. The authors suggest that there are few meaningful applications of podcast technology in K-12 economic instruction. They identify two factors that contribute to this difficulty; first, teachers are not aware of instructional opportunities that podcasting provides. Second, they may lack the technological knowledge to create podcasts themselves or to facilitate podcast creation by their students. Swan et al. briefly describe three approaches using podcasts that are featured on the Econocast website. They offer the website as a means to "minimize technical barriers" to allow teachers to worry less about the challenges of podcast production and consider more deeply the content and pedagogy connections (p. 150).

Lee (2008) points out that a challenge to the application of TPCK theory to social studies is the variety of subjects structures that make up social studies. To help educators, he identifies ten pedagogical actions that provide a framework for integrating technology, one of which specifically "encourages economic literacy through the use of technology." (p. 131)

Lee (2008) suggests that integrating technology into economic instruction develops skills for students that are necessary to effectively use digital sources and resources to make wise decisions. This is important because in 2010, much of personal financial decision making is conducted in a technologically enhanced system of transactions, tracking, and security (Hira,

2009). Consumers are also increasingly responsible for managing all aspects of their budgets. This environment not only necessitates improved financial literacy and decision making, but expects the individual to be savvy enough to navigate and access accounts and be smart about the reliability of other sources of financial information.

While the potential of improving social education through technology appears favorable, it is not clear whether the practice and pragmatic aspects are bearing out the vision and whether the efforts are even worthwhile (Cuban, 2001; Hew & Hara, 2007; Hofer & Swan, 2006). Despite the availability of technology in the classroom and the National Council for the Social Studies (NCSS, 2006) position statement and guidelines for technology, teachers in the field of social studies do not appear to be (a) integrating technology to the same degree or rate as their colleagues in other disciplines (Zhao, 2007) or (b) integrating new strategies to standard methods of instruction (Lucey & Grant, 2010; VanFossen & Waterson, 2008).

LITERATURE

The literature on integrating technology in personal finance and economics has been described as falling into three types of categories. These groupings include literature that extol the potential of technology integration (cheerleading), provide personal accounts (on how to), and empirically explore the use of technology in a social studies, economics, business, or consumer family science context (Friedman & Hicks, 2006; Friedman & VanFossen, 2010).

Potential of Technology

Despite the sparseness of empirical evidence that technology is effective in discipline specific settings, social studies teachers continue efforts to enhance instruction with technology to help them achieve the primary goal or purpose of social studies instruction "to help young people develop the ability to make informed and reasoned decisions for the public good as citizens of a culturally diverse, democratic society in an interdependent world" (NCSS, 2006, p. 5). Efforts to achieve these goals frame much of the technology integration discussion found in the literature today. Intertwined in the technology discussion of many social studies scholars are the glimpses and visions of the potential or promise that technology will enhance, enrich, improve, and change education for the better (Berson, 1996; Hofer & Swan, 2006; Mason et al., 2000)

To find examples of this first category of literature that advocate the use of a technology, an educator need not look any further then the magazine, newsletter, or latest e-mail from their professional associations to locate articles extolling the virtues of the latest web-based learning tool or the next ubiquitous technology. Examples of these are in practitioner-focused publications, such as *Social Education* (NCSS) (Ferrarini & Calhoun, 2007; Swan et al., 2010) and *Inside the Vault* (Federal Reserve Bank) (Federal Reserve Bank of St. Louis, 2010). These articles are valuable, as they serve to summarize and review; they constitute mostly positive critiques and are reported to be used as resources for preservice teacher education (Risinger, 1999).

Personal Accounts

While there are examples of personal accounts in the broader social studies technology integration literature (see Hofer & Swan, 2006; Whitworth & Berson, 2003), there are far fewer examples in the personal finance and economics area. The article by Swan et al. (2010) mentioned above would be considered a personal account of the use of technology to teach economics or personal finance.

Evidence of Impact on Learning

Overall, there are very few studies that specifically test the effectiveness of technology integration in economic or financial education at the K-12 level (Harter & Harter, 2010; U.S. Government Accountability Office, 2011; Way & Wong, 2010) or even more broadly in social studies literature (Friedman & VanFossen, 2010; K. O. Swan & Hofer, 2008; Whitworth & Berson, 2003). One of the longest running technology-enhanced programs for investor education has been *The Stock Market Game* (www.stockmarketgame.org —a program of the Securities Industry and Financial Markets Association—SIFMA since 1977). It is among the most popular web-based programs for teaching personal finance. The premise of this project-based learning program is to (a) provide students the experience of managing a portfolio of stocks and (b introduce students to aspects of real-world investing.

In 1996, the Stock Market Game added a web-based program where students could manage their portfolios online (Cox, 1997). This change enabled the program to offer students the opportunity to buy and sell in real-time trading and to access a wealth of financial information online. In the 2000s, this Internet game provided students with an added source for their information-collection strategies on current events as well as a range of economic and financial analyses about individual stocks, the market, and the economy.

Walstad and Buckles (2008) reviewed results from the NAEP test in economics, and noted that participation in a stock market game was the only significant program that positively impacted students' scores on the test. Mandel (2009) reported similar findings in his analysis of Jump$tart surveys. Most recently, Learning Point Associates (Hinojosa et al., 2009) completed a study funded by the FINRA foundation on the effectiveness of the Stock Market Game on students' knowledge of financial literacy and mathematics. The results from the randomized control trial of 568 classrooms found a significant correlation between students' participation in the program and positive results on measures of financial knowledge and mathematics.

Yet, the Stock Market Game program is not without criticism. Some have suggested the program is flawed in its approach and teaches students the wrong things, including day trading, misperceptions of market cycles, and unrealistic expectations of returns (Maier, 2002; Quinn, 2004). However, these observations are at most anecdotal, with little research based evidence provided to support their claims.

Unfortunately, no other technology enhanced strategy for teaching personal finance has been studied at the K-12 level. In the absence of empirical research on the effectiveness of technology integration efforts, there are other means by which a teacher can assess the quality of a resource. For example, Carroll, McKenna, and Bickle (2001/2002) asked students and financial professionals to evaluate financial websites for use in financial literacy education. Today, websites such as www.econedreviews.org or www.econedlink.org allow visitors to review or contribute feedback or criticism of an educational resource. Comments on these websites add to the personal accounts of technology and are helpful in navigating the mass of online financial education materials. Yet, the dearth of research-based accounts in this area underlies the importance of additional research (Friedman & VanFossen, 2010; McCormick, 2009; K. O. Swan & Hofer, 2008).

Overview of Technology Integration in Financial and Economic Education

There are many technology enhanced resources, tools, and strategies that will support a teacher in teaching personal finance to his/her students. Before choosing a particular tool, teachers should consider what they hope to achieve by integrating technology. M. D. Roblyer (2006) summarized four reasons (to motivate students, to enhance instruction, to increase productivity, and to learn and develop information age skills) for the use of technology in teaching and learning (p 18). Table 11.1 provides examples of computer and web based instructional tools along with brief explanations of the potential reason for integration. For teachers to be able to use these resources most effectively, they must consider the context and strategy they will employ to integrate. In the next section, we discuss these web-based resources and a pedagogical approach to enhance their integration.

Table 11.1. Select Examples of Technology Tools for Teaching and Learning Personal Finance

Tool	*Type of Tool*	*Potential Reason for Use (Other Reasons May Apply)*
Spreadsheets	Software tool	Learn and sharpen information age skills. Can be used to help students track income and expenses in a budget. Many are also capable of calculating statistics. Students may use a predesigned worksheet created by the teacher, from a file template included in a program such as Microsoft Excel, or students can create one.
Podcasts and webinars	Multimedia	Learn and sharpen information age skills. A teacher can use a podcast to create or link to one created by an "expert" and provide students a way to receive content outside of class. Software such as Audacity allows students to record and edit their own audio files and share them with others.
Web-based games and simulations	Internet	Enhance instruction. Web-based games and simulations are readily available from sources such as financial institutions, U.S. federal government agencies, as well as nonprofit organizations. These are often short activities that can complement face-to-face instruction or provide motivation to further explore a concept. Some features include self-guided tutorials (ING Direct's Planet Orange, U.S. Bank's Escape from Knab), knowledge quizzes (Visa's Financial Football / Soccer, newmoney.gov's new note interactive quiz), simple manipulatives (EconEdLink's compound interest calculator), and simulations (CEE's Genirevolution, SIFMA's Stock Market Game). Other sites like finviz.com and finance.yahoo.com enable students to visual and research financial data.
Serious Games	Software tool	Motivate students. Games such as The Sims, The Tycoon series (Roller Coaster, Lemonade, etc.), prompt use of financial literacy skills to survive and complete the objectives of the games. For example, in The Sims, a player is unable to accumulate possessions without sufficient income. These games allow students to apply knowledge to constructed environments that mirror some real-world interactions.
Digital resource libraries	Internet	Increase teacher productivity. Websites, such as EconEdLink, the Jump$tart Coalition clearinghouse, and TeacherTube, provide access to lessons (print and digital) that can be used to teach concepts.

Motivation

Keller (1987) described four components of what influences learning motivation, (1) gaining attention, (2) demonstrating relevance, (3) building confidence, and (4) creating a sense of satisfaction. His ARCS (attention—relevance – confidence—satisfaction) model is used by instructional designers to enhance the motivation of learners. Financial education websites provide a means of motivating students to engage in the discovery and application of financial education concepts. Further, for motivation in financial and economic education, the potential use of online games and simulations seems promising. Shaffer, Squire, Halverson, and Gee (2005) contended that games allow students to "learn by doing" (p. 108). They also suggested that epistemically-framed games develop students' understanding of how to think and act in a community of practice. In the context of financial education, games they enable students to build knowledge of financial decision-making concepts may help inform their notion of how to live and thrive in a market economy. Games and simulations also have the capability to present instruction using a structured inquiry approach (Zhao, 2007). Some other examples of games that allow for application of financial decision-making are described below.

Websites such as Escape from Knab (www.escapefromknab.com) and Planet Orange (www.orangekids.com) use fantasy to engage students. In both simulations, a student takes on the role of a space adventurer or astronaut. Another element of motivation that is included is student control. The student is able to determine what choices s/he makes along the path s/he takes through the program. On the first website, they find themselves stranded on the planet Knab (bank spelled backwards). In order to leave the planet, they must apply some basic financial decision-making skills as attempt to earn $10,000 in 6 months by obtaining a job and managing their finances carefully. Students become astronauts and visit Planet Orange to complete financially-themed missions. Money (Obux) can be earned by reading the pages and completing the submissions. Additional money and a badge may be earned by students who demonstrate their financial knowledge by successfully completing a quiz at the end of the mission. The money they earn may be used to buy additional items for the spaceship or to play other games on the site.

Another example of a simulation that takes place in a more realistic setting is Moneytopia (http://apps.finra.org/moneytopia/moneytopia.html). While this game was designed originally for members of the military and their families, this would be appropriate for high school students. In this game, the player selects a character, a few friends, and a long term goal (Big Dream). The player is required to allocate his/her income to certain items such as a residence, transportation, and wardrobe. Optional items may also be purchased, such as entertainment items for the player's virtual home. When the simulation begins, the player must make a variety of financial decisions, many involving how s/he will spend or save his/her money. A dashboard enables the player to track his/her financial progress and allocate his/her disposable income to checking, saving, and investing accounts or to payment of loans (credit, auto, home). Random events occur as the simulation progresses, and the player must monitor sources of information send to him/her through the virtual mail, phone, and computer items tools in the program. This requires the player to adjust their decision making as time in the game passes.

Sports themed lessons are a good way of capturing a student's attention and the Financial Football/Soccer (www.practicalmoneyskills.com/games/trainingcamp/ff/) game does this by connecting with student's passion for professional football and soccer. In 2004, Visa released this web-based assessment game built around a football theme that featured NFL teams. This multiple choice quiz gave students the opportunity to compete against each other, taking on the identity of their favorite NFL teams as they tested their financial knowledge. In 2008, Visa added a financial soccer edition and expanded marketing of the game internationally. This game appeals to students' interest in arguably the two most popular sports, football (United States) and soccer (worldwide). In 2011, a mobile app version of the game was available as well.

Enhancing Instruction

Gen i Revolution. In 2009, the Council for Economic Education released the web-based personal finance game Gen i Revolution (http://genivevolution.org). This game was developed with funding from FINRA and was based on a CEE publication *Learning, Earning and Investing*. In this game, the goal is for the player to solve a series of personal finance related missions. In each mission, the player selects a team of operatives that may help him/her solve the challenges in the mission. The missions contain tutorials that provide the background knowledge the player needs to solve the mission. Interactive questions and financial calculations give the player an opportunity to earn points as s/he progresses through the missions.

Success Street. This online game, available through the National Endowment for Financial Education (NEFE) website, is a complement to the NEFE High School Financial Planning program. It allows students to compete in one of eight games to apply their knowledge of personal finance. In the game Deal on Wheels, the player explores insurance scenarios as they relate to the purchase and ownership of a vehicle.

Increase Student and Teacher Productivity

For a teacher beginning to examine how to integrate technology enhanced strategies, knowing where to start can be challenging (Loibl, 2010). There is no shortage of resources, activities, and ideas for teaching personal finance available on websites for teachers of economics and personal finance. These sites are provided by a wide range of organizations and institutions. The following is a description of two key websites and the digital resources found on them.

Jump$tart Coalition website (www.jumpstart.org). The Jump$tart website is really a very good starting point for most financial educators. Among the resources available on the site are the *National Standards in K-12 Personal Finance Education* (JumpStart Coalition for Personal Financial Literacy, 2007), a clearinghouse of materials, and Reality Check. The clearinghouse is a searchable database of materials for teaching. A review of the clearinghouse reveals over 200 resources that are interactive and/or accessible on a website. Many of these technology-enhanced resources provide self-directed tutorials or digital copies of lesson plans (html or pdf versions) that can be downloaded for use in grades K-12. Reality Check is an online calculator that helps student's estimates the amount of income necessary to support the type of lifestyle components entered. It also provides some suggestions for the types of occupations that earn the amount of income required.

EconEdLink (www.econedlink.org). Teachers also have access to free lessons via the Internet through sites like Thinkfinity (formerly Marco Polo). The Council for Economic Education is the economic and financial education partner for Thinkfinity and produces the website econedlink.org . The econedlink.org website has grown considerably since its inception in the late 1990s and now offers over 1,200 lessons, links to online data sources, lessons, interactives, video clips, and calculators that are appropriate for use in K-12 instruction.

Financial education websites are provided by a range of financial institutions, government agencies, and other organizations. In addition to the Jump$tart clearinghouse, these sites are often featured in resource lists for teaching personal finance included in numerous published articles and reports advocating the teaching of these concepts (Adams & Raines, 2010; Ferrarini & Calhoun, 2007; Frederichs & Rohrke, 2002; Schug & Lopus, 2008; VanFossen, 2003). Teachers should be mindful and consider the certain features, including availability of self-directed lessons, calculators, games, interactives, simulations, and quizzes as well as commercial objectives or biases.

Learn and Sharpen Information Age Skills

Off-the-shelf (Microsoft Office) and cloud-based (Google Docs) productivity tools can be a means for students to apply knowledge in the creation of financial documents. As mentioned above, the use of spreadsheets to construct and track budgets allows students to manipulate data and construct "what-if" scenarios based on possible changes. The spreadsheet tool included in Google Docs allows students to not only enter and calculate financial information, but with the use of a formula in the data cell, (GoogleFinance, "GOOG," "price"), students can integrate current stock market price information. This type of application enables students to see an example of how data can be dynamically integrated from an online source.

Finally, using software such as Audacity (often available for free on the web), students can create their own presentations or explanations of a concept in a podcast. In addition, with a web, flip, or phone camera, digital video is easily captured, edited, and embedded in a presentation file or shared online (Call, Swan, & Hofer, 2009; K. Swan et al., 2010). This provides students with the opportunity to learn how to create and communicate knowledge digitally.

Future Opportunities

What can we expect in the future? Change in technology is the one constant that is likely to continue. As technology evolves and instructional innovation progresses, the opportunities for enhancing personal finance instruction with technology will likely continue.

Increased use of video. Goffe and Sosin (2005) identified the use of video as a promising addition to an instructor's tool kit. In 2010, this seems to have come to fruition with the explosion of video-sharing sites, such as YouTube, Teacher Tube, and Vimeo. Digital video libraries services like Discovery Education have made the creation, sharing, and accessibility even easier. As mentioned, multimedia video production by students is likely to increase given the number of authoring and editing programs available at little or no cost. As students become more comfortable with video production, they will also need to be versed in the privacy considerations of video sharing.

Distance education. It seems very likely that personal finance education will increasingly be delivered to students via online means. Distance learning in elementary and secondary schools continues to grow in number of students enrolled and in expansion of course offerings. In the fall of 2008, forty two percent of public schools reported they provided access for students to online distance learning (Gray, Thomas, Lewis, & Tice, 2010). The enrollment in these offerings is expected to grow for the foreseeable future (Picciano & Seaman, 2009).

There are some concerns about the rapid growth of online learning opportunities. Shanahan and Brenden (2006) suggest that distance environments for teaching economics fail to promote higher order thinking by students enrolled. Johnson, Burnett, and Rollings (2002) compared outcomes from a face-to-face and online section of a high school consumer economics course. They found students in the online section scored significantly higher on the end-of-course test than those in the face-to-face section. This study is only one of a few that have looked closely at economic or personal finance distance education at the K-12 level. Without sufficient evidence that these environments produce superior outcomes compared to face-to face-classes, it is understandable that teachers of these courses invest little in the redesign of their courses to adapt better to online environments.

Online communities. For teachers in particular, the expansion of social networks for professional development may help to enhance content knowledge and practice. Online communities of practice provide an environment for sharing best practices and resources. Team Fin Lit (indianafinlit.ning.com) is a web-based online community created as a joint venture of the Indiana Department of Education and the Indiana Secretary of State to provide an online community for teachers in Indiana.

Mobile applications. As smart phones/interactive tablets become more prevalent, they may provide yet another tool for teaching personal finance. Already, one can find a multitude of consumer decision-making calculators and programs such as an expenditure tracker, tip calculators, grocery list aggregators, and sale alert programs. In addition, access to a range of economic data is readily available through apps such as Economy from Cascade software. There are also general financial literacy apps available, such as (a) the Financial Football website from Visa mentioned earlier, which also has a mobile app and (b) the self-guided tutorial Financial Literacy from 9magnets, LLC. The rate at which mobile devices are used for instruction will likely hinge on school administrators' attitudes and schools' policies on student access to wireless and cellular networks during the school day.

Implications for Practice

Before effective integration of technology can be expected, the barriers that may prevent teachers from being successful should be considered. For example, Gayton (2008) revealed in a study of three business teachers that despite technology training, the teachers experienced some difficulty integrating technology effectively in their instruction. While the teachers understood how to use the technology, they appeared to lack a full grasp of effective methods of integrating technology and pedagogy. Furthermore, these are some of the factors that have been reported by researchers related to the beliefs and pedagogical perspectives of teachers. While low and high levels of student learning are enabled by technology integration, those teachers who gravitate towards student-centered instruction may be more likely to integrate technology (Ertmer, 2005). Ertmer also suggested that it is not possible to "overestimate the influence of teacher beliefs" (p. 36). Part of the challenge for integration of technology in the social studies, according to Doolittle and Hicks (2003), is that technology integration in the social studies has been haphazard and not grounded or linked to pedagogical theory background.

To further help understand the difference between teacher beliefs and practice, a useful question to ask is "How teachers use technology in instruction?" Yali Zhao (2007) conducted a study that examined how social studies teachers who employ intensive technology integration perceive technology integration, how these teachers integrate technology in their social studies classroom, and how the technology affects their classroom practice (p. 314). Teachers in the study cited increased efficiency as an important reason to use technology. Other reasons cited in the Zhao study were to enhance instruction, relax instruction, or for a change of pace. VanFossen and Waterson's (2008) replication of VanFossen's (1999a) study of Internet use by social studies teachers found that social studies teachers in Indiana used a particular technology, the Internet, for both lower and higher level applications. While more schools in 2005 compared to 1999 were wired for Internet connections and had additional computer facilities, teachers still were not using the Internet to a satisfactory degree. Lack of training was a commonly cited barrier, but less a factor in 2005 than 1999. In both studies, the most commonly cited use was for "glorified information gathering" (VanFossen & Waterson, 2008, p. 144). Surprised by the results, given the increased access to equipment and comfort with the technology, VanFossen and Waterson concluded that other barriers may be in play. They also felt results supported Peg Ertmer's (2005) assertion that pedagogical beliefs may play a key role in teacher's integration of technology in the classroom and should be investigated further.

Conclusion

Despite an increase in the availability of computer- and web-based financial and economic education resources, evidence of significant successful integration of instructional technology is lacking. The plethora of web-based resources are as unlikely to have an impact on teaching personal finance as have the assorted print materials if current practice in economics and personal finance mirrors the experience from the broader social studies field. The challenge for educators is to work to improve understandings of effective integration strategies through research. This evidence can then be used to better inform instructional technology design and best practice. For financial education efforts to be successful, teachers must be grounded in smart technology knowledge, strong financial and economic knowledge, and effective pedagogical practice.

DISCUSSION QUESTIONS

1. Consider your own experience with how you have learned about personal finance. What gaps may exist between modern realities of financial management and decision making and how the content is being taught today?
2. What barriers to technology integration do you perceive in financial education? How would you classify them: pedagogical knowledge, content knowledge, and/or technology knowledge?
3. Consider the advantages and disadvantages to integrating a program like the Stock Market Game in terms of content, instructional strategy, student motivation, and class time. What implementation strategies can be employed to mitigate concerns?
4. What instructional planning strategies can be used to adapt to the next generation of instructional technologies?
5. What security or privacy issues should be considered prior to the teaching of a technology-enhanced financial literacy unit or lesson? How may instructors present guidelines for students regarding how they deal with sensitive personal and family financial information? To what extent should guidelines consider the unique features of mobile devices (cameras, ability to lock the screen with a password) and how should these be discussed with students?

MODEL LESSON

Apps-o-nomics

Suggested Grade Levels: 6-12
Objectives:

(a) Students will identify ways that an app can be helpful in making financial decisions.
(b) Students will use a mobile device to locate and evaluate a financial education app.
(c) Students will use a mobile device to locate and evaluate a financial news app.
(d) Students will develop criteria that a consumer should use when considering the purchase of a mobile app.
(e) Students will identify and locate apps that may be used by a consumer to improve their financial decision making.
(f) Students will compare the features and benefits apps including such as cost, accessibility, and privacy.

Related Personal Finance Standards

Jump$tart National Standards in K–12 Personal Finance Education

Financial Responsibility and Decision Making

Standard 1: Take responsibility for personal financial decisions.

Standard 2: Find and evaluate financial information from a variety of sources

Standard 3: Summarize major consumer protection laws.

Standard 4: Make financial decisions by systematically considering alternatives and consequences.

Standard 5: Develop communication strategies for discussing financial issues.

Standard 6: Control personal information.

Planning and Money Management

Standard 4: Apply consumer skills to purchase decisions.

Materials:

- This activity can be completed with or without access to mobile devices such as an iPod Touch, iPad, or smartphone (like an iPhone or Droid). Teachers are discouraged from lending their own phones to students to use in this lesson. If a teacher wishes to demonstrate aspects of this lesson using their own phone, s/he may use a device that can project their actions to a screen in front of the entire class. Students may also access information about apps from multiple websites.
- Data from the Consumer Electronics Show compiled by the *Washington Post* http://www.washingtonpost.com

Procedures:

1. Ask students how many of them have a cell phone or mobile computing device, such as a laptop, tablet or netbook, or a multimedia portable device (e.g., an iPod Touch).
2. Ask students what percent of people in the United States own cell devices, or mobile devices, or use cell and mobile devices to connect to the Internet.

    - According to data from the Consumer Electronics Show compiled by the *Washington Post* in 2011, 64% of households were expected to own a mobile device; 36% of households were expected to own smartphones; 91% of households were expected to own standard cell phones; and 51% of households owned MP3 players. (See article at www.washingtonpost.com/wp-srv/special/business/a-gadgets-life.)
    - According to a 2010 Pew Internet Survey, 40% used a cell phone to connect to the Internet, send e-mail, or send instant messages; 47% used a laptop or tablet. (See article at http://www.pewinternet.org/Reports/2010/Mobile-Access-2010.aspx.)
    - For further description / explanation of devices, see entries in Wikipedia.

3. Ask students to explain what an “App” is for a mobile device, such as an iPod, iPhone, or other smartphone device.

- An app is a computer software program that is designed for a cell phone or other mobile device. App is short for application.

4. Ask students what types of apps are available.

   - Possible answers include games, social network, e-books, news, and personal productivity (to do lists).
   - Lists and reviews of apps can be accessed on app store/market websites. In 2011, the largest of these store/market websites were provided by companies Apple and Android. Use a search engine to locate these websites or other websites that list and review apps.

5. Ask students to identify criteria they use when deciding what app to purchase or download.

   - Possible answers may include cost, types of features, reliability of the app (e.g., it does not crash often), online/offline functionality (some apps only work when a cell or wifi connection is present), trustworthiness, and privacy.

6. Ask students to identify sources of information to learn about apps.

   - Suggestions from friends.
   - Suggestions from the app market / store (e.g., the Apple App Store suggests other apps based on previous apps downloaded).
   - Random searches via a search engine or app market/store search feature.
   - Reviews or news stories.

7. Ask students to explain the pros and cons of these sources of information.

   - Explain to students that some apps can be used to help with financial decision making.

8. Ask students to brainstorm what types of apps might help a person when s/he is making personal financial decisions.

   - Budgeting

- (apps that allow a user to enter and categorize income and expenses)
- Comparison shopping
- (apps that aggregate prices of goods and/or services, scan product barcodes)
- Making payments
- (apps for mobile banking access, electronic fund management —PayPal, credit card readers)
- Tracking and managing account balances
- (apps for mobile banking and financial institution access, enable a user to check balances, transfer funds)
- Financial and consumer news
- (apps from financial news websites including market summaries, track stock prices and other economic indicators)
- Financial education
- (apps for mobile financial learning)

9. The next section involved locating and evaluating apps based on the criteria established earlier. The procedures below are listed based on the availability of computers or devices.

10. Procedure for activity with student device:

    - Divide students into groups of 2 or 3, depending on the number of devices.
    - Assign or allow students to choose a type of app they will locate and evaluate. You may want to make sure multiple categories are represented. Categories can include those from the list brainstormed in Number 8. Additional possibilities may include the following categories:

        - Financial responsibility
        - Decision making
        - Earning income
        - Careers
        - Budgeting or managing money
        - Borrowing or credit
        - Risk management or insurance
        - Saving
        - Investing
        - Financial news
        - Financial education

- Determine ahead of time if you want students to only review descriptions of the apps or if they may download the app onto their device during class. Some apps are not free.

11. Modification of procedure for activity with only a teacher device available:

    - Instead of dividing students into groups, the teacher can display the device using a document camera.
    - Students can explore and search for apps using information available on an app-related website.

12. Procedure for activity with no device, but computer access:

    - If a device or the ability to project the device screen is not available, students can still explore and search for apps using information available on an app-related website.

13. Assessment

    - Working in groups of 2 or 3, students design a new app related to financial literacy or financial decision making.
    - The design can be done on a storyboard created on paper or digitally using a slide presentation software program such as PowerPoint.
    - Students should consider how they might integrate the following features:
        - User interface
        - Data source
        - Integration with other services
        - Cost
    - Students present their designs in class or post them on a wiki to share electronically.

REFERENCES

Adams, M. E., & Raines, P. (2010). *Indiana middle school business curriculum resources for personal financial literacy.* Retrieved from https://learningconnection.doe.in.gov

Bernanke, B. (2010). Fostering financial literacy. Retrieved from http://www.federalreserve.gov/newsevents/speech/bernanke20100413a.html

Berson, M. (1996). Effectiveness of computer technology in the social studies: A review of the literature. *Journal of Research on Computing in Education, 28*(4), 486-499.

Braunstein, S., & Welch, C. (2002). Financial literacy: An overview of practice, research, and policy. *Federal Reserve Bulletin, 88*. Retrieved November 14, 2010, from http://federalreserve.gov/pubs/bulletin/2002/1102lead.pdf

Bucks, B. K., Kennickell, A. B., Mach, T. L., & Moore, K. B. (2009). Changes in U.S. family finances from 2004 to 2007: Evidence from the Survey of Consumer Finances. *Federal Reserve Bulletin, 95*, A1-A55.

Call, C., Swan, K. O., & Hofer, M. (2009). Hot off the presses: Podcasting for the economics classroom. *Social Studies Research and Practice, 4*(2), 145-151.

Carroll, J. B., McKenna, J., & Bickle, M. C. (2001/2002). Youth financial education web sites: Evaluating value and appeal. *Journal of Consumer Education, 19/20*, 70-77.

Cole, S., & Shastry, G. K. (2009). Smart money: The effect of education, cognitive ability, and financial literacy on financial market participation [Working Paper]. *Harvard Business School Working Paper n. 09-71*.

Council for Economic Education. (2010). *Voluntary national content standards in economics 2nd Edition*. New York, NY: Council for Economic Education.

Cox, A. C. (1997). Using the stock market game in the social studies classroom. *Social Education, 61*(6), 347-350.

Cuban, L. (2001). *Oversold and underused: Computers in the classroom*. Cambridge, MA: Harvard University Press.

Doolittle, P. E., & Hicks, D. (2003). Constructivism as a theoretical foundation for the use of technology in social studies. *Theory and Research in Social Education, 31*(1), 72-104.

Duke, E. (2010, April 8). *The importance of financial education*. Paper presented at the Jump$tart Coalition Investing in Our Future: Financial Education and Washington Event, Washington, D.C.

Ertmer, P. A. (2005). Teacher pedagogical beliefs: The final frontier in our quest for technology integration? *ETR&D, 53*(4), 25-39.

Federal Reserve Bank of St. Louis. (2010). Featured resource: Econ Ed Live! *Inside the Vault, 14*(2), 1-12. Retrieved from http://www.stlouisfed.org/publications/itv/

Ferrarini, T. H., & Calhoun, J. (2007). Cool websites and other technology resources for teaching about the United States economy. *Social Education, 71*(2), 87-91.

Frederichs, M., Lena, R., & Rohrke, A. (2002). Guide to finanancial literacy resources. Retrieved from http://www.frbsf.gov/community/webresources/bankersguide.pdf

Friedman, A. M., & Hicks, D. (2006). Guest editorial: The state of the field: Technology, social studies, and teacher education. *Contemporary Issues in Technology and Teacher Education, 6*(2), 246-258.

Friedman, A. M., & VanFossen, P. J. (2010). The Internet in social studies classrooms. In R. Diem & M. J. Berson (Eds.), *Technology in retrospect: Social studies in the information age 1984-2009* (pp. 51-74). Charlotte, NC: Information Age Publishing.

Gayton, J. (2008). Understanding teaching with the Internet in business education. *The Delta Pi Epsilon Journal, 50*(1), 31-44.

Goffe, W., & Sosin, K. (2005). Teaching with technology: May you live in interesting times. *Journal of Economic Education, 36*(3), 278-291.

Gray, L., Thomas, N., Lewis, L., & Tice, P. (2010). *Educational technology in U.S. public schools: Fall 2008* (NCES 2010-034) Retrievedf from http://nces.ed.gov/pubsearch/pubsinfo.asp?pubid=2010034

Greenspan, A. (2003). The importance of financial and economic education and literacy. (Raising interest in economics). *Social Education, 67*(2), 70-71.

Hammond, T. C., & Manfra, M. M. (2009). Giving, prompting, making: Aligning technology and pedagogy within TPACK for social studies instruction. *Contemporary Issues in Technology and Teacher Education, 9*(2), 160-185.

Harris, J., Mishra, P., & Koehler, M. (2009). Teachers' technological pedagogical content knowledge and learning activity types: Curriculum-based technology integration reframed. *Journal of Research on Technology in Education, 41*(4), 393-416.

Harter, C., & Harter, J. F. R. (2010). Is financial literacy improved by participating in a stock market game? *Journal for Economic Educators, 10*(1), 21-32.

Hew, K. F., & Hara, N. (2007). Empirical study of motivators and barriers of teacher online knowledge sharing. *Educational Technology Research and Development, 55*(6), 573-595.

Hinojosa, T., Miller, S., Swanlund, A., Kelly, H., Brown, M., & O'Brien, B. (2009). *The Stock Market Game™ study: Brief report*. Washington, DC: FINRA Investor Education Foundation.

Hira, T. K. (2009). *Personal finance: Past, present and future. Networks Financial Institute Policy Brief 2009-PB-10*. Retrieved from http://www.networksfinancialinstitute.org/Lists/Publication%20Library/Attachments/153/2009-PB-10_Hira.pdf

Hofer, M., & Swan, K. O. (2006). Standards, firewalls, and general classroom mayhem: Implementing student-centered technology projects in the elementary classroom. *Social Studies Research and Practice, 1*(1), 120-144.

Hung, A. A., Mihaly, K., & Yoong, J. K. (2010). Federal financial and economic literacy education programs, 2009 *RAND Corporation technical report series* (pp. 1-108). Santa Monica, CA: RAND Corporation, RAND Labor and Population.

Hung, A. A., Parker, A. M., & Yoong, J. K. (2009). Defining and measuring financial literacy *Rand Corporation Working Paper WR-708*. Santa Monica, CA: RAND Corporation, RAND Labor and Population.

International Society for Technology in Education. (2007). *National educational technology standards for students*. Washington, DC: International Society for Technology in Education.

International Society for Technology in Education. (2008). *National educational technology standards for teachers*. Washington, DC: International Society for Technology in Education.

International Society for Technology in Education. (2009). *National educational technology standards for administrators*. Washington, DC: International Society for Technology in Education.

Johnson, D., Burnett, M., & Rollings, P. (2002). Comparison of Internet and traditional classroom instruction in a consumer economics course. *Journal of Family and Consumer Sciences Education, 20*(2), 20-28.

Johnson, E., & Sherraden, M. S. (2007). From financial literacy to financial capability among youth. *Journal of Sociology & Social Welfare, 34*(3), 119-146.

JumpStart Coalition for Personal Financial Literacy. (2007). *National standards in K-12 personal finance education* (3rd ed.). Washington, DC: Author.

Keller, J. M. (1987). Strategies for stimulating the motivation to learn. *Performance + Instruction, 26*(8), 1-7.

Lee, J. K. (2008). Toward democracy: Social studies and TPCK. In A. (Ed.), *The Handbook of Technological Pedagogical Content Knowledge for Educators* (pp. 129-144). New York, NY: Routledge.

Loibl, C. (2010). A look inside: teacher information search for personal finance instruction. *International Journal of Consumer Studies, 34*(3), 287-297. doi: 10.1111/j.1470-6431.2010.00867.x

Lucey, T. A. (2007). The art of relating moral education to financial education: An equity imperative. *Social Studies Research and Practice, 2*(3), 486-500.

Lucey, T. A., & Grant, M. (2010). Using technology to prepare critically thinking global citizens. *Social Studies Research and Practice, 5*(3), 119-138

Lusardi, A. (2011). *Americans' financial capability. National Bureau of Economic Research Working Paper Series. No. 17103.* Retrieved from http://www.nber.org/papers/w17103

Lusardi, A., Mitchell, O. S., & Curto, V. (2010). *Financial literacy among the young: Evidence and implications for consumer policy.* Retrieved from http://www.dartmouth.edu/~alusardi/Papers/Financial_literacy_young.pdf

Maier, M. H. (2002). A critical review of Learning from the Market: Integrating the Stock Market Game across the curriculum. *The Journal of Economic Education, 33*(1), 83-88.

Mandell, L. (2008). Financial literacy of high school students. In J. J. Xiao (Ed.), *Handbook of Consumer Finance Research* (pp. 163-183). New York, NY: Springer.

Mandell, L., & Klein, L. S. (2009). The Impact of Financial Literacy Education on Subsequent Financial Behavior. *Journal of Financial Counseling and Planning, 20*(1), 15-24.

Mason, C., Berson, M. J., Diem, R., Hicks, D., Lee, J. K., & Dralle, T. (2000). Guidelines for using technology to prepare social studies teachers. *Contemporary issues in technology and teacher education, 1*(1), 107-116.

McCormick, M. H. (2009). The effectiveness of youth financial education: A review of the literature. *Journal of Financial Counseling and Planning, 20*(1), 70-83.

National Council for the Social Studies. (2006). *Technology position statement and guidelines A position statement of National Council for the Social Studies.* Retrieved from http://www.socialstudies.org/positions/technology

National Council on Economic Education, National Association of Economic Educators, & Foundation for Teaching Economics. (1997). *Voluntary national content standards in economics.* New York, NY: National Council on Economic Education.

Picciano, A. G., & Seaman, J. (2009). *K–12 online learning: A 2008 follow-up of the survey of U.S. school district administrators.* Retrieved from http://sloanconsortium.org/publications/survey/k-12online2008

Quinn, J. B. (2004, March 1). Kids will be... daytraders? *Newsweek, 143*, 47.

Remund, D. L. (2010). Financial literacy explicated: The case for a clearer definition in an increasingly complex economy. *Journal of Consumer Affairs, 44*(2), 276-295.

Risinger, C. F. (1999). Teaching students financial literacy using the internet. *Social Education, 73*(2), 92.

Roblyer, M. D. (2000). The national educational technology standards (NETS): A review of definitions,implications, and strategies for integrating NETS into K-12 curriculum. *International Journal of Instructional Media, 27*(2), 133-146.

Roblyer, M. D. (Ed.). (2006). *Integrating educational technology Into teaching* (4th ed.). Upper Saddle River, NJ: Prentice-Hall.

Schug, M., & Lopus, J. (2008). Economic and financial education for the 21st Century. *Social Education, 72*(7), 359-362.

Shaffer, D. W., Squire, K. R., Halverson, R., & Gee, J. P. (2005). Video games and the future of learning. *The Phi Delta Kappan, 87*(2), 104-111.

Shanahan, M., & Brenden, G. (2006). Teaching and learning economics at a distance. In W. E. Becker, M. Watts & S. R. Becker (Eds.), *Teaching Economics: More Alternatives to Chalk and Talk* (pp. 133-150). Northhampton, England: Edward Elgar.

Sosin, K. (1997). *Impact of the web on economics pedagogy.* Paper presented at the Allied Social Sciences Association, New Orleans, LA. Retrieved from http://ecedweb.unomaha.edu/ksosin/webteach.pdf

Swan, K., Hofer, M., Swan, G., & Mazur, J. (2010). The production, consumption, and distribution of economic podcasts. *Social Education, 74*(3), 148-151.

Swan, K. O., & Hofer, M. (2008). Technology and social studies. In I. Levstick & C. Tyson (Eds.), *Handbook of Research in Social Studies Education* (pp. 307-326). New York, NY: Routledge.

US Government Accountability Office. (2011, June). Financial literacy: A federal certification process for providers would pose challenges (Pubication No. GAO-11-614). Retrieved from www.gao.gov/new.items/d11614.pdf

VanFossen, P. J. (1999a). An analysis of the use of the Internet and World Wide web by secondary social studies teachers in Indiana. . *The International Journal of Social Education, 14*(2), 87-109.

VanFossen, P. J. (1999b). The national voluntary content standards in economics. *ERIC Digest.* Retrieved from http://www.ericdigests.org/1999-4/economics.htm

VanFossen, P. J. (2003). Best practice economic education for young children? It's elementary. *Social Education, 67*(2), 90-94.

VanFossen, P. J., & Waterson, R. A. (2008). "It is just easier to do what you did before...": An update on Internet use in secondary social studies classrooms in Indiana. *Theory and Research in Social Education, 36*(2), 124-152.

Walstad, W. B., & Buckles, S. (2008). The National Assessment of Educational Progress in economics: Findings for general economics. *American Economic Review: Papers & Proceedings, 98*(2), 541-546. doi: 10.1257/aer.9#.2.541

Way, W. L., & Wong, N. (2010). Harnessing the power of technology to enhance financial literacy education and personal financial well-being: A review of the literature, proposed model, and action agenda *Center for Financial Security WP 10-6*. Madison, WI: University of Madison Wisconsin.

Whitworth, S. A., & Berson, M. J. (2003). Computer technology in the social studies: An examination of the effectiveness literature (1996-2003). *Contemporary Issues in Technology and Teacher Education, 2*(4), 472-509.

Wilson, E., & Wright, V. (2010). Images over time: The intersection of social studies through technology, content, and pedagogy. *Contemporary Issues in Technology and Teacher Education, 10*(2), 220-233.

Zhao, Y. (2007). Social studies teachers' perspectives of technology integration. *Journal of Technology and Teacher Education, 15*(3), 311-333.

CHAPTER 12

MAPPING FINANCIAL FUTURES AND DEVELOPING SOCIAL CAPITAL

Decision-Making About Career, Specialization, and Interest Rates

Mary Frances Agnello and Andrea L. Knapp

Economic literacy is an important aspect of education for the American populace. Unfortunately, K-12 schools fare poorly in their efforts to teach children and youth about related tenets (Bernanke, 2006). Even though policymakers argue that financial literacy is important, national economic policies and practices represent determinants of the general public's financial possibilities. Pursuing financial literacy, in and of itself, represents an insufficient strategy for improving society because the economic decisions made by key policymakers affect the financial decision-making contexts for all. Professionals in the discipline of economics see a need for economic literacy, in essence, a strong grasp within the field and in the public of domestic and international economic systems and their interrelationships (The Federal Research Bank of Minneapolis, 2011).

Reframing Financial Literacy: Exploring the Value of Social Currency, pp. 235–252

The Jump$tart Coalition for Personal Financial Literacy (2007b) defines financial literacy as "the ability to use knowledge and skills to manage one's financial resources effectively for lifetime financial security" (p. 1). However, while the term itself is easily defined, implementation of the underlying concepts is not. This chapter focuses on the evolution of financial literacy teacher education, particularly informed by four standards from the Council for Economic Education and Jump$tart that align well with a discussion of social capital, a concept developed by Pierre Bourdieu (1986). It is posited that youth can be coached and prepared to develop their social currency that leads to sounder financial decision making. It is believed that K-12 students with financial literacy knowledge, skills, and dispositions are more prepared to be self-sustaining and productive citizen workers. The chapter concludes by relating the standards described herein to the need for social networking as a critical component of social capital development.

CURRICULUM STANDARDS

Research on Teacher Knowledge

Financial literacy is a relatively new concept in the K-12 curriculum; in fact, federal efforts to improve financial knowledge and practice commenced with the Excellence in Economic Education Act (2004), yet inconsistent state legislation has directed financial literacy education (Lucey & Maxwell, 2009). Financial literacy education has evolved from a largely private concern to a national public policy issue as it has become increasingly clear that individual financial decisions collectively affect the national economy (Way & Holden, 2009). Relying on teachers to support and teach financial literacy in the curriculum assumes that teachers have a good understanding of how to implement the teaching guides that others create. Research findings show that teachers feel that they have a basic understanding of financial literacy as revealed by the *Pollinate* study (Otter, 2010), yet as indicated by Way and Holden (2009), few teachers fee prepared to teach financial literacy.

The Otter study, in addition that of Wilhelm and Chao, (2005) revealed that teachers are interested in teaching financial literacy and that they consider it a professional need for them to be able to teach financial literacy adequately. Roughly three years before the *Pollinate* study in 2007, the Networks Financial Institute at Indiana State University conducted a study of national K-12 financial literacy. This institute was funded by the Lilly Endowment Inc. in October 2003 to provide financial leadership for Indiana. The survey revealed obstacles to successful implementation of financial literacy in the classroom, which included a lack of financial and professional support. Wilhelm and Chao (2005) found that most K-12 educators who teach financial literacy topics use a combination their own and trade developed materials, as well as online lessons.

Efforts in several domains have furthered educational efforts in financial literacy and researching the phenomenon. The California Council on Economic Education has taken a step in the right direction to boost teachers' confidence in managing their own finances and to transfer that expertise to classroom teaching (California Council, 2008). Three-day financial literacy training was offered by the Iowa State Savings Bank to improve knowledge, skills, and confidence to teach financial education in middle and high schools (Iowa State, 2010). Way and Holden (2009) used a novel approach to reaffirm that teachers are ill- prepared to teach the subject matter. The Networks Financial Institute found that "middle and high school teachers are more likely to teach financial literacy topics compared to K-5 teachers" (Networks Financial Institute, 2007, p. 7), and that "most K-12 non-financial literacy teachers believe math is the subject area where financial literacy topics would be most valuable" (p. 12). Interestingly, the *Pollinate Survey* notes that "teachers ... believe personal finance instruction should begin in elementary school" (Otter, 2010, p. 2), in addition to believing that "the best way to deliver personal finance instruction is through both a stand-alone course and embedding concepts in other courses" (p. 2). In-depth comparison would be necessary to determine what, if any, variables existed in the surveys creating such differences (e.g., the timeframe of 2007 versus 2010 or the national sample of teachers versus California only, etc.). The varying views only reinforce the debate surrounding where and when financial literacy should be introduced. Teaching financial literacy is vital, yet the lack of formal professional development to assist teachers in achieving this end presents a quintessential paradox.

Teacher Preparation

By incorporating the financial literacy standards into the economics curriculum via the social studies curriculum, educators are poised to teach financial literacy within the existing curriculum. Alignment of two sets of standards: the 2007 Jump$tart Coalition for Personal Financial Literacy's *National Standards in K-12 Personal Finance Education* and the 2010 Council for Economic Education's *Voluntary National Content Standards in Economics* is one strategy for furthering the goals of instruction in financial literacy. These standards clearly outline fundamental financial topics and the impact those topics have on everyday lives. *The National*

Standards in K-12 Personal Finance Education "trace a path to a minimal level of competency upon completion of high school" (Jump$tart Coalition, 2007b, p. 3) and are divided into six overarching categories. While all categories and standards deserve attention, financial responsibility and decision making and income and careers are the two standards chosen to develop and discuss here. Children who receive an allowance for the first time weigh how to handle their newfound income; so does the high school student working a part-time job and planning to buy a car, as well as the college graduate in a poor economy with student loans and without a steady job. Decision making can greatly affect income and should be taught early and emphasized frequently, thus encouraging the development of invaluable analytical skills and other thought processes applicable to a plethora of daily activities.

Modeling for Teacher Preparation

The Jump$tart Standard 1 (taking responsibility for personal financial decisions) and Standard 4 (making financial decisions by systematically considering alternatives and consequences) under the category of financial responsibility and decision making reflect the need for students to firmly grasp that resources are limited and choices inevitable. From fourth graders meeting the Standard 4 expectation of ranking "personal wants/needs in order of importance" (Jump$tart Coalition, 2007b, p. 9) to 12th graders explaining via Standard 1 "how individuals demonstrate responsibility for financial well-being over a lifetime" (Jump$tart Coalition, 2007b, p. 8), continuous reinforcement assists students in comprehending that they will not be fiscally responsible until such time as they truly take ownership of the role of catalyst in their own financial outcomes. Serving as a fiscal agent of change is readily apparent when considering a career path. Standard 1, part of the Income and Careers section, states students explore career options" (Jump Start, etc.), yet perhaps one of the most important decisions individuals can make is deciding what to be when they "grow up." The overall competency suggests that one should "use a career plan to develop personal income potential" (Jump$tart, 2007b, p. 11), and this, too, relates to additional Council for Economic Education standards including specialization (standard 6) and interest rates (standard 12)

(http://www.councilforeconed.org/ea/standards/standard.php?sid=6 , and

http://www.councilforeconed.org/ea/standards/standard.php?sid=12 respectively).

Specialization helps students view themselves as future producers and workers and recognize they will earn more by specializing in doing the things they can do well and that entail the least sacrifice in forgone opportunities. There is an important connection between (a) decision making, whereby people and organizations decide what is profitable and what is not, and (b) income, which involves employers being willing to pay higher wages and salaries to those employees who can produce more or better goods or services in a given amount of time. Therefore, the Jump$tart objectives for (a) 4th graders to be able to "give an example of how an individual's interests, knowledge, and abilities can affect career and job choice" (Jump$tart Coalition, 2007b, p. 11); (b) 8th graders to be able to "give an example of how education and/or training can affect lifetime income" (p. 11); and (c) 12th graders to be able to "analyze how economic, social-cultural, and political conditions can affect income and career potential" (p. 11) underscore the complexity of financial literacy while simultaneously highlighting the interconnectedness among the standards and their applicability to everyday decisions.

As students begin to comprehend the inherent relationship between decision making, income, and specialization, it behooves the student and the educator to include one final content standard in this particular mix: interest rates. While the 2010 Council for Economic Education Standard 12 (interest rates) may not be the most readily apparent standard to complement the previously discussed standards, it intuitively ties together the four standards into one comprehensive lesson. Because "it is important for students to understand the incentive effects of interest rates" (Council for Economic Education, 2010, p. 29), upon completion of content Standard 12, students should be able to "explain situations in which they pay or receive interest, and explain how they would react to changes in interest rates if they were making or receiving interest payments" (p. 29).

Teaching about interest rates as stand-alone items is an important lesson, but effective financial literacy education must be considered in multiple settings from multiple viewpoints. When is money paid as interest a good investment? When is it wasteful? If interest is paid on student loans, it can be an investment. If student loan or credit card interest is being paid for pizza delivery, could the money have been better spent on homemade pizza, supermarket pizza, or healthier less expensive cuisine? What is the difference in the two scenarios—student loan interest as investment versus student loan being spent unwisely? Could one say the same for a student loan made for a student who parties all semester rather than engaging in academics? Interest rates also align well with the idea of developing social capital—in the form of parents' investing money and time into their children's education (Bourdieu, 1986). For the purpose of self-development or the acquisition of goods and services, the cost of borrowing money over the long-term (e.g., student loans) or for the short-term (e.g., credit cards) is a force with which individuals must reckon, particularly in a consumer society.

Figure 12.1 illustrates the relationship among these standards, with the 2007 Jump$tart categories and standards serving as focal points and the 2010 Council for Economic Education standards as supports. From students contemplating a career path to adults considering a career change, the diagram below reflects standard, possible thought processes involved in making such important decisions. While people possess unique ideas that pertain to where they want to go and how they want to get there, all can employ these various standards in order to analyze their respective futures. Perhaps, if approaching the topic in this manner is inappropriate as deemed so by the professional judgment of the teacher, other strategies can be used to teach the same concepts. For example, is getting an expensive loan ahead of payday a good way to expend interest? Is mortgaging one's car for emergency cash a good way to finance unforeseen expenses? Not only do such thinking exercises reflect the value of studying financial literacy and the impact that financial literacy can have on the lives of students and nonstudents alike, they also create an environment in which the value of social currency can be explored with the understanding that "various social groups value financial topics differently" (Lucey & Maxwell, 2009, p. 224). Furthermore, to the extent that financial literacy is omitted from the curriculum and that this omission prevents all K-12 students from considering their potential choices, there is a need for educators to embrace financial literacy with students. In addition to an obvious subject area like social studies, financial literacy links conveniently with mathematics instruction; it also is an area around which students can write essays in language arts. Many aspects of science, technology, engineering, and mathematics (STEM) present possibilities for financial literacy explorations as well.

Learning about money, comprehending its workings, calculating its growth, and considering the relationship between wealth accumulation and working capital are important lessons in financial literacy mastery. Working with students to conceptualize their financial futures in these domains broadens their financial literacy; however, developing financial literacy does not guarantee that students will apply the knowledge, skills, and dispositions needed to create the networks needed for financial success. The second part of this paper will focus on social capital, its definition, and its development. It advocates the engagement of students in money matters through development of social networks (social capital) that produce money or currency (capital).

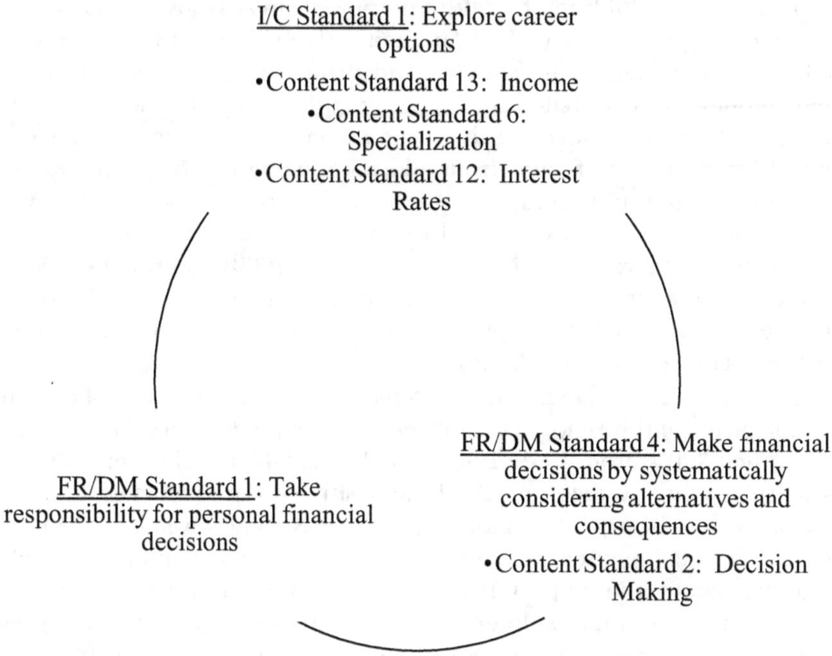

Figure 12.1. Relationships among responsibility, decision-making, and career standards.

SOCIAL CAPITAL AS FINANCIAL LITERACY

Defining Social Capital

> A student's creativity can only ever be a self-creation. Only rhetorical exuberance can lead one to forget what makes the very definition of the student's role: to study is not to create something but create oneself; it is not to create a culture, still less a new culture, but create one's capacity to be, at best a creator of culture, or, in most cases an informed user or transmitter of a culture created by others, that is, a teacher or specialist. More generally, to study is not to produce, but to produce a capacity to produce. (Bourdieu & Passeron, 1979, p. 55)

Pierre Bordieu's social research led to his hypothesis of social capital, which explains the unequal opportunities, in school and in postschool years, for students from families of different classes (Bordieu, 1986; Bourdieu & Passeron, 1979). Taking into account Bourdieu and Passeron's quote from above, students can develop their capacity to produce. In so doing, they learn the skills that are needed to network and build social capital that the children of wealth and power already possess. This viewpoint differs from that of human capital theories which consider only educational monetary investments and profits or resources convertible into money. A view that dismisses intangible capital overlooks a most important feature of social capital—the phenomenon of its transmissibility and the reliance of gains from education being based heavily upon a family's invested cultural capital (Bordieu, 1986, p. 48). Social currency or social capital is a form of capital defined by Bourdieu (1986) and discussed by several recent scholars (e.g., Putnam, 2000). Bourdieu's (2008a) work also shows cultures in crises, and with fastidious detail, he chronicles the position of social science with respect to political action as played out between France and her colonies.

Bourdieu's ground breaking works have influenced the work of current sociologists, anthropologists, cultural workers, educators, and others (Bourdieu & Passeron, 1979; Bourdieu, 2008a, 2008b). They lend a social science insight that defies much of the positive surface media coverage of the attributes of capital economies, or at least they reveal some of the tradeoffs in competitive versus cooperative economic communities. His findings about the importance of social capital resonate in current research reports. Today's domestic and international environments present social, political, and economic differences defined by geographic places, settings, and circumstances in which different social groups operate sometimes with anonymity and other times for community connection (Blokland & Savage, 2008; Hsung, Lin, & Breiger, 2009; Radcliffe, 2006).

Developing Social Capital

In a reframed view of the four financial literacy concepts discussed herein (i.e., taking responsibility for personal financial decisions, making financial decisions, deciding what kind of specialization in which to focus one's educational efforts, and paying interest rates), students should be able to make informed and well-considered decisions. Building on social capital, students need to be able to make sense of which and how many resources they possess in their families, schools, churches, neighborhoods, businesses, and other arenas involved in commercial and noncommercial exchange (Nisbet, 2002). How do educational standards reinforce related skills and understandings by focusing learning only on reading, writing, math, technology, and science? What other basic skills are being forgotten? What about the basic skills and understandings behind building shelters and homes, cultivating food, connecting ecologically to the earth, and building community networks (Radcliffe, 2006)? In K-12 and in postsecondary education, students construct their understandings of concepts and in the best of learning environments, apply, evaluate, and create social capital in interaction with the various disciplines (Radcliffe, 2006). They would be asked to tie these skills to the standards in the subject areas of focus in K-12 education. Informed deliberations about students' future educations, lives, ability to make informed decisions, and interest rates connect to forces often beyond individuals' control, as well as to those within the realm of personal power (Hsung, Lin, & Breiger, 2009). Furthermore, K-12 students can begin to distinguish between and among the situations over which they have more and less control.

Some forces beyond personal control include the market value of work or the income remuneration that individuals earn for certain jobs and/or professional skills, along with interest rates determined by the Federal Reserve and banks. The desire to produce and be productive harnessed with educational foundations for financial literacy can inform students about their possible futures. Some connected questions informed by social capital might include: Whom do students dream of becoming? How might students' decisions affect themselves and others? Is the cost benefit of optimum and desired goals worth the cost of getting there? How do good and bad decision-making affect the health and wealth of individuals and communities? What are the students' skills and talents? What do students need in order (a) to prepare themselves to become productive citizen workers and (b) to specialize? What is needed and desired by students (a) to provide necessities to their families and (b) to engage in social networks (Bourdieu, 2008b; Blokland & Savage, 2008; Radcliffe, 2006)? What can be done to strengthen or weaken students' opportunities for personal development and achievement?

Some scenarios to consider in the building and maintaining of social capital entail assumptions of ethical practices among those individuals in whom fiduciary trust has been placed, as well as how citizens can take social action to address those situations in which that trust has been violated. Such social responsibilities associated with citizenship also assume political action on the part of citizens to ensure that those in whom public welfare has been entrusted do what they should and act in ethical ways (Vassallo, 2010). A politically engaged citizenry is required to make certain that some of these ethical ideals are attained (Nisbet, 2002). A socially and economically engaged citizenry is vital, for it must ask questions and take actions through political networks, strengthened by formal and informal social and economic connections. In addition, this citizenry must consider personal, community, and greater social needs as advocated by Nisbet. Although Nisbet's work is considered politically conservative, his view of democracy and democratization has interesting parallels to the teachings of Paulo Freire (1970), often associated with leftist politics.

Cultural literacy as advocated by Freire (1970) promoted the understanding of an individual's place in the larger social order. Through transformative education, the teacher and student, utilizing strategies recommended by Freire, are able to work toward improving/increasing students' abilities to change their social and economic circumstances. Freire's vision is useful for developing students' understanding of their place in the world, engaging students in communities and groups, developing students' talents, helping students make plans, creating opportunities for students, and ultimately developing social capital (Agnello, Sarria, & Slater, 1996).

A disconnect in the relationship between the civil society and the international arena occurs in the contradiction between human needs and postindustrial nations' overutilization of resources, particularly in the United States. In "Economics in a Full World" Daly (2005) elaborates on the limits to growth and the need for us to understand that the world food supply (provided by fishing and the use of many natural resources) cannot continue indefinitely. Coming to ecological terms with the limits to growth has been discussed for 3 decades, and yet the idea has not gained much American public attention because of the need for the capitalist economy to promote the buying and selling of goods and services that are beyond those "needed" (Agnello & Lucey, 2008, 2010). As shortages become more apparent and publicized, many groups of people are prepared to work for saner and safer ways to grow and prepare food (Gussow, 2001), as well as to invest in slow but sound endeavors like sustainable agriculture (Tasch, 2008), which is already being practiced in many parts of the world (Radcliffe, 2006).

In many other countries, social capital found in pockets of rural and urban poverty has been studied to discover that such factors as dispositions, skills, tastes, experiences, family, church, community, social and association networks, educational access, job and economic opportunities, and job and economic properties do indeed make a difference in the acquisition of wealth, respect, and position. These same factors are also pertinent to survival in some cases (Hsung, Lin, & Breiger, 2009; Radcliffe, 2006). Some of the messages from international researchers of social capital include the importance of local, state, and national culture (with a focus on the local culture and on rigorous, yet responsive educational systems) in fueling local economies (Hsung, Lin, & Breiger, 2009; Olaniran & Agnello, 2008; Radcliffe, 2006; Agnello, Sarria, & Slater, 1996). Also included in the international discourse on developing social capital is an imperative (a) to pay homage to indigenous peoples who have been on a sustainable track for centuries and (b) to call attention to the disruption that capitalism, globalization, and political strife cause these populations (Radcliffe, 2006). And yet, developing nations are intent on accommodating change, particularly with respect to providing the best possible education for their young by adopting a Western and often a United States model of schooling that promotes competition and capitalism, usually to the detriment of these groups.

The United States also faces serious problems with respect to ensuring optimal education through public schooling, one of the highest priorities of the nation. Assessment systems have been very flawed with regard to developing advanced critical thinking skills and dispositions, as well as moral and ethical aptitudes and applications (Apple & Jungck, 1990; Gilligan, Ward, Taylor, & Bardige, 1988; Kincheloe, 1995). Particularly with regard to the underclasses, new perspectives on state assessment systems in the U.S. reinforce the importance of working with teachers in classrooms to address the needs of students, many of whom lack the social capital of fluency in the dominant standard language (Collins, 1991). Newly prepared educators will be asked to build on students' existing language strengths, to evaluate knowledge separate from language, and to use assessment to better accommodate learning (National Research Council, 2010a, 2010b). Aligning the development of social capital to technological, financial, scientific, and other kinds of literacy holds promise for developing citizen workers who are prepared for intensified cycles of economic change.

Conclusion

Utilizing student propensity to network socially with technological tools, students and teachers should deliberate the social, economic, and political trends in society (Agnello, 2001). Orienting children and youth to think about their financial futures as part of the local, state, national, and international future builds a foundation upon which to consider personal goals, assets, and strategies for attaining stability in the financial arena, as well as how to think about providing drinking water and food for the world's population (Agnello & Lucey, 2008, 2010). Simulations of social and economic networking are feasible activities in all the curricular disciplines. Enhancing speech, theatrical, and kinesthetic abilities in learners, as well as the core disciplines of language arts, science, math, and social studies, engages future citizen workers in development of their social currency. They are then more adept at attaining success and asserting themselves in making sound decisions as they entertain career options, specialize, and take responsibility for financial decisions building and exercising their social capital as power. "Moving literacy from isolated skills to personal, cultural, and sociopolitical exercises of public life, students and teachers can rewrite the discourses of [financial] literacy"

(Agnello, 2001, p. 188). The importance of teacher learning in educational reform is critical (Smylie, 1996). The transformation of student potential into human and social capital relies on educators who understand the complexity of their mission and their call to ethical and moral undertakings as molders of future citizens.

DISCUSSION QUESTIONS

1. Explain why you agree or disagree with the following statement: It is critical to teach financial literacy in several subject areas in the curriculum.
2. Discuss which standard referenced in this chapter you think is most essential to (a) teaching financial literacy and (b) understanding financial literacy. If you choose the same standard for each part of this question, discuss why. If you choose a different standard for each part of this question, discuss why.
3. Why do you think financial literacy is not part of the secondary economics curriculum?
4. What kinds of social currency are possessed by your family and by the students in your neighborhood school?
5. How do the concepts of financial literacy and social currency overlap? What kinds of basic skills and understandings support learning in both areas?

MODEL LESSON

What Do I Want to Be When I Grow Up (and How Do I Plan to Get There?)

Suggested Grade Levels: 10, 11, 12

Objective:

(a) Students will consider the costs of their decisions as well as what kinds of opportunities they might seek

Related Standard:

SS.D.1.2.1. The student understands that all decisions involve opportunity costs and that making effective decisions involves considering the costs and the benefits associated with alternative choices.

Materials:

- Mix of songs that mention work, such as the following selections:
    - "She Works Hard for the Money" (Donna Summer)
    - "Five O'clock World" (The Vogues)
    - "Nine to Five" (Dolly Parton)
    - "Take this Job and Shove It" (Johnny Paycheck)
    - "Shiftwork" (Kenny Chesney)
- Handout from: http://www2.ed.gov/print/students/prep/college/consumerinfo/questions.html

Procedures:

(a) Opening Activities

1. Open the lesson with the following discussion question: How can you best prepare yourself for your future? Play the song(s).
2. To support the discussion question, have students consult the following website: http://www2.ed.gov/print/students/prep/college/consumerinfo/questions.html
3. Discuss: How will you determine what is necessary for you to prepare for your future career or profession?
4. Discuss: What resources are necessary to attend a university or some other path to career preparation?
5. Discuss: How will you obtain these resources?
6. Discuss: What impact will your social networks (such as family, friends, neighborhood, etc.) have on your ability to prepare for your future?
7. Discuss: Based on what it will cost to attain your goals, what kind of benefits will you have?

(b) Developmental Activities

1. Teacher pre- and postinterest and activity surveys can measure student development. Students and teachers brainstorm and discuss the following ideas and concepts. Pre- and post-activity questionnaires will be administered by the teacher to the students. (The questionnaires can be comprised of all of these concepts or contain only one).

- Consider choices—What are choices you have, make, and might make?
- Goal setting—How do you set goals?
- Time line—Discuss a schedule in which you have planned to achieve a goal and set forth time allocated to achieve the goal.
- Plan to achieve goals—What are your plans to achieve your goals?
- Plan to finance goals—How do you plan to finance your goals?

(c) Closing Activities

1. Students work individually or in groups.

    - Students present a budget detailing how they plan to finance their career or professional choices.
    - Students explain their choices verbally and in writing.

(d) Summary and Assessment

1. Consider the following two scenarios and discuss how financial literacy and social currency factor into each student's planning.

    Student A:

    I would really like to attend Island University in Hawaii. How fun it would be to study on the beach! I might get homesick though; I wonder how quickly I could fly across the country from Hawaii on a moment's notice and what would that roundtrip airfare cost—not to mention out-of-state tuition? I know I will need loans to help pay for college, no matter where I go. My family will help me pay, but I'm not sure how far I can get in Hawaii based on what I've made working at the local grocery store. I want to be an accountant, but Island University's focus is on marine life, not numbers. I could get a scholarship there if I had an interest in studying dolphins, but that doesn't help when I want to study numbers. Actually, I don't want to be *just* an accountant, I want to be a forensic accountant and work for the IRS. I bet with that level of knowledge and exposure to the IRS, I could get a job anywhere! That would be exciting … though after graduation, I will need to think about the loans I need to repay. I know it will be more (thanks to interest), and the longer it takes me to pay them off, the more I will pay. I am not happy about that. Would I be better off attending college closer to home?

Student B:

I don't see what the big deal is about college. I don't really want to attend, but everyone talks about it like I should. So maybe I should at least think about it. I guess that is the decision I need to make—do I want to attend college? I could get a job selling computers at the electronics store downtown, and I don't need a degree for that. There is a guy who started there and worked his way up pretty quickly because he does have a special certificate in computers, and the company helped pay for it. So if I got a loan, worked part-time, and went to college part-time, and with the company's help, I bet I could make it work. But it would take a little longer, which is okay, since I'd be getting experience from the store as well as from school. I was reading the brochure from this one local college, and they offer a lot of programs in computers; I'd have so many options of areas in which I could become an expert, and then the company would not want to lose me. So they would pay me more! And if they didn't, I could take my certification elsewhere and make more money. If I work really hard, I could even put some of that higher salary in a savings account and get interest on it, so I'd be saving even more for my future.

2. Pose the following discussion question: What are the important steps to take or factors to consider when planning for a career and/or profession?
3. Instruct students to design a checklist of things to do and/or think about as they plan a career/profession. Then individual students can evaluate themselves using the checklist—checking things they have already done and/or thought about.
4. Pose the following discussion question: What kinds of social capital (social, familial, neighborhood networks) do you have that do not have a monetary value but which is still very valuable?
5. Instruct individual students to create a summary table and/or creative poster that reveal community, family, and student assets.

REFERENCES

Agnello, M. F. (2001). *A postmodern literacy policy analysis*. New York, NY: Peter Lang.

Agnello, M. F., & Lucey, T. A. (2010). Citizenship and critical economic literacy: Vitalizing economics standards for system change. *Social Advocacy and Systems Change*, *2*(1), 11-43.

Agnello, M. F., & Lucey, T. (2008). More than "Water under the bridge": Initiating a critical democratic interpretation of economic education. *International Journal of Critical Pedagogy*, *1*(2), 105-128.

Agnello, M. F., Sarria, M., & Slater, R. (1996, Spring/Summer). Educating the poor: Literacy, educational leadership and democracy. *Research and Policy Report Series*, *4*(2). College Station: Race and Ethnic Studies Institute, Texas A & M University.

Apple, M., & Jungck, S. (1990). You don't have to be a teacher to teach this unit: Teaching, technology, and gender in the classroom. *American Educational Research Journal*, *27*(2), 227-251.

Bernanke, B. (2006). Financial literacy. Testimony before the Committee on Banking, Housing, and Urban Affairs of the U.S. Senate. Retrieved on December 9, 2011 http://www.federalreserve.gov/newsevents/testimony/bernanke20060523a.htm

Blokland, T., & Savage, M. (2008). *Networked urbanism: Social capital in the city*. Hampshire, England: Ashgate.

Bourdieu, P. (2008a). *Political interventions: Social science and political action*. New York, NY: Verso.

Bourdieu, P. (2008b). *The bachelors' ball: The crisis of peasant society in Bearn*. Chicago, IL: The University of Chicago Press.

Bourdieu, P. (1986). The forms of capital. In J. E. Richardson (Ed.), *Handbook of theory of research for the sociology of education* (pp. 241-58). New York, NY: Greenwood Press. (R. Nice, Trans.)

Bourdieu, P., & Paseron, J.C. (1979). *The inheritors: French students and their relation to culture*. Chicago, IL: The University of Chicago Press.

California Council on Economic Education. (2008). *CCEE quarterly update*. Retrieved from http://www.ccee.org/downloads/newsletters/CCEEQuartely_110708.pdf

Collins, J. (1991).Hegemonic practice: Literacy and standard language in public education. In C. Mitchell & K. Weiler (Eds.), *Rewriting literacy: Culture and the discourse of the other* (pp. 229-254). New York, NY: Bergin & Garvey.

Council for Economic Education. (2010). *Voluntary national content standards in economic*, (2nd ed.). Retrieved from http://www.councilforeconed.org/ea/standards/standards.pdf.

Daly, H.E. (2005). Economics in a full world. *Scientific American*, *293*(3), 100-107.

Excellence in Economic Education Act of 2004, 20 USC 7267). *No Child Left Behind*.

The Federal Reserve Bank of Minneapolis. (2011). *Economic Literacy Action Steps*. Retrieved on from http://www.minneapolisfed.org/news_events/events/

Freire, P. (1970). *Pedagogy of the oppressed*. New York, NY: Seabury Press.

Gilligan, C., Ward, J. V., Taylor, J. M., & Barige, B. (Eds.). (1988). *Mapping the moral domain: A contribution of women's thinking to psychological theory and education*. Cambridge, MA: Harvard University Press.

Gussow, J. D. (2001). *This organic life: Confessions of a suburban homesteader*. New York, NY: Chelsea Green.

Hsung, R. M., Lin, N., & Breiger, R. L. (Eds.)(2009). *Contexts of social capital: Social networks in markets, communities, and families*. New York, NY: Routledge.

Iowa State University Extension. (2010). *Extension News*. Retrieved from http://www.extension.iastate.edu/news/2010/may/080301.htm.

Jump$tart Coalition for Personal Financial Literacy. (2007a). *Jump$tart!: Financial smarts for students*. Retrieved from http://jumpstart.org/assets/files/standard_book-ALL.pdf.

Jump$tart Coalition for Personal Financial Literacy. (2007b). *National standards in K-12 personal finance education*, (3rd ed.). Retrieved from http://www.jumpstart.org/national-standards.html

Kincheloe, J. (1995). *Toil and trouble: Good work, smart workers, and the integration of academic and vocational education*. New York, NY: Peter Lang.

Lucey, T. A., & Maxwell, S. A. (2009). Preservice elementary teachers' confidence teaching about money. *Curriculum and Teaching Dialogue, 11*, 221-237.

National Research Council. (2010a). *Language, diversity, school learning, and closing achievement gaps: A workshop summary*. Washington DC: The National Academies Press.

National Research Council. (2010b). *Best practices for state assessment systems, Part 1: Summary of a Workshop*. Washington DC: The National Academies Press.

Networks Financial Institute at Indiana State University. (2007). *National K-12 financial literacy qualitative & quantitative research*. Retrieved from http://www.networksfinancialinstitute.org/SiteCollectionDocuments/NationalK12FinancialLiteracyStudy.pdf

Nisbet, R. (2002). *Conservatism: Dream and reality*. New Brunswick, NJ: Transaction.

Olaniran, B., & Agnello, M.F. (2008). Globalization, educational hegemony, and higher education. *Multicultural Education and Technology Journal*, *2*(2), 68-86.

Otter, D. (2010). Teacher attitudes and beliefs about teaching financial literacy. *Pollinate, the Teacher Financial Literacy Project*. Retrieved from http://www.pollinateproject.org/pdf/DanOtter_Pollinate_Research_June2010.pdf

Putnam, R. D. (2000). *Bowling alone: The collapse and revival of American community*. New York, NY: Simon and Schuster.

Radcliffe, S. A. (2006). *Culture and development in a globalizing world: Geographies, actors, and paradigms*. London: Routledge.

Smylie, M. A. (1996). From bureaucratic control to building human capital: The importance of teacher learning in education reform. *Educational Researcher, 25*(9), 9-11.

Tasch, W. (2008). *Investing as if food, farms, and fertility mattered*. New York, NY: Chelsea Green.

Vassallo, F. (2010). *France, social capital and political activism*. New York, NY: Palgrave Macmillan.

Way, W. L., & Holden, K. C. (2009). Teachers' background and capacity to teach personal finance: Results of a national study. *Journal of Financial Counseling and Planning, 20,* 64-78.

Wilhelm, W. J., & Chao, C. A. (2005). Personal financial literacy: Shaping education policy. *The Delta Pi Epsilon Journal, XLVII,* 20-35.

CHAPTER 13

USING ART AND COMMUNITY INVESTIGATION TO MOTIVATE PRESERVICE TEACHERS' LEARNING AND TEACHING OF SOCIAL AND ECONOMIC/ FINANCIAL JUSTICE ISSUES

Thomas A. Lucey and James D. Laney

Preparing preservice teachers (PSTs) who appreciate their roles as agents for social justice, in general, and economic/financial justice, in particular, represents a moral challenge. In an education climate that emphasizes mathematics and literacy, additional instructional strategies are needed to stimulate PST's deeper awareness and reconciliation of social justice's abstract and concrete elements.

In abstract, social justice represents a procedural conception that concerns the governance of personal interactions. There is a vision or ideal that largely eludes PSTs. While they grasp the theoretical conceptions argued in their preparation settings, such as Freire's Critical Pedagogy, their daily commonsense experiences provide a background of disinformation that requires modification to challenge the generally accepted traditional "grammar" of schooling (Tyack & Tobin, 1994). This education

Reframing Financial Literacy: Exploring the Value of Social Currency, pp. 253–277

structure employs hierarchical decision-making processes and perpetuates classist social patterns. Educators tend to shape student learning within this framework, rather than guiding student thinking that encourages social change. Teacher preparation programs motivate students by priming their interest in social change, but may limit these efforts to teaching of conceptions but not their applications.

In its concrete form, social justice represents a tangible concept on a personal scale. Individuals have opportunities to (a) experience vicarious and/or real-life situations or environments that may be socially unjust and (b) make choices about whether to address the injustices that may be present, immediate, or systemic. To accomplish these processes, educators should consider using instructional tools that enable students to (a) experience both the concrete and abstract nature of social justice and (b) realize its relevance to their professional practice. Reynolds and Brown (2010) conclude that the preparation of teachers for social justice represents an endeavor of introspection, collaboration, and foresight, thus indicating that the efforts needed to develop socially just teachers are involved and complex.

Nucci's (2001) differentiation between morality (behaviors related to human welfare) and social convention (normative behaviors that are agreed upon) conveys the importance of social justice to the education community by reaffirming the fallacies of conduct that derive from commonsense thinking. Behaviors that society accepts can both support or marginalize human welfare. Movement towards a socially just society requires the development of behaviors that support the welfare of all societal members, not just those of a favored or dominant culture or class of citizens. Patterns of social injustice, such as racism, classism, sexism, and ablism, involve regular patterns of judgment and ill behavior towards particular groups of people that society agrees upon. These actions do not benefit the victims; thus, they are not moral. A socially just or moral community values input from all societal stakeholders and equitably weighs the ideas of all.

Conceptions of a good citizen involve more depth than simple compliance with social rules and expectations. Westheimer and Kahne's (2004) explication of three good citizen models (i.e., responsible, participatory, and justice-oriented) illustrates the challenges of fostering a comprehensive approach to developing participatory democratic citizens in an environment that advocates adherence to a school system that purports itself as meeting everyone's needs. While schools are proficient at developing responsible and participatory citizens, efforts to prepare justice-oriented citizens are not surprisingly lacking. The systemic reform orientation of justice-oriented citizens threatens power hierarchies of schools and districts. As described by Tyack and Tobin (1994), existing K-12 learning structures (i.e., the lock-step, graded school) result from efforts to standardize student learning into a more efficient learning process. These graded structures and processes superseded the nongraded ones which respected individual students' development. Additional literature affirms that schools continue discrimination among students, as evidenced by patterns of re-segregation that yield disparate learning conditions among the haves and have-nots (Kozol, 2005; Oakes & Lipton, 2007; Orfield & Yun, 1999).

STATEMENT OF THE PROBLEM

The current study interprets how PSTs in social studies methods courses at two higher education institutions responded to a learning experience that was designed to stimulate their awareness and interest in teaching their students about social justice issues, in general, and economic/financial justice, in particular. The learning experience used art-based instructional tools to motivate PSTs community investigation of social justice issues and their development of age-appropriate lessons based on their findings.

Specifically, the current study describes the participants' (a) dispositions towards social and economic/financial justice and (b) confidence in their own arts-based teaching skills, inquiry-based teaching skills, and social justice teaching skills before, during, and after participating in a sample art-based lesson on social and economic/financial justice and a community inquiry project related to a social justice issue. A survey was administered to students at the beginning of the semester, after experiencing (as students) an art-based lesson that introduced general conceptions of social and economic/financial justice, and after their generation and demonstration (as teachers) of research-based lessons and social action plans related to particular community issues/challenges with social justice implications.

LITERATURE

There appears to be resistance on the part of many elementary PSTs to consider social justice topics beyond what society conventionally accepts (Lucey, 2008). The difficulty of teaching for social justice presents a multifaceted challenge (Cochran-Smith et al., 2008; McDonald, 2005; North, 2008). In a climate where a predominately White middle class teaching population lacks the financial, contextual, and cultural knowledge and skill base to effectively teach and fully empathize with underrepresented students, teacher educators are called upon to teach candidates ways to facilitate authentic classroom discussion and expression of social issues in order to foster respectful teaching-learning processes.

Preparation Issues

Recent works document PSTs' difficulties viewing social studies and democratic processes from a perspective of social action/engagement (Carr, 2008; Lucey, in press). They also illustrate the challenges that teacher educators face developing candidates who can recognize the need to value diversity within society and critically think about how their professional practice relates to associated dispositions. A problem in teaching for social justice involves the development of teacher preparation programs that recognize the need to address unjust dispositions that candidates may bring to their programs. Research literature suggests that candidates' views derive from a variety of contexts and experiences that may marginalize efforts to teach about social justice issues (Garmon, 2004, 2005; Villegas, 2007). In the views of these candidates, social justice issues may contradict "commonsense" (Tupper, 2008) ideas that represent readily accepted, but unsubstantiated, beliefs about social processes or cultural groups. As Tupper explains, "In North America, these stories tell us that: we live in a democracy; that universal citizenship exists, and that as citizens of a democracy, we enjoy the same rights and freedoms" (p. 73). Members of the dominant culture accept these social myths because they benefit from patterns of injustice that occur. Those who are dominated or oppressed realize the falseness of these views because their experiences with systemic sexism, racism, classism, and forms of discrimination invalidate such claims. Such beliefs serve to perpetuate structures designed to maintain the power of the dominant culture (Sleeter, 1994) and may remain unchecked unless candidates experience conditions that enable them to personally connect with the injustices and modify their behaviors to affect change (Trout, 2009). These conditions may be provided both within and outside the classroom.

The Role of Art in Teaching for Social Justice

Art, in all of its many forms, represents an appropriate instructional tool for fostering candidates' appreciation and empathy for social justice issues because of its ability to trigger affective and emotional responses among those who encounter it. This experience not only results through observation (such as attending a concert or visiting a gallery), it also occurs through discussion, creation, and display/performance of art works (Booth, 1997). Teacher-led debriefings or interactive discussions inform discussion participants about the social context behind works of art and the meanings intended by the music composer or visual artist. Through creation and display/performance, the student creators and observers learn about the tools and strategies artists use to express ideas about a topic. The displaying and sharing of original artworks on similar ideas/topics also serves to summarize and bring closure to the whole experience. The activities described above provide opportunities for discussing, developing, and sharing artworks that reflect social justice ideals.

The value of these strategies may extend to the promotion of learners' ability to relate art metaphors to society. Booth's (1997) view of art as a process of envisioning various metaphors in daily experiences conveys a vision of individuals realizing the various roles that are played out in society and how one relates himself/herself to those roles. This ideal is akin to a broad view of spirituality (Kessler, 2008; Lucey, in press), which interprets the spiritual self as representing a sense of social identity within the contexts of others, as opposed to a narrow, mystical interpretation. Gibson (2010) calls for a holistic interpretation of nature and the environment, rather than a human-centered interpretation. In other words, humans should recognize a balance of place within the global environment, learning to care for, rather than control it. Instructional use of art may serve as a vehicle for stimulating awareness of this responsibility among educators.

In a sense, these new visions of society harken back to representations of the Homeric period (Macintyre, 1984), in which human existence was viewed as a story that one inhabited. The challenge of developing candidates who teach for social justice involves both prompting them to develop an artistic vision of society and the artistic tools for changing that vision into one of mutual respect that benefits all participants.

Service Learning

Getting students to acknowledge this responsibility requires facilitation of their immersion in experiences that prompt reflection on mutual support within a community. According to Cuban and Anderson (2007), the manner by which a participant views a service learning experience relates to the project's outcomes. When providing students with community mentors, the manner by which the mentor interprets his or her role in regard to the student and project bears greatly on the way the student may respond to the experience (Swaminathan, 2007). Planning the community experience requires that the teacher or instructor consider both the structure of the assignment and the dispositions of community liaisons with which students will interact. Such decisions may determine whether participants view their community experiences through a justice-orientation, rather than a responsible or participatory lens (Westheimer & Kahne, 2004).

The study described herein conveys the attitudes towards social justice and related teaching strategies of PSTs as they progress through their undergraduate social studies methods courses. The project featured (a) sample lessons that used works of art as organizing centers for introducing social-justice related ideas, (b) a community inquiry project that prompted their research and investigation of solutions to social injustices, and (c) development of original lesson plans and social action plans on social-justice-related issues. It provided opportunities for participants to (a) critically contemplate the ways that their communities respond to unjust social conditions and (b) creatively develop educational experiences for elementary and middle school students to learn about social justice and social action.

RESEARCH QUESTIONS

The research questions for the study were as follows: (1) Do PSTs' dispositions towards social and economic/financial justice improve/change as they experience arts-based instruction and a community inquiry project centered on social and financial/economic justice issues? (2) At the end of the study, how did the PST participants perceive art as a content vehicle for teaching about social and economic/financial justice? (3) At the end of the study, how did the PSTs perceive the teacher's role in teaching for social justice and social action?

METHODOLOGY

Sample

The study involved three sections of undergraduate social studies methods courses at two universities. One elementary social studies methods course was taught at a southern suburban institution, and two sections of a middle-level social studies methods course were taught at a Midwestern institution in a midsized community. There were 77 students within the three course sections of which 49 completed all three surveys and 27 completed all multiple choice items across all three administrations.

Instrument

The *Survey of Pre-service Teachers' Social Justice, Art, and Music Attitudes* was developed for this study by the two authors. It consisted of 59 items that interpreted respondents' agreement with statements that concerned (a) their confidence in teaching using inquiry, (b) their confidence in teaching using art-based activities, (c) their confidence in teaching about social justice, (d) their own personal economic/financial justice dispositions, (e) their own personal social justice dispositions, and (f) their own personal social justice teaching dispositions. Interitem correlation alphas during the first administration of the subscales presented below ranged from .583 (Inquiry and Social Justice Teaching Confidence) to .910 (Social Justice Dispositions). The alphas for the items that comprised the inquiry subscale increased to .91 and .98 during the second and third administrations, respectively. Similarly, the alphas for the items that comprised the Social Justice Teaching Confidence subscale increased to .70 and .73 during the second and third administrations, respectively.

The instrument also contained two open response items. The first asked respondents for their "thoughts about the effectiveness of art forms as content vehicles for exploring social issues." The second sought information about teachers' "responsibilities for prompting their students' community involvement."

Procedure

The instructional phase of this research project consisted of two parts. The first part employed three arts-related activities to stimulate PSTs' awareness of and interest in diversity-related and social justice-related issues/problems. The three activities were Cultural Spaces (McCarter, 1994), Self as Other (Pedelty, 2001), and a third activity that used the Discipline-Based Arts Education approach (Laney, 1996).

In the third activity, described in detail in Lucey and Laney (2009), the instructors played two pieces of music. For this study, the lesson employed "This Land Is Your Land," by Guthrie (1940/1997) and "Sacrificial Culture," by Lamm and Van Eps (1999), which are songs that feature content related to economic/financial diversity and economic/financial injustices. Each musical work was paired with an art image that served to visually interpret the music. The lesson used a picture of George Segal's "The Breadline," a bronze sculpture that depicts several men waiting for handouts at a soup kitchen, as the image for Guthrie's song. The activity also employed Francis Bacon's "Lying Figure" (1966), a modernistic painting of a grotesque, suffering figure on a table, as the partner work for Lamm and Van Eps' song. The Guthrie/Segal pairing presented the social justice concept in a literal and concrete way, whereas the Lamm and Van Eps/Bacon pairing constituted a much more interpretive, symbolic, and abstract representation.

As each song played in the third activity, the instructor distributed the song's lyrics to his students. After discussing the song and artwork using questions/tasks from three art disciplines (art history, art criticism, and aesthetics) and providing background information on the artworks and artists, the instructors divided their students into small groups to make art (i.e., to compose and perform an original song about a selected social justice issue and then create and display a supporting work of visual art). In other words, the students were asked to produce their own works of art that constituted vehicles of social protest against some perceived social injustice.

This activity provided a classroom motivator for students' pursuit of a longer-term community inquiry project. For this long-term project, students (a) selected a social issue related to social injustice for their group to investigate, (b) interviewed two community leaders about the problem and their recommendations for its solution, (c) obtained published statistics related to the conditions causing the problem, (d) collaborated online with students in other classes who were researching the same problem, and (e) developed an action plan (i.e., an upper elementary or middle school lesson plan featuring arts integration and a social action follow-up activity) based on their findings. The project culminated with demonstrations of classroom activities that used works of art and the Discipline-based Art Education approach for promoting upper elementary and middle school students' (1) understanding of social issues/problems relating to social justice and (2) participation in social action in response to identified social injustices.

The students completed the *Survey of Pre-service Teachers' Social Justice, Art, and Music Attitudes* three times during the project—at the outset of the semester, at the conclusion of the instructor's sample lesson based on the Discipline-based art education model, and at the conclusion of the class meeting in which research findings and student-generated instructional activities were shared with all other students in the class.

Analysis

The researchers performed both quantitative and qualitative analyses of data. Because of the convenience nature of the sample, responses to items formatted in a Likert-style scale were limited to descriptive analysis.

Responses to the two open response items were coded for observed patterns. Themes in these patterns were explored between and within survey administrations.

RESULTS

This section provides the findings from the study and consists of two parts. The first part provides descriptive mean statistics that convey the participants' confidence in the use of inquiry and art-based lessons over the three administrations of the survey. It also interprets changes in dispositions related to social justice, inquiry, and arts-based teaching/learning. The second section provides an analysis of changes in comments that respondents made about their arts-based teaching/learning experiences with social justice and about their ideas concerning a teacher's responsibility for teaching about social justice.

Confidence and Dispositions

Table 13.1 shows the results of the three survey administrations, with *lower* numbers on the 5-point Likert scale indicative of *better* confidence or dispositions. By the end of the study, respondents indicated that they had more confidence in teaching with inquiry processes and in using art within their teaching. They also expressed more confidence in teaching about social justice. Specifically, respondents' confidence in teaching with art increased noticeably over all three administrations of the survey. Confidence in teaching with inquiry increased similarly to that of teaching with art; however, the increase was less pronounced because respondents initially had a fairly high level of confidence in teaching with inquiry. Confidence in teaching about social justice increased between the first two survey administrations; however, it did not change between the second and third survey administrations.

Social justice dispositions and social justice teaching dispositions generally improved from the first to second survey administrations, but declined between the second and third administrations of the survey (especially with respect to social justice teaching disposition, with dispositions returning to just above the starting level). Economic/financial justice dispositions stayed about the same from the first to the second survey administration, but declined by the third survey administration.

Table 13.1. Mean Confidence Teaching Art, Inquiry and Social Justice and Mean Dispositions Towards Social Justice, Economic Justice, and Teaching Social Justice (1 = Strongly Agree; 5 = Strongly Disagree)

	Adm. 1	*Adm. 2*	*Adm. 3*
Confidence Teaching Inquiry	2.49	2.01	1.88
Confidence Teaching Art	2.90	2.17	1.78
Confidence Teaching Social Justice	2.50	2.15	2.15
Social Justice Dispositions	1.90	1.77	1.83
Economic/Financial Justice Dispositions	2.13	2.12	2.24
Social Justice Teaching Disposition	2.20	1.91	1.99

Effectiveness of Art and Responsibility for Teaching About Social Justice

The second part of the survey contained two open-response items. This section describes the patterns of responses among those who provided responses to the questions during all three survey administrations.

Effectiveness of art forms as content vehicles for exploring social issues. Respondents generally affirmed the worth of these tools throughout the three administrations. For example, one student initially reflected "Art reflects life, so a lot of art tells a story or pertains to important historical eras. I believe using it as a content vehicle will lead to higher levels of thinking." For the last survey administration, the same student wrote "I think they are great because each piece of artwork has so much to say about the time when it was created. It also conveys social issues, depending on the art work." This student initially possessed a great appreciation for art, which was reinforced through the course activities and project.

One respondent did not initially express positive views of art use. S/he disclosed, "I'm not sure" at the first survey administration. This uncertainty dissipated to an acknowledgement of the importance by the time of the second survey administration; however, at the third administration the student's position was reversed, "I thought they were okay, but not that useful."

Some students conditioned their appreciation with each successive administration. During the final administration, several respondents attributed the effectiveness of art to the quality of the planned lesson and asserted that art should not be overly emphasized. For example, one student was very positive about art use at the beginning of the course, stating that "Art is useful to explore social issues because you can examine art from different social statuses." This appreciation was also present after the Discipline-Based Art Education Model demonstration: "Art is a good way to explore social issues, because it can represent different social circumstances." After completion of the community inquiry project and related lesson demonstration, the disposition was tepid: "Art is okay, but should not be the focus of a social studies class."

Similarly, another student initially expressed positive impressions, "I think art forms help people to see things they aren't familiar with." These feelings were expanded upon during the second administration: "Art forms bring to light many social issues that students may not think about every day. They provide a window to look through and learn about other cultures and time periods that students may not experience otherwise." The final administration yielded a less encouraging response: "Art forms are good stimulations for exploration; however, I don't think they should be the main content vehicles."

Social justice and social action teaching responsibilities. Comments about teachers' responsibilities in teaching for social justice and social action changed somewhat during the three survey administrations. Many respondents affirmed these responsibilities during all three administrations. For example, one student initially commented as follows:

> I believe teachers are in a place to make a real difference. I believe that teaching children the importance of being a positive community participant is one of the best ways to start making a difference in the social issues of today. I also feel this helps give a sense of self-worth to people, and I think children need all of that they can get.

This student realizes the teacher's power to shape student development and recognizes a responsibility for using that influence to affect just communities. This disposition was also evident during the second administration, during which s/he commented, "I believe the teacher is a positive role model in all children's eyes, and so they should do everything in their power to develop active members of society." During the final survey, the message was concise, yet the disposition the same: "I believe they are in a place to make a difference, and they should."

Another student initially reflected, "teachers have a responsibility to get students motivated to help in communities. This will make the community better, the student and the school." During the second administration, a similar response occurred: "a teacher should recommend that students get involved in their communities. It will help students." The final reflection was nearly identical: "It is important to have teachers get students involved in their community. It will help them in the future."

Some students expanded their views of responsibilities as the project progressed; for example, one respondent initially commented,

> Teachers should make children aware of who they are as individuals and what effect they have in their community. Teachers should be responsible for offering chances for their students to be involved in their community. I feel you should create a classroom community so children can see how it is to be a part of a grander scheme.

This student clearly possesses a pro-social disposition that advocates teacher's efforts to build students' sense of identity through development of healthy community. During the second administration, this position changed to a broader sense of community responsibility: "I believe teachers have a lot of responsibility to at least make their students and parents aware of community involvement opportunities so that they may know what's going on." The position was affirmed during the third administration: "Teachers are probably the second (or first) most important person for getting children involved in their communities."

Similarly, another respondent reflected, "I believe teachers have a great responsibility in promoting their students' community involvement. Teachers should be examples of active community members and inspire their students to do the same." This assertion was followed by the second survey administration comment: "I think teachers share the majority of the prompting, but parents should be responsible, too." The third survey administration comment, "Teachers should be a major influence on this issue to their students," reaffirms the initial disposition.

Those who considered responsibilities for teaching about social justice as being supplemental to other areas or as optional were more elaborate in their responses with each survey administration. For example, one student remarked, "Teachers can present opportunities for community involvement, but beyond that there lie few responsibilities." During the second administration, this position was reaffirmed, "I think that they can discuss it and encourage it, but it should not be a responsibility." Finally, the student commented, "Responsibility falls on extracurricular duties or another class based on being a citizen (maybe a good citizen/model citizen class) rather than grouped into regular curriculum." Over the project, this student's positions about teaching and social justice became more adverse.

DISCUSSION

While quantitative data indicate that PSTs' confidence in their own art-based and inquiry-oriented teaching skills increased over the three survey administrations, the qualitative analysis suggests that the experience also prompted solidification of positive views/perceptions concerning art-based teaching and social justice teaching. Although many respondents appeared initially receptive to the experience, the prolonged or recurring exposure to art and social justice themes challenged the patience of some students.

This situation may reflect a resistance on the part of students to experiencing or having repeated exposure to new ideas and/or sensitive social issues. It may relate to literature that concerns the commonsense (Tupper, 2008) and dispositions (Garmon, 2004, 2005; Villegas, 2007) that students bring into programs and their resistance to being inundated with new instructional ideas. Through this assignment, students experienced repeated exposure to art-based instruction and social justice issues, perhaps to the point of over-saturation. While coursework included various social studies topics/issues, the social justice theme was pervasive throughout the course. Other art forms and inquiry-based instructional methods were employed in the course to broaden views of other social studies areas and the interconnectedness of social science disciplines. For example, a simulation of early nineteenth century voluntary and involuntary immigrations to the United States conveyed the relationships between citizenship, economics, and geography, and prompted students to consider the bias of textbook immigration coverage. By modeling art-based strategies that invited student exploration of broad social understandings, the course also prompted them to reconsider some of the social "facts" to which they had become accustomed.

These results augment Lucey's (2008) report that teacher candidates appreciate the conceptual view of social justice and the advocating of its general ideals (e.g., equality and fairness for all), but resist exploring the systemic causes of and/or possible solutions to social injustices that require them to rethink their own lifestyles. Lucey's findings derived from a lesson that only involved music, rather than visual and music combinations. In addition, the current study contained a research (i.e. community inquiry) component that Lucey's study did not. The current findings indicate that art-based class discussions, supplemented by community research, may affirm the surface appreciation for social justice conceptions, but they may also reinforce some candidates' negative core dispositions. Additional research is needed to determine how these activities and projects may be used to change student attitudes in more dramatic, positive, and permanent ways.

In general, PST participants improved their dispositions towards social justice and social justice teaching by the end of the study. On the other hand, dispositions towards economic/financial justice declined somewhat by the end of the study. An explanation for this finding may be found in some anecdotal evidence from instructors' observations of students in the lesson-generation phase of the project. Students who were asked to investigate and write lessons about social justice issues related to economic/financial topics (e.g., homelessness or generational poverty) tended to express the greatest discomfort and uncertainty with their assigned tasks. They also required the most instructor-assistance in coming up with content and age-appropriate works of art and activity ideas for their original lesson plans and social action plans.

Limitations. This study employed a convenience sample from two institutions, and the researchers selected the activity, music, and images. The third survey administration at one institution occurred in a class that combined two sections. The merging of the two sections for this meeting allowed members of each section to see each other's work, but the additional time needed to demonstrate lessons caused the meeting to exceed the scheduled time and reduced the number of students who completed the survey. Conducting this research using different art/music pairings in the model lesson could influence patterns of student interest and/or receptiveness to the material. Alternative timings of survey administrations could also prompt different results

Conclusion

This study found that a convenience sample of PSTs gained more confidence in using art and inquiry processes by experiencing a sample lesson focused on Discipline-based Art Education model (Laney, 1996) and by participating in a related community investigation project. Positive dispositions towards (a) the use of art and (b) teachers' responsibilities in teaching for social justice and social action appeared to intensify somewhat during the project, although some individual students' negative dispositions seemed to be reinforced.

The importance of art as an instructional tool to prompt affective learning with PSTs cannot be denied; perhaps the question to consider relates to what emotions the art triggers and the relationship of classroom instruction and content to patterns of individual emotions. If teacher education involves a process of preparing teachers to build just classroom communities, respect for dispositions that are antithetical to social injustices should be promoted. Social justice involves a process of respecting all people. The basis of this respect lies in an acknowledgement that behavioral decisions are driven by fate of origin and not from unbridled freedom of will. To bring about these social conditions, classrooms should provide opportunities for students to discuss social issues, acknowledge alternative viewpoints, examine the prompting contexts, and derive appropriate solutions that respect the needs of all community stakeholders. Works of art evoke emotional responses and offer great potential as content vehicles for introducing PSTs and elementary/middle school students to concepts of social and economic/financial justice, while community inquiry holds promise for translating social justice ideals into social action. The modeling of the just community should begin in the school classroom.

DISCUSSION QUESTIONS

1. What emotions do you feel when you experience or create art/music? How do these emotions relate to your perceived artistic/musical ability? What art/music genre do you value? To what extent do your artistic/musical values relate to "common sense" tastes in art/music?
2. To what extent was community part of your teaching or learning? How was your relationship with community defined through these processes?
3. Consider the three citizen types described by Westheimer and Kahne (2004). What are some examples of how art might be used to foster each of the three citizen types that these researchers mention (i.e. responsible, participatory, and justice-oriented)?
4. What ideas, concepts, or issues within financial education lend themselves to visual and/or musical representation? What popular or well-known songs or visual works of art can you think of that could be used as content vehicles for teaching about financial education topics?
5. What is economic/financial justice? What economic/financial injustices exist within today's society? What traditional financial education topics relate to such injustices?

MODEL LESSON

Rich Man, Poor Man

Suggested Grade Levels: Grades 4-8 (and above)

Objectives:

(a) To consider reasons why some people are rich and others poor.
(b) To differentiate between planned and market economies.

(c) To recognize public transportation as a social and economic/financial justice issue.
(d) To understand the rationale for governments to sometimes intervene and modify the what-to-produce and for-whom-to-produce decisions in a market economy.
(e) To research/compute the impact of transportation costs on one's personal financial budget.
(f) To realize citizens' right to devise and initiate action that counters unjust social conditions.

Related Standards:

Jump$tart National Standards in K–12 Personal Finance Education

Financial Responsibility and Decision Making

Standard 2: Find and evaluate financial information from a variety of sources.

Standard 4: Make financial decisions by systematically considering alternatives and consequences.

Income and Careers

Standard 1: Explore career options.

Standard 2: Identify sources of personal income.

Standard 3: Describe factors affecting take-home pay.

Planning and Money Management

Standard 1: Develop a plan for spending and saving.

Standard 5: Consider charitable giving

Materials:

- Dorothea Lange's photograph "Towards Los Angeles, California" (http://www.flickr.com/photos/library_of_congress/3549663710).
- Background information on Dorothea Lange and her photographs (http://myhero.com/myhero/hero.asp?hero=d_lange).

- Bob Miller's song lyrics for "The Rich Man and the Poor Man" (http://www.folkarchive.de/rich.html).
- Recording of Bob Miller's song "The Rich Man and the Poor Man" (http://www.rhapsody.com/bob-miller).
- Blog on public transportation as a social and economic/financial justice issue (http://worldsofmegraves.wordpress.com/2010/11/12/public-transportation-social-justice-one-nation).

Teacher References:

- Cohen, R. D., & Samuelson, D. (1996). *Songs for political action.* Bear Family Records, p. 64.
- Kourilsky, M. L. (1996). *Economics: Debriefing teachable moments.* Kansas City, Missouri: Ewing Marion Kauffman Foundation, pp. 99-103.
- Stevens, R. J., & Fogel, J. A. (2009). Comparing FSA photographs by Ben Shahn: A lesson in media literacy. *Middle Level Learning: Supplement to National Council for the Social Studies Publications, 35*(May/June), 2-9.

Procedures

(a) Opening Activities (based on ideas from Stevens & Fogel, 2009):

1. Teacher tells students that they are going to use their observational and inference-making skills to analyze a photograph.
2. Show the students Dorothea Lange's photograph entitled "Towards Los Angeles, California" (http://www.flickr.com/photos/library_of_congress/3549663710). The photograph depicts two migrant works carrying suitcases and walking along a remote, deserted section of highway. The photograph also shows a billboard in the distance with a picture of a middle-class gentleman riding in a train; the billboard reads, "Next time try the train. Relax. Southern Pacific." Ask students to make a three-column chart of the people, objects, and activities that they readily observe in the photograph.
3. Ask students to make inferences about the photograph based on the following questions: (1) When and where was the photograph taken? (2) What are the people in the photograph doing? Why? (3) Why do you think the photograph was taken?
4. For the purpose of inquiry, ask students to list any unanswered questions they have about the photograph.

5. Provide students with background information (or ask students to research background information) about Dorothea Lange, her photographs, and the Great Depression/Dust Bowl era (using http://www.myhero.com/myhero.asp?hero=d_lange and other resources).
6. Ask students to compare the information provided/found with their original inferences about the photograph. Which inferences were supported/rejected?
7. Based on the information provided/found, ask students to answer the following questions: (1) Who was Dorothea Lange? (2) For whom was Dorothea Lange working? (3) What mood/message was Dorothea Lange trying to communicate in "Towards Los Angeles, California"? What artistic/compositional elements help convey that mood/message? (4) If you could compose a new title for Dorothea Lange's photograph, what would it be?
8. Distribute the lyrics of Bob Miller's 1932 humorous protest song "The Rich Man and the Poor Man" (http://www.fokarchive.de/rich.html; Cohen & Samuelson (1996, p. 64).

> There's just two kind of people, the sinner and the saint;
> There's one that gets and always got while the other poor one ain't.
> Oh, the rich man drives his Lincoln past the red light with a grin,
> And the poor man follows right behind in his little hunk of tin.
> There's a motorcycle copper following upon their trail;
> Oh, the rich man tears his ticket, but the poor man goes to jail.
>
> Oh, the rich man takes the high road anywhere that he may go,
> But when the poor man's travelin' he must always take the low.
> So if you're rich you'll travel snug as peas are in the pod;
> Oh, the rich man rides a cushion and the poor man rides the rods.
>
> Oh, the rich man when he's ailing stays at home and calls the doc,
> But the poor man has to go to work, be in time to punch a clock.
> The rich man takes his medicine, has his doctors and his nurse;
> So the rich man he gets better but the poor man he gets worse!
>
> Oh, the rich man steals a million from the bank that he controls,
> While the poor man steals a loaf of bread or a penny's worth of rolls. They take them to the courthouse, one is laughing, one's in tears;
> Oh, the rich man gets an apology while the poor man gets ten years!

Oh, the rich man gets a lawyer and the lawyer pleads his case,
While the poor man asks for sympathy but of that there is now trace.
So if you're rich don't worry but the poor must give up hope;
Oh, the rich man gets acquitted while the poor man gets the rope!

Oh, the rich man when he kicks off has a casket made of gold,
While the poor man has a wooden box and his grave looks mighty cold.
The rich man gets a sermon but here's one thing that's sure,
When the rich man takes that last long ride he's as much dead as the poor!

9. Play Miller's song (http://www.rhapsody.com/bob-miller) as you show Dorothea Lange's "Towards Los Angeles, California." Ask students to compare the messages of the song and photograph. Is the song meant to be funning, serious, or both? What is its purpose?

(b) Developmental Activities

1. Lead a guided discussion using the following questions: (1) Why are some people rich and others poor? (2) Are all wealthy people smart and good? Are all poor people less intelligent and less deserving? If so, why? If not, why not? (3) How should the resources of a country be distributed? Equally? Or in accordance with each individual's efforts at making it on his/her own? (Kourilsky, 1996).
2. Provide students with information on alternative economic systems (i.e. a planned economy versus a market economy). Explain that in a *market system* those individuals who own resources that are most in demand will have the highest incomes. The economic decisions of what to produce, how to produce, and for whom to produce are determined by the interaction of producers (suppliers) and consumers (demanders). *Private property, competition, and consumer sovereignty* are key sub-concepts in a market-system model (Kourilsky, 1996). Ask students to brainstorm and research jobs that are high-paying versus low-paying and explain why some people have greater incomes than others. Then ask students to reflect on future job possibilities for themselves. What special knowledge/skills and education/training are needed for each of these jobs?
3. Explain that in a *planned economy* scarce resources or productive means are held in common, with one planner or a group of plan-

ners making the economic decisions of what to produce, how to produce, and for whom to produce. Planner decisions can be made based on self-interest or the wants of the population as a whole.

4. As Kourilsky (1996) suggests, have students role play a planned economy by pretending each class member owns an equal portion of the tissue paper in the classroom art supply cupboard. It is the opinion of one class member that the tissue paper should be used for producing colorful, laminated bottles. Whom must that individual convince? How could that individual get what s/he wants? What process will the class use in making the for-whom-to-produce decision? Also have the students role play a market economy. Pretend that one individual student in the class privately owns several pieces of tissue paper. S/he wants to use the paper for producing colorful, laminated bottles. Whom must that individual convince? How will s/he go about deciding how to allocate the finished laminated bottles? Ultimately, what will determine the amount of money s/he makes? To what extent do you think that these decisions are fair or just?
5. Define the terms *social justice* and *economic/financial justice* for the students. Ask students how Dorothea Lange's "Towards Los Angeles, California" and Bob Miller's "The Rich Man and the Poor Man" relate to these concepts. Point out that public transportation constitutes a social and economic/financial justice issue. Because of inadequate public transportation, many people who are trying to get a job may not be able to get to that job. Because of racism, economic injustice, and/or other historic factors, some public transportation systems may not adequately meet the needs of all its citizens, especially low-income, minority, and other under-represented groups such as the handicapped, young, and elderly. (For more details on this often over-looked aspect of social and economic/financial justice, see the following blog site: http://worldsofmegraves.wordpress.com/2010/11/12/public-transportation-social-justice-one-nation/.)
6. Inform the students that in a market economy, as we have in this country, governments sometimes modify the what-to-produce and for-whom-to-produce decisions (Kourilsky, 1996); for example, a government may choose to provide convenient and affordable public transportation for all its citizens. To what extent does public transportation affect the life choices of those who depend on it? What choice in medical care does a person who depends on public transportation have? Ask students to describe other ways

in which governments and or individuals/groups in the private sector could help poor people such as those depicted in Lange's photograph and Miller's song.

(c) Closing Activities

1. Direct students to generate their own visual works of art and/or songs that have themes similar to Lange's "Towards Los Angeles, California" and Miller's "The Rich Man and the Poor Man." Ask students to select popular, modern-day songs to go with Lange's photograph and/or with their own visual works of art; then have them explain/defend their choices. As an example, note that the drawing (Figure 13.1) at the end of this chapter, entitled "Two Different Lives," was produced by a high school student. The student wrote the following explanation of her visual work of art and choice of song:

   > I think this song "Fireworks" by Katy Perry relates to my picture. It is saying everyone is special in [his/her] own way, and no one is more important than anyone else. Just because someone has less or more money than someone else doesn't mean they should be treated [as] lower or higher class. Each person is [his/her] own person and should be loved for who [s/he is].
   >
   > Social justice is about every single person getting the same rights and payment. This really hasn't ever been true. In history, so many people have unequal rights. Some examples are during World War [II]. African Americans and Mexican Americans had to go into the war. Many didn't agree because they didn't have their own rights and were going to go take a bullet for someone [else's] freedom. It wasn't [only] that occasion, too; there were a lot of times [since] the world began we have had social justice issue problems.
   >
   > So my picture shows one [person's] hand with money and [a] credit card in another [person's hand]. It shows one person with a smaller living and another person with more money. It represents that the person with more money doesn't have to carry or save cash like the other person. This shows that social justice is needed, but not everyone can see that because they are caught up with everything else in their life.

2. Assign each student the task of interviewing at least one parent to find out how the parent gets to work, how much the transportation costs, and what the parent's monthly/yearly income is. Have the students calculate the transportation-to-work costs for each

week, month, and year. What percentage of the parent's income do these costs represent? What implications does this information have for personal/family budgetary planning? How might your lifestyle change if a different percentage of your parents' income was devoted to transportation?

3. Instruct students to research public transportation issues/problems in the local area. What are the types of public transportation that exist in your communities? To what extent is this situation related to social and/or economic/financial justice? Is there a need for social action? What is government doing? What are private individuals/groups doing? Is there anything meaningful that the students could do (e.g., writing letters to government officials and/or creating an advertising campaign to promote adoption of public-transit-related legislation or to promote public awareness of the availability and/or benefits of convenient, safe, and affordable public transit)?
4. Have students devise and implement an appropriate social action project in response to an identified social issue/problem. During the developmental process, prompt students to envision responsible, participatory, or justice-oriented responses to the situation. What are the risks and rewards of each alternative? Who benefits from each solution and who pays the cost? What do their discussions tell about why social justice may be elusive? How might efforts for social justice change to overcome this elusiveness?

(d) Summary and Assessment

1. Observe students' comments during guided, in-class discussions. Did the students grasp the concepts of what makes people rich versus what makes people poor, high-paying versus low-paying jobs, planned versus market economy, public transportation as a social and/or economic/financial justice issue, etc.?
2. Evaluate students' visual and/or musical works of art. Were students able to generate art products that reflected the concepts taught? Were students able to correctly describe, orally or in writing, the concepts behind their art products?
3. Evaluate students' research on transportation-to-work costs as a budgetary consideration. Were students able to correctly identify and calculate these costs and to describe the impact on the personal/family budget?

Figure 13.1. Two different lives.

4. Debrief students on their social action efforts. Did their efforts have any noticeable, measureable impact? What evidence can students cite?

REFERENCES

Bacon, F. (1966). *Lying figure* (Painting).

Booth, E. (1997). *The everyday work of art.* Naperville, IL: Sourcebooks.

Carr, P. (2008). Educators and education for democracy: Moving beyond "thin" democracy. *Interamerican Journal of Education for Democracy, 1*(2), 147-165.

Cochran-Smith, M., Shakman, K., Jong, C., Terrell, D. G., Barnatt, J., & McQuillan, P. (2009). Good and just teaching: The case for social justice in teacher education. *American Journal of Education, 115*, 347-377.

Cuban, S., & Anderson, J. B. (2007). Where's the justice in service learning? Institutionalizing service-learning from a social justice perspective at a Jesuit university. *Equity and Excellence in Education, 40*(2), 144-155.

Garmon, M. A. (2004). Changing pre-service teachers' attitudes/beliefs about diversity: What are the critical factors? *Journal of Teacher Education, 55*(3), 201-213.

Garmon, M. A. (2005). Six key factors for changing pre-service teachers' attitudes/beliefs about diversity. *Educational Studies, 38*(3), 275-286.

Gibson, J. W. (2010). *A reenchanted world: The quest for a new kinship with nature*. New York, NY: Metropolitan Books/Henry Holt and Company

Guthrie, W. (1997). This land is your land, *This Land Is Your Land: The Asch Recordings, Vol. 1* [CD]. Washington, DC: Smithsonian Folkways. (Original work published in 1940)

Kessler, R., (with Fink, C.) (2008). Education for integrity: Connection, compassion, and character. In L. P. Nucci & D. Narvaez (Eds.), *Handbook of moral and character education* (pp. 432- 456). New York, NY: Routledge.

Kozol, J. (2005). *The shame of the nation. The restoration of apartheid schooling in America*. New York, NY: Crown.

Lamm, R., & Eps, J. V. (1999). Sacrificial culture. *In My Head* [CD]. New York, NY: Mystic Music & Entertainment.

Laney, J. (1996). Developing your own integrated art-social studies lessons using the discipline-based art education model. *Children's Social and Economics Education, 1*(1), 89-91.

Lucey, T. A. (2008). Fence sitting: Pre-service teachers' agreement with tenets of economic responsibilities and social justice. In C. J. Craig & L. F. Deretchin (Eds.), *Imagining a renaissance in teacher education: Teacher education yearbook XVI* (pp. 237-251). Lanham, MD: Rowman & Littlefield.

Lucey, T. A. (in press). Conceptions of democratic essence: Pre-service teachers' interpretations of democratic principles and their connections to social justice, economic class, and spirituality/religion. D. Zyngier & P. Carr (Eds.), *Can education make a difference? Experimenting with, and experiencing democracy in education.* Charlotte, NC: Information Age Publishing.

Lucey, T. A., & Laney, J. D. (2009). This Land Was Made for You and Me: Teaching the concept of social justice in the elementary and middle school grades. *The Social Studies, 100*(6), 260-272.

MacIntyre, A. (1984). *After virtue* (2nd ed.). Notre Dame, IN: Notre Dame Press.

McCarter, R. (1994). *Cultural spaces*. Retrieved from http://www.eduref.org/cgi-bin/printlessons.cgi/Virtual/Lessons/Social_Studies/Sociology/SOC0006.html

McDonald, M. A. (2005). The integration of social justice in teacher education: Dimensions of prospective teachers' opportunities to learn. *Journal of Teacher Education, 56*(6), 418-435.

North, C. E. (2008). What is all this talk about "social justice"? Mapping the terrain of education's latest catchphrase. *Teachers College Record, 110*(6), 1182-1126.

Nucci, L. P. (2001). *Education in the moral domain*. Cambridge, England: Cambridge University Press.

Orfield, G., & Yun, J. T. (1999). *Resegregation in American schools*. Retrieved from http://civilrightsproject.ucla.edu/research/k-12-education/integration-and-diversity/resegregation-in-american-schools/orfiled-resegregation-in-american-schools-1999.pdf

Oakes, J., & Lipton, M. (2007). *Teaching to change the world* (3rd ed.). New York, NY: McGraw-Hill.

Pedelty, M. (2001). Self as other: An intercultural performance exercise. *Multicultural Education, 8*(3), 29-32.

Reynolds, R., & Brown, J. (2010). Social justice and school linkages in teacher education programmes. *European Journal of Teacher Education, 33*(4), 405-419.

Sleeter, C. E. (1994). Resisting racial awareness: How teachers understand the social order from their racial, gender, and social class locations. In R. A. Martuesewicz and W. M. Reynolds (Eds.), *Inside/out: Contemporary critical perspectives in education* (pp. 239-264). New York, NY: St. Martin's Press.

Swaminathan, R. (2007). Educating for the "real world": The hidden curriculum of community service-learning. *Equity & Excellence in Education, 40*(2), 134-143.

Trout, J. D. (2009). *Why empathy matters. The science and psychology of better judgment.* New York, NY: Penguin Books

Tupper, J. A. (2008). Interrogating citizenship and democracy in education: The implications of disrupting universal values. In D. E. Lund & P. R. Carr (Eds.), *Doing democracy. Striving for political literacy and social justice* (pp. 71-84). New York, NY: Peter Lang.

Tyack, D., & Tobin, W. (1994). The "Grammar" of schooling: Why has it been so hard to change? *American Educational Research Journal, 31*(3), 453-479.

Villegas, A. M. (2007). Dispositions in teacher education: A look at social justice. *Journal of Teacher Education, 58*, 370-380.

Westheimer, J., & Kahne, J. (2004). What kind of citizen? The politics of educating for democracy. *American Educational Research Journal, 41*(2), 237-269.

CHAPTER 14

HOME INTERACTIONS, IN THE CONTEXT OF LEARNING ABOUT NUMBERS 1-100

How Do Romanian Parents Teach Place Value to Their Children?

Madalina Tanase

This chapter describes the home interactions between first-grade Romanian children and their parents, in the context of learning about numbers 1-100. The author wanted to account for the real life applications of learning numbers 0-100 (why numbers are important, how knowing numbers may help children later on in life, etc.). Numbers are everywhere, and in order to lead a healthy, successful life, people need to possess the skills to interpret and manipulate these numbers. Children use numbers in formal and informal ways when they count, play games, or go shopping. Moreover, teenagers and adults use numbers when dividing the bill three ways at a restaurant; reading and understanding nutrition labels; estimating tips, sales prices; and reading maps (Quantitative Literacy Design Team, 2001).

In teaching children about numbers, money can be used as a manipulative that bridges students' everyday lives to school curriculum, thereby

Reframing Financial Literacy: Exploring the Value of Social Currency, pp. 279–303

connecting mathematics to personal finances. Young children have a natural curiosity about money: a 3-year old, for example, "is ready to understand what money does and is ready to start earning it" (Godfrey, 1995, p. 52). Parents and teachers need to capitalize on this interest and expose children as early as possible to personal finance education, creating opportunities that allow students to apply mathematics knowledge in the real world, understanding that "financial literacy lies in mathematics in the real world and in the contexts of their students" (Maxwell, 2008, p. 161). For example, in grades K-2, teachers can use money to teach students about place value, as the U.S. currency follows the base-10 system notation (Brenner, 1998). If children are taught financial management at an early age, they become less vulnerable in the marketplace as they develop into teenagers and young adults (Martin & Oliva, 2001). Even small tasks, such as teaching children how to count money and to make change, may have long-lasting effects on the financial decisions children make when they become teenagers and adults (Maxwell, 2008).

Teaching mathematics as a discipline that has little application outside the school should therefore be a thing of the past (Carnevale & Desrochers, 2003; Gutierrez, 2002; Wiest, Higgins, & Frost, 2007). Teachers need to abandon conventional mathematics teaching (i.e., using rote memorization to teach students rules and procedures), for it only applies to a few technical professions. This kind of mathematics teaching does not "adequately prepare students for their personal or vocational lives" (Wiest et al., 2007, p. 47), as it cannot be applied to everyday contexts. In order to make mathematics meaningful, teachers and parents should include tasks that relate to children's everyday lives (Brenner, 1998), in an effort to help children develop critical thinking skills (i.e., asking questions, critiquing the information they hear and read about, and engaging students in activities that allow them to apply mathematical problem-solving skills within real-life contexts). These skills will impact the students on a personal and civic level. On a personal level, youth and young adults will be able to make sound financial decisions (Quantitative Literacy Design Team, 2001). On a civic level, students will understand issues of power, agency and oppression, seeing themselves as "part of the solution to injustice, both as youth and as they grow into adulthood" (Gutstein, 2003, p. 38).

LITERATURE

Researchers (Aubrey, Bottle, & Godfrey, 2003; Barta & Schaelling, 1998; Kline, 1998; Sarama & Clements, 2006; Whyte & Bull, 2008) have interpreted the ways students learn about numbers for some time. Foundational skills, such as counting and the ability to understand and represent numbers, develop before formal instruction and undergird mathematics skills when school begins (Jordan, Kaplan, Ramineni, & Locuniak, 2008; Whyte & Bull, 2008). Moreover, counting ability constitutes the basis of arithmetic for all children (Butterworth, 2005). Due to the relevance of number acquisition at an early age and its connection with later mathematics achievement, researchers (Blevins-Knabe & Musun-Miller, 1996; Ramani & Siegler, 2008; Siegler & Ramani, 2009; Whyte & Bull, 2008) advocate for parental involvement in mathematics games and activities before formal school instruction.

Using Manipulatives to Teach Counting

Counting and representing numbers constitute the foundation for computation skills and mental mathematics (Kline, 1998; Richardson, 1997; Xin & Holmdal, 2003). Researchers (Jordan et al., 2008; Siegler & Ramani, 2008; Whyte & Bull, 2008) have investigated some of the resources parents use to teach numbers. While many of these counting resources are significant, this chapter will focus only on three: the use of games, money, and fingers.

Engaging children in number games has been found to enhance children's understanding of numbers (Barta & Schaelling, 1998; Siegler & Ramani, 2009; Whyte & Bull, 2008). As games help children learn to estimate, predict, and plan, teachers and parents should increase the use of games, enabling children to "experience and explore mathematics within the context of culture" (Barta & Schaelling, 1998, p. 388). Researchers (Siegler & Ramani, 2009; Whyte & Bull, 2008) have discussed the benefits of engaging preschool children in linear number board games. Games help children understand a combination of spatial, temporal, kinesthetic and verbal cues. Studies (Ramani & Siegler, 2008; Siegler & Ramani, 2009) indicate that preschool students from low-income backgrounds who play linear number board games, rather than circular board games or other numeric activities, improve their understanding of basic number skills, such as counting and numerical identification. Such games may therefore narrow the gap in numerical knowledge that students from different socioeconomic status (SES) backgrounds have when they begin school.

Considered "a bridge between everyday life and school" (Brenner, 1998, p. 89), money is another important manipulative to teach children how to count. Researchers (Martin & Oliva, 2001; O'Neil & Brennan, 1997) discuss the significance of teaching children about money from an early age, as children have a natural curiosity about money. Parents and teachers can use this curiosity to teach young students how to shop, to give and receive change.

In a study that investigated the inclusion of everyday mathematics into instruction, Brenner (1998) found that as early as preschool, children could identify dollars and quarters and understand their value. By the end of second grade, the children had a stronger knowledge about money, grasping the relationship between dollars and cents. Brenner found that students with the most everyday experience in using money were disadvantaged at school because of the way the topic of money was discussed in the textbook (as a topic with little applicability to real life). Children shopped with their parents outside of school, using real money, counting it, and giving and receiving change. In school, children recognized textbook pictures of coins. Brenner discussed the need for everyday mathematics to be included in the curriculum more effectively.

Wadlington and Wadlington (2008) further discussed the use of money with students with mathematical disabilities in an effort to make abstract mathematics concepts more concrete, being more effective than worksheets. Perry (2000) explained the use of money in class to reinforce counting skills. Students role-played going to the store and took turns (a) selling and buying products, (b) giving change from $1, $5, $10, and $20, and (c) being able to beat the cash register's time. As young as three, children begin to exert their shopping power (Godfrey, 1995), and their first exposure to learning about money is through their parents. Accordingly, Martin and Oliva (2001) advocated helping children learn about money at home as early as possible, as this is a basic life skill.

The fingers represent other manipulatives that parents use to teach their children about numbers. Ardila (1993) discussed the use of fingers in counting, as they provide a natural scaffold for calculation that fits the base-10 number system. In analyzing the appropriateness of timing for finger use, Jordan et al. (2008) found a positive correlation between use of fingers and accuracy of number combination in kindergarten and first grade. However, the same study indicated a negative correlation when the participants were second grade students. This study warrants the conclusion that while teachers should encourage kindergarten students to use their fingers to count as they develop accuracy with number combinations, older students should be taught to do mathematics in their heads and rely less on their fingers.

Consequently, parents and teachers need to understand the importance of using manipulatives in order to help develop their children's fluency with numbers (Kline, 1998). To reach this goal, they need to provide their children with opportunities to work with concrete materials, such as board games or fake money, as they learn to count. The use of such concrete materials helps children understand abstract concepts that they experience in their daily lives (Westling & Fox, 2000).

Home Practices and the Impact on Student Learning About Numbers

Researchers (i.e., Aubrey et al., 2003; LeFevre, Polyzoi, Skwarchuk, Fast, & Sowinski, 2010; Pan, Gauvin, Liu, & Cheng, 2006) have investigated the types of interactions that take place between parents and their children in order to account for the opportunities children have to learn numbers at home. These studies have revealed three types of home interactions that involve numbers: (a) direct versus indirect practice, (b) formal versus informal instruction, and c) calculation versus noncalculation activities.

Aubrey et al. (2003) analyzed formal and informal opportunities to learn about numbers by observing a family with two children, Child H and Child L. Informal opportunities were the times when mathematics was part of the child's everyday life, as mother and child played games and participated in household activities that provided the child with the opportunity to count. For example, child H counted the knives and forks while laying the table, followed recipes, and weighed things out. On the other hand, Child L and her mother engaged in a more formal interaction, as the goal was the acquisition of counting and arithmetic skills. Child L counted and played card-matching games and puzzles, but she was not engaged in informal household activities. Although the findings do not link these informal interactions with better number skills, they point to the difference in parental teaching styles. Teachers should consider these different types of interactions, as some students and parents may not be familiar with the "play pedagogy" teachers may use in their classrooms.

In a cross-cultural study, Pan et al. (2006) analyzed the involvement of Chinese and American parents and children in calculation and noncalculation activities. Calculation activities involved number computations, as students added, subtracted, divided, and multiplied. When parents and children were involved in noncalculation activities, children usually counted, read numbers, and measured amounts. Chinese students had a better numerical knowledge, overall, which was directly linked to the school-oriented mathematics knowledge their mothers exposed them to through the calculation activities.

LeFevre et al. (2010) found that parents of primary grade students were involved in direct and indirect mathematics activities. The direct activities were the ones in which children memorized math facts, did mathematics in their head, and counted money. In indirect mathematics activities, parents and children played games, measured ingredients for cooking, and sorted collections of objects. Both types of interactions had a positive impact on children's understanding of numbers. However, the researchers reported that a more direct exposure to mathematical content led to better early numeracy skills. Parental positive attitudes towards mathematics also contributed to the better number acquisition of their children; the parents who were more confident in their ability to teach their children mathematics engaged their children more in number activities.

These studies shed more light on the different types of parental interactions that occur at home, in an attempt to engage children in number learning activities. In order to make mathematics meaningful, teachers should pay attention to their students' differing exposure to numbers, in trying to incorporate the everyday mathematics students learn at home (through counting objects, shopping, playing games) in the school curriculum (when teaching addition, subtraction, etc.). On the other hand, these studies indicate that if parents involve their children in direct mathematics activities (i.e., formal activities, calculation activities), where children add, subtract, use money, and play card-matching games, these activities lead to stronger early numeracy skills.

Frequency Versus Nature of the Interaction

While the above studies discussed the types of interactions that take place between parents and their children in the context of learning about numbers, questions still remained whether the nature of these interactions or the frequency with which parents are engaged in number activities with their children have a stronger influence on number acquisition.

Blevins-Knabe and Musun-Miller (1996) investigated the types and frequency of number-related behaviors U.S. preschool children and their parents engaged in at home. The researchers found a high positive correlation between the level of mathematics activities, the time spent on engaging children in number activities (counting, keeping score in games, reading numbers on road signs), and scores on a test of mathematics ability.

Zhou et al. (2006) found that children with good number skills were exposed to experiences involving numbers at home, with counting being the most common event that occurred in these interactions. Investigating the extent to which parents engaged in mathematical games with their children, the researchers found that Chinese parents used math in their play (counting, ordering) more than Canadian parents. Not only the amount of time, but also the nature of the interaction, seemed to be different, as more Canadian students stated they did not like mathematics activities and tended to be more distracted than their Chinese counterparts during their interactions with parents.

In another study, Pan et al. (2006) stressed the significance of the nature of the interaction versus the amount of time spent doing number exercises. Investigating the type of interaction between mothers and 5-year old and 7-year old children from China and the U.S., the researchers found that, overall, Chinese mothers engaged more in teaching school-oriented mathematics knowledge (computations) than did the U.S. mothers. This study concluded that the type of mathematics that parents teach children has more impact in promoting the mathematics competence of preschool children than the time parents spend teaching their children about numbers. This may explain the superior performance of Chinese students in school mathematics.

The aforementioned studies concerned the importance of involving students in number-related activities at home, prior to school instruction. Whether informal or formal interactions benefit children more is still a topic of investigation, as are the nature and the frequency of these interactions. Parents may use different manipulatives to teach their children about numbers. Researchers agree that home environment is crucial to preschool children's experience with the world (Whyte & Bull, 2008) and that parents are influential in their children's number acquisition (LeFevre et al., 2010). In order to learn more about the ways parents teach their children about numbers, the current study analyzed the knowledge Romanian parents have about numbers and how they apply this knowledge when involving their children in number acquisition activities.

METHODOLOGY

The data used in this chapter are part of a larger study (i.e., Tanase, 2008) which focused on the interactions between students, teachers, and parents and the impact these interactions had on student learning of place value concepts.

Participants

Four first grade teachers, their students, and the students' parents participated in this study. The students came from two old schools in a large city in southeast Romania--Iorga and Delavrancea Elementary.[1] Iorga was considered the higher performing school in this study, as Iorga students had won more awards in mathematics competitions, and they scored generally higher than Delavrancea students in the national mathematics competition. The annual national competition is held at the end of eighth grade, as students transition to high school.

Students. The total number of students in this study was 64. There were 36 students at Iorga, 24 in the veteran teacher's class (Ms. Ionescu) and 12 students in the novice teacher's class (Ms. Ali). There were 28 students at Delavrancea, 18 in the veteran teacher's class (Ms. Popescu) and 10 students in the less experienced teacher's class (Ms. Reiz).

In terms of SES, more students came from families with an average income ($100 per capita monthly) than from families with large incomes (over $200-$300 per capita monthly). There were 70% students from families with an average income and 30% from large income-families. A school break-down shows an equal amount of students coming from average and large income families, namely 70% average income families and 30% large income families.

Parents. The researcher sent questionnaires to the parents to gather demographic information, including income and education level, as well as information on parents' involvement with their children's homework. Thirty-eight families who were sent the questionnaires returned them and agreed to be further interviewed. The researcher randomly selected eight parents, two in each class, for interviews.

The researcher collected information about the parents' level of education to account for the differences in the learning opportunities they provided their children. Higher education was considered a post high school or college degree, while average education was considered a high school degree. At Iorga, 42% of the parents held a higher education degree. They were all the parents of the students in Ms. Ionescu's class. Only one parent at Delavrancea held a higher education degree, the parent in Ms. Popescu's class.

Table 14.1. Participant Data

Teachers	*Teaching Experience*	*# of Students in Each Class*	*Student Test Grades* *A*	*D*	*Income* *Large*	*Average*	*% of Parents With a High Degree*	*Average Degree*
			Iorga					
Ionescu	21 years	24	65%	15%	15%	85%	52%	48%
Ali	4 years	12	50%	10%	40%	60%	0%	100%
			Delavrancea					
Popescu	23 years	18	65%	5%	11%	89%	11%	89%
Reiz	9 years	10	30%	30%	0%	100%	0%	100%

Data Collection and Analysis

The following questions guided this study: (1) What do Romanian parents know about numbers 0-100, and (2) What opportunities to Romanian parents create at home for their children to learn about numbers? In order to answer these questions, the researcher gathered the data from student tests and homework and parental questionnaires and interviews. Descriptions of the data sets are provided below.

Student tests. Students were assessed on their understanding of place value concepts after classroom instruction. The researcher coded the test exercises as higher order and lower order thinking exercises, following the model of two U.S. mathematics textbooks, *Investigations in Number, Date and Space* (Foresman, 2004), and *Everyday Mathematics* (Bell & Bell, 2004).

Student homework. The researcher collected the work students had completed at home and categorized the types of exercises into lower order thinking and higher order thinking concepts. Homework was considered correct and complete when all the problems were solved without error and incorrect and/or incomplete when there were errors in the workbooks and/or not all exercises were solved. Artifacts from homework expanded over a month's period. The researcher considered only the homework assigned following the first teaching of the base 10 numbers up until and including the last teaching of base 10 numbers.

Parent questionnaires. The questionnaires contained items that requested demographic information, as well as information regarding the degree of parental involvement in their children's education. The responses enabled the researcher to understand what type of knowledge parents had about place value concepts as well as how this knowledge impacted their children's learning.

Parent interviews. The researcher asked the parents to describe the learning opportunities they provided for their children in order to foster the learning of base 10 numbers. The researcher coded parental definitions and understanding of place value concepts as strong (if parents understood the nature and significance of base 10 numbers) or weak (if parents could not define base 10 numbers and/or they did not understand why these numbers were significant). The researcher also coded the types of parent-children interaction as strong (if parents went beyond help with homework and created their own assessments) and weak (if parents only helped/checked their children's homework).

FINDINGS

In order to understand the impact of parental knowledge of base 10 numbers on children's learning, the researcher analyzed the parental questionnaires and interviews. The first part of the findings section discusses the Romanian parents' knowledge of numbers 0-100, while the second part accounts for the learning opportunities the Romanian parents created to teach their children about numbers.

Parental Understanding of Numbers 0-100

Findings reveal that parents of students in the better performing classrooms at both schools generally had a clearer understanding of the nature and the significance of place value concepts than did parents in both average performing classrooms. For example, parents of students in the veteran teachers' classrooms defined base 10 numbers as "all positive and whole numbers, higher than 0;" "all numbers comprised between 0-100;" and "the basis of mathematics." These answers show that parents in both Ms. Ionescu and Ms. Popescu's classrooms identified base 10 numbers as numbers 1-100, and described these numbers as being both positive and whole, reflecting at least a basic understanding of base 10 numbers. On the other hand, parents in the less experienced teachers' classrooms at both schools stated they did not know what these numbers represented: "Something that you must learn, to count them, to subtract them;" "I don't know what to tell you." The parents' vague knowledge about base 10 numbers is reflected by the fact that they could neither identify the base 10 numbers, nor describe them. This may be directly related to the students' scores on the final test, as students in both these classrooms scored generally lower than their peers.

Moreover, parents in the veteran teachers' classrooms at both schools understood the applicability of learning about numbers: "these numbers represent the cornerstone of mathematics ... when [children] go past 10, they start to learn mathematics;" "Everything depends on these numbers, [for] they are the basis of math and, generally speaking, [of] everyday life, too;" "It is the most important thing; everything is up to 100 in real life, even counting money." These parents further believed it was important to learn these numbers because children "deal with these numbers all their [lives], using them with other subjects as well" and because these numbers will provide children with "a complete image of what follows, number order in general, negative numbers." On the other hand, parents in the less experienced teachers' classes at both schools provided more general answers regarding the importance of learning about numbers: "It will be good for them later;" "Learning is important, [for] they need to know [how] to count forwards and backwards;" "They need to know these numbers to do well in life."

Parents' knowledge of base 10 numbers was directly related to the comfort level they experienced when helping their children learn base 10 numbers before and after school instruction. At Iorga, parents who had a stronger understanding of place value concepts also felt at ease helping their children learn numbers before and after class. Survey data show that 60% of the parents in Ms. Ionescu's classroom (the veteran teacher) were comfortable with base 10 numbers. The interviewed parents stated that they helped their children understand these concepts both before and after the teacher taught them. Parents in Ms. Ali's class were less comfortable with base 10 concepts, and this lack of comfort was also evidenced in the lesser support they provided their children before and after the teacher taught them.

At Delavrancea, 55% of the surveyed parents in the veteran teacher's classroom (Ms. Popescu) were comfortable with base 10 numbers. These parents stated that they tried to help their children before and after the teacher addressed the concepts in class. On the other hand, the parents in the less experienced teacher's class (Ms. Reiz) were the least comfortable with place value concepts, as only one of the parents stated she was very comfortable to teach these notions to her child. This confirms the findings of LeFevre et al. (2010) that parents who were more confident in their ability to teach their children mathematics engaged their children more in number activities.

Help With Numbers 0-100

In order to account for the type of interactions that took place between parents and their children, the researcher asked the parents to describe the learning opportunities created at home, as well as the resources they used. At Iorga, parents in the veteran teacher's class (Ms. Ionescu) stated that in order to make sure their children understood these concepts before class, they played games that involved counting (e.g., Monopoly), practiced all the time, and gave children a lot of examples with numbers. One parent commented on the ways numbers were part of her daughter's everyday life, discussing the importance of explaining what these numbers represented: "There always had to be an explanation for what was happening around her, so whenever she encountered numbers, we discussed what these numbers represented." The other parent commented on the importance of helping his son distinguish between numbers: "I explained the difference between tens and units so he can distinguish between numbers, and I used money to teach numbers." After Ms. Ionescu addressed the concepts in class, the interviewed parents stated that they practiced more with numbers and were involved in helping children with the homework. Parents created their own worksheets to explain numbers and continued to involve the children in games that used counting, addition, and subtraction of numbers.

An analysis of student homework in Ms. Ionescu's class found 75% of the homework requirements to be correct. Parental support with number learning may also be reflected in the final test scores, as 65% of the students in Ms. Ionescu's class earned a grade of A, and only 15% earned a grade of D or below. Both of the parents interviewed felt confident that they helped their children learn numbers: "He finished the math test in 15 minutes and got 100% correct answers, so I think I did a good job;" "I did help her, [for] I asked her questions and I made her count." When present, parental support had a positive impact on student learning.

On the other hand, parents of the students in Ms. Ali's class, the novice teacher at Iorga, did not engage their children in number learning before classroom instruction. For fear they might teach these concepts incorrectly, the parents only got involved after the teacher taught the numbers 0-100 in class. The interviewed parents stated that they followed the teacher's model, reading their children's notes from class and re-explaining the concepts as the teacher did. For resources, the parents used manipulatives (i.e., money, sticks, and fingers) to count numbers: "We use money. My daughter likes to buy snacks from the school store; so I give her money, and I ask her: What can you buy with 10, Roni?;" "We used sticks and fingers to count backwards and forwards from 1-100."

When interviewed, both parents in Ms. Ali's class believed they helped their children learn the numbers "well enough." However, test results show that the students in Ms. Ali's class made more mistakes than did Ms. Ionescu's students. The lack of support before classroom instruction about numbers may explain the poorer results of the students in Ms. Ali's class. This result supports previous research findings (Siegler & Booth, 2004; Whyte & Bull, 2008) that discuss the importance of involving children in experiences with numbers outside school (i.e., playing games, counting objects). Such experiences may facilitate an increase in familiarity with numbers.

Moreover, even if the students' homework in Ms. Ali's class was generally correct, the notions that were reinforced at home were of the same lower difficulty level as the notions the teacher addressed in class. The teacher did not challenge her stronger students, keeping all her students at the same level. The frequency and the quality of parental support were directly correlated to student learning of place value. When parents had a more fragmented understanding of base 10 numbers and only got involved with homework after Ms. Ali taught these numbers in class, their children had a weaker understanding of numbers, as shown in the test results.

At Delavrancea, one of the parents in the veteran teacher's class stated she did not teach the numbers to her daughter before Ms. Popescu addressed them in class, for fear she would teach them incorrectly: "It made no sense; the teacher teaches them differently in class; she knows how to teach them; we only help with homework." After the teacher taught numbers, this parent stated that she mostly followed the teacher's and the textbook's models, using sticks and fingers to help her daughter learn the numbers. The other interviewed parent in Ms. Popescu's class stated she had helped her son both prior to and after class instruction to make sure he had an understanding of the numbers. As resources, this parent developed her own worksheets and also used the textbook to explain numbers to her son. Both interviewed parents in Ms. Popescu's class believed they helped their children understand numbers: one commented, "He will study them in class with his teacher, and he will understand them even better then;" the other remarked, "I helped her as much as I could." Despite the fact that 65% of the students in both veteran teachers' classrooms earned an A on the final test, Ms. Popescu's students were tested on less complex concepts than were Ms. Ionescu's students at Iorga.

When interviewing the two parents in Ms. Reiz's classroom at Delavarncea, the researcher learned that both parents created experiences for their children to learn about numbers before instruction. The parents in the less experienced teacher's class stated that they created opportunities for their children to learn about numbers before class instruction: "I taught her to count them backwards and forwards to make sure she [was] prepared before school starts." They also stated they helped with homework after the teacher taught the numbers in class, using the textbook, abacus, and sticks. Despite the parent-children interactions in number-learning activities before and after school instruction, only 30% of Ms. Reiz's students earned a grade of A on the final test. When asked to state whether they felt they helped their children learn the numbers, both parents in Ms. Reiz's class confessed they were not sure: "I don't know; I may not have done a good job at explaining them to her; young people [i.e. the teacher] tend to explain in different ways." In this case, the nature of the interaction, and not the frequency with which parents helped their children, seems to have had a stronger impact on student learning (Pan et al., 2006). Because the parents did not feel as confident to help their children with these concepts, the students in Ms. Reiz's class developed a fragmented understanding of base 10 concepts.

Overall, parents who possessed a stronger knowledge base of mathematics were more comfortable with their ability to help their children master more complex notions. For example, the parents in both veteran teachers' classrooms at both schools involved their children both before and after school instruction on base 10 numbers; this involvement included activities meant to facilitate and reinforce their children's number acquisition. These parents played board games with their children and created their own teaching resources (i.e., worksheets). Conversely, parents in the novice teacher's classroom at Iorga lacked confidence in their ability to provide their children with the support needed; therefore, they got involved less at home before Ms. Ali addressed the concepts in class for fear of making mistakes, and they only followed the teacher's pattern when helping at home. The way these different types of home interactions impacted student learning is reflected in the way students performed on the final test. When parents designed their own instructional activities and engaged children in number games, their children's understanding of numbers increased.

When asked about their involvement with their children's learning at school, the interviewed parents at both schools stated they felt comfortable with the way the teachers addressed the concepts in class, and they did not have any suggestions for the teachers. All parents also stated that their only involvement with their children's learning took place at home and was undertaken with the purpose of strengthening and diversifying the concepts taught in class. More parents in the veteran teacher's class at Iorga stated that Ms. Ionescu urged them to get involved in their children's learning at home, provided support with the homework, assigned general rules, and told parents to challenge their children as much as they could. This might have motivated the parents to get more involved at home and to help with their children's homework. However, this support was not enough to enhance all students' learning, for 15% of Ms. Ionescu's students earned a grade of D or below on the final test.

Opportunities were not always created by the teachers to involve parents in classroom instructions, leaving the parents with a limited understanding of what goes on in class in terms of teaching and learning mathematics. However, even when teachers (e.g., Ms. Ionescu) invited parents to participate in mathematics classes, due to time constraints and other personal reasons, the parents did not take advantage of the teacher's offer. The reluctance to get involved in their children's learning past the level of simple support with homework may be due, in general, to parental beliefs that they cannot impact curriculum and school instruction in any way. Even when parents had a strong mathematics knowledge and felt comfortable with their ability to help their children master place value concepts, they stated they did not want to get involved because (a) it was not their profession and (b) they thought they could not significantly or meaningfully impact curriculum or teaching. These beliefs may be due, in part, to parents' own experience with school. If their own experience was not a positive one, parents tend to be less likely to want to get involved in their children's learning at school (Bloom, 2009). Moreover, parents may be uncertain of the role they can play in their children's learning at school (Nakagawa, 2000), or they may perceive their contribution to the school environment as being irrelevant and not valued (Matuszny, Banda, & Coleman, 2007).

DISCUSSION AND CONCLUSIONS

This study found that parental engagement in children's learning of numbers, prior to school instruction, generally enhanced children's understanding of numbers in the veteran teachers' classrooms at both schools. For example, when parents engaged their children in experiences involving numbers (e.g., the parents in Ms. Popescu's class using money to buy snacks, or the parents in Ms. Ionescu's class doing mental mathematics while playing counting games and counting objects), students' understanding of numbers increased. However, despite the fact that 65% of the students in both veteran teachers' classrooms scored A on the final test, the findings indicate that 15% of Ms. Ionescu's students and 5% of Ms. Popescu's students still failed the final test, earning a grade of D or below. Moreover, despite the fact that parents in Ms. Reiz's class stated they helped their children learn about numbers both before and after school instruction, overall, the students in the less experienced teacher's class at Delavrancea scored the lowest of the four classrooms on the final test.

These findings warrant the following conclusions: firstly, the lower results in the final test are explained by the difference in the learning opportunities created at home by parents. These different opportunities may be the direct result of a lower SES status, and they confirm Mandell's (2008) findings. Mandell reported that students from lower income households scored lower on the Jump$tart 1997, 2000, 2002, 2004, and 2006 financial literacy surveys than their peers who came from households that had higher incomes.

Second, parental level of education is directly related to the SES of the family, as data indicate that parents in both of the less experienced teachers' classrooms at both schools had a lower level of education and overall had a lower SES than the parents of the students in the veteran teachers' classes at both schools. Students enter school with different levels of understanding about numbers, and students from lower-income families (e.g., the students in Ms. Ali's and Ms. Reiz's classrooms) are deprived of the learning opportunities that may benefit their peers from middle level families (Ramani & Siegler, 2008). This conclusion has implications for teachers and parents as described below.

Teachers should acknowledge the importance of the different learning experiences their students had prior to school instruction. Second, teachers should relate their students' everyday mathematics experiences to the school curriculum, connecting the concrete to the abstract. By making mathematics meaningful, teachers engage students with mathematics that relates to their own lives and their family's experiences (Malloy, 2002) in an attempt to narrow the achievement gap between students from lower-level families and their peers from richer households (Ramani & Siegler, 2008). On the other hand, parents need to be aware that they are a vital link in helping with their children's number acquisition before formal school instruction (Aubrey et al., 2003; Clark, 2001; Ramani & Siegler, 2008). As such, they need to engage their children in games involving numbers and introduce them to money as a tool to teach about place value.

Since the ability to understand numbers empowers individuals, teachers and parents need to help their children develop critical thinking and problem-solving skills. This goal can be achieved by enabling students to make connections between mathematics principles and real-life scenarios, by centering the curriculum around questions and interests students have about their lives in order to help them learn "who they can and they cannot be in the world" (Vasquez, 2004, p.86). On a personal level, possessing this ability to understand and interpret numeric information translates into power, enabling individuals to lead more successful lives. On a civic level, mathematically literate individuals may use mathematics as a tool to combat social injustices and make the world a better place, not only for themselves, but for the ones around them (Weist et al., 2007). It starts with being able to count (Butterworth, 2005).

DISCUSSION QUESTIONS

1. What are your memories of how your parents taught you mathematics? What resources or tools were used? What was available? How did resource availability relate to your family's social and economic status?
2. Describe the patterns of interaction between your parents and your teachers with regard to your learning of mathematics. How might they relate to your confidence in understandings of the subject?
3. In what ways can parents (a) show their children they value their education, and (b) instill a love for learning?
4. To what extent may parents' attitudes about mathematics influence their children's attitudes about mathematics?

5. In what ways can teachers help their students' parents get more engaged in their children's learning, both at home and at school?

MODEL LESSON

Shopping at 99 Cent Stores

Grade Levels: K-1st

Objectives:

(a) Students will buy and sell goods of a value up to 99 cents;
(b) Students will compare amounts to prices and count on from prices to find change.

Related Standards

National Council for Teachers of Mathematics

Algebra Pre-K-2

1. Use concrete, pictorial and verbal representations to develop an understanding of invented and conventional symbolic notations.

Number and Operations K-2

1. Develop understanding of the relative position and magnitude of whole numbers and ordinal and cardinal numbers and their connection.
2. Count with understanding and recognize "how many" in sets of objects.
3. Use multiple models to develop initial understanding of place value and the base -10 numbers.

Jump$tart National Standards in K–12 Personal Finance Education

Financial Responsibility and Decision Making

Standard 1: Apply reliable information and systematic decision making to personal financial decisions. Take responsibility for personal financial decisions.

Standard 4: Apply reliable information and systematic decision making to personal financial decisions. Make financial decisions by systematically considering alternatives and consequences.

Materials

- The teacher will create three shops or shopping stations in the classroom where students will use fake money (pennies, nickels, dimes, and quarters) to buy and sell different goods
- Toy-shop merchandise that students can practice selling and buying from their toy-shop (up to 99 cents)
- Inventory sheet for small group work
- Bingo grid for individual work
- Bunny Money (by Stephen Krensky & Emily Bolam, Simon & Schuster Children's Publishing, 2011)

People Involved (The activity involves children practicing selling and buying goods at three different centers. Three adults will need to supervise these centers.)

- Teacher
- Teacher aide
- Parent volunteer

Procedures

(a) Opening Activities

1. The teacher reviews the value of pennies, nickels, dimes, and their use for buying and selling goods and services. The teacher discusses how many pennies may be exchanged for a nickel and a dime and introduces another coin of greater value, the quarter. The teacher shows pictures of a quarter and distributes bags of fake dimes, nickels, pennies, and quarters to students to look at and compare.

(b) Developmental Activities

1. After discussing the use of money in buying objects/toys, the teacher reads the students a story that involves money, Bunny Money (Krensky & Bolam, 2011). In this story, four little bun-

nies want to buy a hat for their mother. The hat costs $1.00. Will they have enough money to buy the hat?

2. The teacher allows the students to practice buying and selling toys they can find in the 99 cent stores, while at the same time learning to give and receive correct change. Students will take turns buying and selling in the three little shops that the teacher has organized in the classroom, using fake money. The teacher, along with the teacher's aide and a parent volunteer (if available), provide assistance when needed until all the students have practiced buying and selling goods worth up to 99 cents.

(c) Closing Activities

1. The teacher assigns students to small groups, and students further develop an inventory for their dream toy-shop with items of their choice. The students label the prices of the toys. The teacher and teacher helpers are there to guide the students when needed. The teacher gives each group a 25-item inventory sheet on which the students either draw or write the name of the toys that their shop sells and the prices for each item.

(d) Summary and Assessment

1. The students will be informally assessed, throughout the duration of the lesson, as they practice selling and buying goods. The teacher, teacher's aide, and/or parent volunteer will be tracking the following behaviors: Was salesperson able to provide correct change by himself/herself? Was the buyer able to calculate what change s/he needed to receive by himself/herself? Was the buyer able to provide the correct change to buy particular items by himself/herself?
2. Group activity: *Nine-Item Inventory Sheet* The students will be assessed formally as they design the inventory sheet in small groups (see sample provided by the teacher). The teacher will collect the 9-item inventory sheet from each group. The teacher will grade the group activity as follows:

   Grading for group activity inventory sheet: The point total for this activity is 10. Students will earn:

   - 10 points if they come up with nine toy items and prices for each of them.
   - 5 points if they only list at most 5 toy items and their prices.

- 1 point if they list at least 1 item and its price.

3. Follow-up Activity with Parental Assistance. At home, students and parents can practice by buying and selling the following merchandise and by using the worksheet described below to keep track of the change they need to receive. They can take turns or play once, allowing the students to sell and decide on the change that needs to be provided.

   The students will be assessed as they fill out the worksheet entitled "Buying Food and Getting change."

   Grading Criteria for Homework:
   6 points: if the students circled the exact change on all items.
   3 points: if the students circled the exact change on at least 3 items.
   1 point: if the students circled the exact change on 1 item.

Group Activity Sheets

Nine-Item Inventory Sheet		
Item	**Name of the Toy**	**Price**
1		
2		
3		
4		
5		
6		
7		
8		
9		

Follow up Activity with Parental Assistance

The following worksheet was retrieved October 30th, 2010 from the following website: http://www.moneyinstructor.com/ws/ws0017a.asp

Buying Food and Getting Change

 5¢  35¢  30¢

 40¢  10¢

Draw an "X" on the change received after buying the items pictured.

Purchase these items.	**Pay.**	**Get change back?**
1. 	50¢	
2. 	50¢	

3. 	50¢	
4. 	75¢	
5. 	50¢	
6. 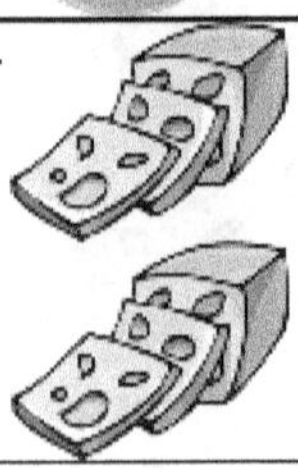	75¢	

NOTE

1. The names of the participants and those of the schools are pseudonyms to protect the participants' identities.

REFERENCES

Ardila, C. (1993). On the origins of calculation abilities. *Behavioural Neurology, 6*, 89–97.

Aubrey, C., Bottle, G., & Godfrey, R. (2003). Early mathematics in the home and out-of-home contexts. *International Journal of Early Years Education, 11*(2), 91-103.

Barta, J., & Schaelling, D. (1998). Games we play: Connecting mathematics and culture in the classroom. *Teaching Children Mathematics, 4*(7), 388-393.

Bell, J., & Bell, M. (2004). *Everyday mathematics. Grade 1*. The University of Chicago School Mathematics Project. Chicago, IL: The McGraw Hill Companies.

Blevins-Knabe, B., & Musun-Miller, L. (1996). Number use at home by children and their parents and its relationship to early mathematical performance. *Early Development and Parenting, 5*(1), 35-45.

Bloom, L. A. (2009). *Classroom management: Creating positive outcomes for all students*. Upper Saddle River, NJ: Pearson Education.

Brenner, M. E. (1998). Meaning and money. *Educational Studies in Mathematics, 36*(2), 123-155.

Butterworth, B. (2005). The development of arithmetical abilities. *Journal of Child Psychology and Psychiatry, 46*(1), 3-18.

Carnevale, A. P., & Desrochers, D. M. (2003). The democratization of mathematics. In B.L. Madison & L.A. Steen (Eds.), *Quantitative literacy: Why numeracy matters for schools and colleges* (pp. 21-31). Princeton, NJ: The National Council on Education and Disciplines.

Clark, M. M. (2001). Challenges and changes in preschool education. *Primary Practice, 28*, 42–47.

Foresman, S. (Ed.). (2004) *Investigations in number, date and Space: Building number sense, Grade 1*. Cambridge, MA: Glenview III.

Godfrey, N. (1995). *A penny saved*. New York, NY: Simon and Schuster.

Gutierrez, R. (2002). Enabling the practice of mathematics teachers in context: Toward a new equity research agenda. *Mathematical Thinking and Learning, 4*(2&3), 145-187.

Gutstein, E. (2003). Teaching and learning mathematics for social justice in an urban, Latino school. *Journal for Research in Mathematics Education, 34*(1), 37-73.

Jordan, N. C., Kaplan, D., Ramineni, C., & Locuniak, M.N. (2008). Development of number combination skill in the early school years: when do fingers help? *Developmental Science, 11*(5), 662-668.

Kline, K. (1998). Kindergarten is more than counting. *Teaching Children Mathematics, 5*(2), 84-87.

Krensky, S., & Bolam, E. (2011). *Bunny Money*. New York, NY: Simon and Schuster.

LeFevre, J. A., Polyzoi, E., Skwarchuk, S. L., Fast, L., & Sowinski, C. (2010). Do home numeracy and literacy practices of Greek and Canadian parents predict the numeracy skills of kindergarten children? *International Journal of Early Years Education, 18*(1), 55-70.

Malloy, C. E. (2002). Democratic access to mathematics through democratic education: An introduction. In L. D. English (Ed.), *Handbook on international research in mathematics education* (pp.17-25). Mahwah, NJ: Erlbaum.

Mandell, L. (2008). Financial literacy of high school students. In J. J. Xiao (Ed.), *Handbook of consumer finance research* (pp. 163-184). New York, NY: Springer.

Martin, A., & Oliva, J. (2001). Teaching children about money: Applications for social learning and cognitive learning developmental theories. *Journal of Family and Consumer Sciences, 93*(2), 26-29.

Matuszny, R. M., Banda, D. R., & Coleman, T. J. (2007). A progressive plan for developing collaborative relationships with parents from diverse backgrounds. *Teaching Exceptional Children, 39*(4), 24-31.

Maxwell, S. A. (2008). Mathematics and financial literacy: Collaboration or conflict? What are mathematics educators' responsibilities? In T. A. Lucey & K. S. Cooter (Eds.), *Financial Literacy for Children and Youth* (pp. 149-169). Athens, GA: Digitaltextbooks.

Nakagawa, K. (2000), Unthreading the ties that bind: Questioning the discourse of parental involvement. *Educational Policy, 14*(4), 443-473.

O'Neil, B., & Brennan, P. (1997). Financial planning education throughout the life cycle. *Journal of Family and Consumer Sciences, 89*(2), 32-36.

Pan, Y., Gauvin, M., Liu, Z., & Cheng, L. (2006). American and Chinese parental involvement in young children's mathematics learning. *Cognitive Development, 21*(1), 17-35.

Perry, B. K. (2000). Patterns for giving change and using mental mathematics. *Teaching Children Mathematics*, 7(4), 196-199.

Quantitative Literacy Design Team. (2001). The case for quantitative literacy. In L.A. Steen (Ed.), *Mathematics and democracy: The case for quantitative literacy* (pp.1-22). Princeton, NJ: The National Council on Education and the Disciplines.

Ramani, G. B., & Siegler, R. S. (2008). Promoting broad and stable improvements in low-income children's numerical knowledge through playing number board games. *Child Development, 79*(2), 375-394.

Richardson, K. (1997). Too easy for kindergarten and just right for first grade. *Teaching Children Mathematics, 3*, 432-437.

Sarama, J., & Clements, D. H. (2006). How children learn about numbers. *Early Childhood Today, 20*(5), 10-11.

Siegler, R. S., & Booth, J. L. (2004). Development of numerical estimation in young children. *Child Development, 75*(2), 428-444.

Siegler, R. S., & Ramani, G. B. (2009). Playing linear number board games-but not circular ones-improves low-income preschoolers' numerical understanding. *Journal of Educational Psychology, 101*(3), 545-560.

Tanase, M. (2008). *The impact of interactive factors on Romanian students' understanding of place value* (Unpublished dissertation). University of Nevada, Las Vegas.

Vasquez, V. M. (2004). *Negotiating critical literacies with young children*. Mahwah, NJ: Erlbaum.

Wadlington, E., & Wadlington, P.L. (2008). Helping students with mathematical disabilities to succeed. *Preventing School Failure, 53*(1), 2-8.

Westling, D., & Fox, L. (2000). *Teaching students with severe disabilities* (2nd ed.). Upper Saddle River, NJ: Merrill/Prentice Hall.

Whyte, J. C., & Bull, R. (2008). Number games, magnitude representation, and basic number skills in preschoolers. *Developmental Psychology, 44*(2), 588-596.

Wiest, L. R., Higgins, H. J., & Hart Frost, J. (2007). Quantitative literacy for social justice. *Equity & Excellence in Education, 40*, 47-55.

Zhou, X., Huang, J., Wang. Z., Wang, B., Zhao, Z., Yang. L., & Yang, Z. (2006). Parent-child interaction and children's number learning. *Early Child Development and Care, 176*(7), 763-775.

ABOUT THE AUTHORS

Mary Frances Agnello majored in French, foreign language education, and government, receiving her bachelor of arts degree from The University of Texas at Austin. After several years of teaching in Houston urban and Texas rural public high schools, she completed a master's and doctor of philosophy in curriculum and instruction at Texas A&M University in College Station, focusing her work in foundations of education and language, literacy, and culture. Dr. Agnello spent 8 years in San Antonio at The University of Texas at San Antonio and at Our Lady of the Lake University working in teacher education, foundations, and educational leadership. Currently she is an associate professor at Texas Tech University in Lubbock. Her research focuses on preservice teachers' knowledge in the social studies curriculum and critical pedagogy.

Alan Bates is an associate professor at Illinois State University. He completed his PhD in child and adolescent development from the University of California at Santa Barbara in 2005. He teaches child growth and development and early childhood math methods for undergraduates and a learning theory course for graduate students. Alan's research agenda focuses primarily on preservice and practicing teachers' mathematics self-efficacy and teaching efficacy, college students' financial morality, and parental involvement in children's cognitive development, specifically in the mathematical domain.

Paul R. Carr is associate professor in the Departments of Sociology and Interdisciplinary Studies at Lakehead University (Orillia), which is about an hour north of Toronto. His research examines critical pedagogy, democracy, peace studies and the media, and his latest book is *Does Your Vote Count? Critical Pedagogy and Democracy* (Peter Lang, 2010). He is co-director of the Global Doing Democracy Research Project.

Weiwei Chen is an economics PhD candidate at the University of Memphis. She has been the research assistant for the analysis of the Tennessee financial literacy education program. Her research interests are in applied microeconomics. Before joining the University of Memphis, she had her MA in economics analysis from the University of Carlos III, Madrid, and BA in economics from Huazhong University of Science and Technology, China.

Catherine (Cathy) Fagan is a lecturer in the School of Education within the College of Social Sciences at the University of Glasgow, Scotland. She teaches on doctoral and masters programmes in education and on under- and postgraduate initial teacher education programmes. Her main research focus is the social, cultural and policy contexts of work-related education and her doctoral studies examined education and work in the contexts of a global knowledge economy, enterprise culture and entrepreneurship. Current research is on values based approaches to financial education programmes and conceptions of future-mindedness in teacher education. She is chair of the International Association for Citizenship, Social and Economics Education (IACSEE) and is editor of that association's international peer-reviewed online journal of the same name (CSEE).

Valerie Farnsworth is a research fellow at the University of Leeds in the School of Education's post-14 education research group where she focuses on curriculum studies. Her main interests are in the relationships between curriculum and knowledge, identity and practice, and political/cultural/social contexts and structures of relations and the ways these relationships mediate post-14 educational policies, professional practices and student learning. She is originally from the United States and moved to England in 2006 after completing her PhD in educational policy studies at the University of Wisconsin-Madison.

Vicki A. Green teaches undergraduate and graduate teachers at the University of British Columbia's Okanagan campus. Her undergraduate students create archival short films on economic history. She completed the stockbroker's course through the Canadian Securities Institute and manages her own financial portfolio. Dr. Green serves on IACSEE journal's editorial board and is a member of the Canadian Federation of Economic Education.

Julia A. Heath is the director of the Center for Economic Education at the University of Memphis. She received her PhD in economics at the University of South Carolina. Dr. Heath received a Visiting Research Fellowship to Princeton University to conduct research in economics education and has published extensively in the area. She has won several teaching awards, including the Carnegie Foundation U.S. Professor of the Year Award for Tennessee. She received the economics discipline's highest award, the Kenneth G. Elzinga Distinguished Teaching Award, and the Educator of the Year Award from the National Association for Financial Literacy, both in 2008. She has also received her University's Thomas W. Briggs Foundation's Excellence in Teaching Award and the Distinguished Teaching Award. She was named the 2006 Financial Educator of the Year by the Tennessee Bankers Association. Dr. Heath is a member of the national board of directors of the Council for Economic Education and is a member of the economics standing committee of the National Assessment of Education Progress.

Andrea Johnson holds a bachelor's and master's degree in sociology from North Carolina A&T State University and North Carolina State University respectively, as well as a doctoral degree in Leadership Studies from North Carolina A&T State University. She is a faculty member in the Department of Sociology and Social Work at North Carolina A&T State University where she teaches a variety of sociology courses. Her research interests are in the areas of social and commercial entrepreneurship, African American wealth attainment, and interpersonal relationships. Dr. Johnson promotes financial literacy on campus as well as in the community by providing a variety of workshops and seminars. In addition to teaching in academia, she has over 14 years combined experience working in nonprofit agencies, managing youth programs, and working with community organizations.

Andrea L. Knapp is the assistant dean of finance and business services with the Texas Tech University College of Education. She received her BBA in Accounting and MBA from Texas Tech University. Her professional experience includes fiduciary oversight of a college; fiscal responsibility for an academic medical practice plan; human resource management; contract negotiation; and strategic planning.

James D. Laney is professor and assistant chair in the Department of Teacher Education and Administration at the University of North Texas in Denton, Texas. He received his doctoral degree in Learning and Instruction, with a minor in curriculum and the study of schooling, from the University of California, Los Angeles. His research and writings are in the areas of generative teaching-learning theory, general social studies education, economics education, aging education, and fine arts integration.

Jennifer Loew studied economic education, economics, and economic and social history at RWTH Aachen University, Germany, receiving her MA degree in 2008. She currently is a research assistant and doctoral student at RWTH Aachen University. Her main roles are as study adviser, lecturer in the domain of teacher education, and developer of teaching materials. Her research foci are in the areas of morality and responsibility in the economic context, moral decision making, moral development, and management development. "Morality and Responsibility—A Theoretical and Empirical Research Concerning Perception and Judgment of Responsibility in the Economic Context" is the title of her PhD research project.

Thomas A. Lucey is an associate professor in the Department of Curriculum and Instruction at Illinois State University in Normal, Illinois. He holds a bachelor's in business administration from the University of Notre Dame and earned his masters and doctoral degree in Instruction and Curriculum Leadership from the University of Memphis. Dr. Lucey teaches social studies methods courses for undergraduates and courses that concern multicultural learning and the education of teachers for graduate students. His research interests concern social studies, financial, and citizenship education and related moral and social justice issues.

Jeff Sanson is the director of programs with the Indiana Council for Economic Education (ICEE) and a PhD student in learning design and technology at Purdue University. His research interests include the design of distance learning environments for teacher professional development and technology integration in economics and social studies. Sanson has designed and developed an online professional development course on teaching personal finance. He has also made numerous presentations to K-12 teachers on effective strategies for enhancing instruction with technology in the areas of personal finance and economics.

Madalina Tanase is an assistant professor in the College of Education, at the University of North Florida. Dr. Tanase works in the Department of Foundations and Secondary Education, where she teaches general methods and classroom management classes. Her research interests include cross-cultural mathematics studies (factors contributing to the success in mathematics, how can we close the achievement gap between students from different countries), epistemological beliefs of teaching and learning (what beliefs do preservice teachers hold when they enter teacher education programs, can these beliefs be changed) and teaching in higher education (classroom management issues)?

Phillip J. VanFossen is the James F. Ackerman professor of social studies education, director of the Ackerman Center for Democratic Citizenship, and associate director of the Purdue University Center for Economic Education at Purdue University. VanFossen is also serving as the Interim Department Head for the Department of Curriculum and Instruction. He is the program author for a recently released high school economics textbook. His research interests include how social studies teachers use the Internet, digital media, and virtual worlds (e.g., MMORPGs such as *World of Warcraft*) in their teaching. He has authored 3 books, numerous chapters, and more than 25 refereed articles on these topics.

Benjamin R. Wellenreiter, EdD, is a social studies teacher at Morton Junior High School, Morton Illinois. Ben has studied school systems in Argentina, the United Kingdom, and South Africa. His research interests include adolescents' social behavior while at school, adolescents' understanding of peer/adult authority structures, social science teaching methods, patriotism in schools, and hidden curricula.

CONTRIBUTING ASSISTANTS

Kelsey Kaatz studies Elementary Education at Illinois State University. She is a native of Coal City, Illinois. Set to graduate in December 2011, Kelsey hopes to find a teaching job for the fall of 2012 school year. After teaching for a few years she plans to return to school to receive her master's degree in education.

Rachel Kinkelar graduated in 2011 with an Early Childhood Education major from Illinois State University. She plans on staying in the central Illinois area and teaching for a few years, then pursuing her master's degree in Early Childhood Education.

Lauren Rivera studies Early Childhood Education at Illinois State University. She is a native of Park Ridge, Illinois.

INDEX

www.ingramcontent.com/pod-product-compliance
Lightning Source LLC
LaVergne TN
LVHW052247200926
848481LV00002B/298
9781617357190